# BYZANTIUM

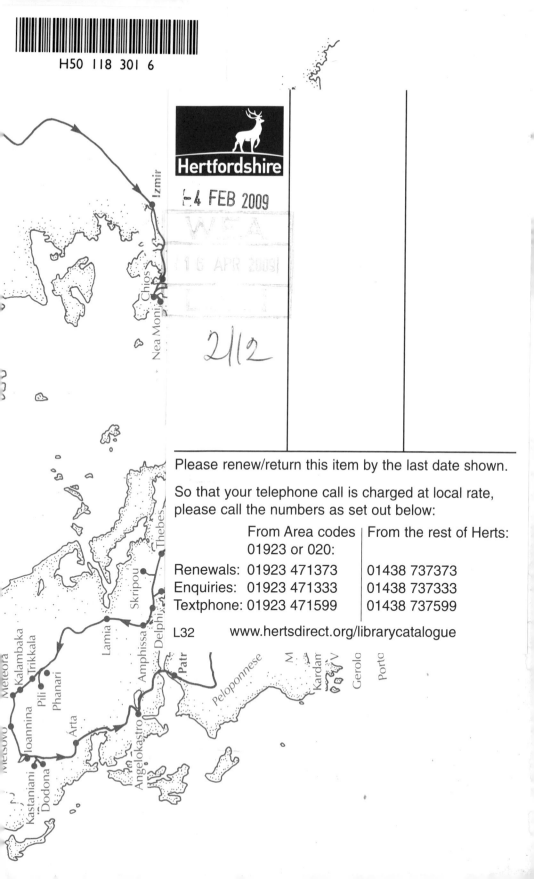

Please renew/return this item by the last date shown.

So that your telephone call is charged at local rate, please call the numbers as set out below:

| | From Area codes 01923 or 020: | From the rest of Herts: |
|---|---|---|
| Renewals: | 01923 471373 | 01438 737373 |
| Enquiries: | 01923 471333 | 01438 737333 |
| Textphone: | 01923 471599 | 01438 737599 |

L32  www.hertsdirect.org/librarycatalogue

# BYZANTIUM

## A journey and
## a guide

Desmond Seward and
Susan Mountgarret

**HARRAP**
London

For Charles and Jane Mowbray

First published in Great Britain 1988
by HARRAP Ltd
19-23 Ludgate Hill, London EC4M 7PD

ISBN 0 245-54637-5

Printed and bound in Great Britain by
Mackays of Chatham Limited

# Contents

Acknowledgements   6

Introduction   7

Prologue – Venice and Ravenna   12

Royal Serbia   38

Old Serbia   60

Macedonia, the debatable land   77

Kastoria and Thessalonica   97

Constantinople, city of the world's desire   117

Chios, the chewing-gum island   143

Byzantine Athens   154

Hosios Loukas and the rock monasteries of the Meteora   168

The Despots of Epirus – Ioannina and Arta   184

The Byzantine Peloponnese   201

Byzantium discovered – the Despots of Mistra   224

Appendix · (Travel, hotels etc.)   240

Bibliography   245

Further reading   248

Glossary   249

Index   251

# Acknowledgements

We are especially grateful to Sir Steven Runciman, who has given us so much advice and encouragement. We would also like to thank in particular Mr and Mrs Nigel Clive, Sir William Deakin, Mrs Tamara Talbot-Rice, Mr and the Hon. Mrs Patrick Leigh-Fermor, Mrs Kenelm Digby-Jones, Mr and Mrs Alexander Calligas of Monemvasia, Mr Paul Canellopoulos, and Dr Kosta Balabanov of the Museum of Macedonia at Skopje.

Among the many other people to whom we are indebted are: the late General Mihailo Apostolski; Mr Dušan Miševski of the Macedonian Institute for the Conservation of Historical Monuments; Igumen Justin of Dečani, Mrs Roksanda Timotijević of Prizren; Fr. Mome Dilevski of Sv Nikita, Brazda; Mr Goce Cakoski of Prilep; Mr Soterios Kissas of the Department of Byzantine Antiquities (Thessalonica); Mrs Aygul Koç of Istanbul; Mrs Chrysanthe Baltoyiannis of the Byzantine Museum at Athens; Mr Christos Papageorgiou and Mr Georgios Botetsios of Arta; and Miss Barbara Papadopoulos of the Department of Byzantine Antiquities (Ioannina).

The extracts from *Black Lamb and Grey Falcon*, by Rebecca West, are reprinted by permission of A. D. Peters & Co. Ltd. The extract from *Sailing to Byzantium*, by W. B. Yeats, is reprinted by permission of A. P. Watt Ltd.

# Introduction

$S$ OMEONE said to us 'Byzantium has vanished, just like Atlantis.' We asked a Byzantinist if this were true. 'No, it isn't, though you can't see Byzantium in museums or at exhibitions,' he told us. 'The great Byzantine art treasures are immovable.' So we gave ourselves 50 days in which to see its legacy. This posed many challenges, the greatest of which was to our historical imagination. Travel is easy nowadays, and virtually nowhere remains unexplored; the only discoveries left for a modern traveller are of the intellectual kind.

Voltaire sneered that the Holy Roman Empire was 'neither holy, nor Roman, nor an Empire.' Byzantium was all three. Its Emperor was the Thirteenth Apostle to his subjects who, whether Greek or Slav, whether from Anatolia or Armenia, called themselves *Romaioi*. Its territories were imperially vast. In its heyday it held sway over Greece and the south western Balkans; over what is now Turkey and over parts of Italy; and, until the rise of Islam, over Egypt, Syria and North Africa.

Its foundation was laid in AD 330 when the Emperor Constantine the Great moved his capital from Rome to the ancient Greek city of Byzantium on the Bosporus. Constantinople, the New Rome, became the centre of an Eastern Roman Empire; while the Western disappeared in 476, this would endure for another thousand years.

The Emperor Justinian (527–65), builder of the mighty cathedral of Hagia Sophia, reconquered Italy, together with North Africa and southern Spain, so that his rule extended from the Straits of Gibraltar to Mesopotamia, and from the Danube to the Sudan. In the late sixth century, however, Lombards overran Italy, Slavs and Avars the Balkans, Persians the East. Although the invaders were defeated, Egypt, Syria and North Africa were lost to Islam in the seventh century, Constantinople itself very nearly falling to the Arabs in the eighth. Byzantium survived, restricted to the Balkans and Anatolia – both of which were continually laid waste by savage tribes – and a handful of Italian cities, Venice and Naples remaining dependencies even after the loss of Ravenna in 752.

From the beginning the Orthodox Church, which is inseparable from Byzantium, developed differently from Western Christianity. Its liturgy and its theology were Greek, its Pope was the Holy Emperor – God's living viceroy on earth, 'the King whom St Peter commanded the Faithful to honour'. During the eighth century it was fiercely divided by a movement known as iconoclasm, which condemned the veneration of icons and which lasted for over a hundred years and destroyed many superb works of art.

At the close of the tenth century and the start of the eleventh the ferocious Emperor Basil II – the 'Bulgar Slayer' – reconquered the western Balkans and strengthened the Byzantine presence in southern Italy. The Empire was as rich and powerful as it had ever been. Its capital was the largest in Europe, with over a million inhabitants. But Basil was succeeded by weak rulers. In 1071 Romanus IV was crushingly defeated at Manzikert by the Seljuk Turks who swarmed into Anatolia. Meanwhile the Normans destroyed Byzantine Italy. The Empire was saved for another century by the Comnenus dynasty, who held the Balkans and began to reconquer Anatolia, containing the Turks and surviving the influx of Western barbarians during the First Crusade. Its last members were no less inept, however, than the heirs of Basil II.

In 1204 the Venetians persuaded the soldiers of the Fourth Crusade to sack Constantinople. The Latin Empire of the East was set up and Greece was divided into Frankish principalities. A number of Byzantine successor states emerged, of which the Empire of Nicaea became the foremost. Nicaea recaptured Constantinople in 1261, but Byzantium never fully recovered. Inexorably the Osmanli

Turks subdued all Anatolia, beginning the enslavement of the Balkans in the fourteenth century. Parasitical Venetian merchants monopolized what was left of Constantinople's trade while bankrupt Emperors indulged in futile civil wars. Only Bayezid's defeat by Tamberlane in 1402 postponed the fall of Constantinople.

Though they were reduced to little more than their capital and the Peloponnese, nevertheless the final rulers of the house of Palaeologus presided over a remarkable Greek renaissance in art and scholarship, in particular at the city state of Mistra, near Sparta. Toward the very end they even began to reconquer northern Greece from the Latins, until stopped by angry Turks. Under different circumstances they might well have restored the Empire. In 1453 Sultan Mehmet II stormed his way into the New Rome, however, and the last Roman Emperor of the East, Constantine XI, sought and met a lonely death in battle at the Romanus Gate. It was the end of a realm which had renewed itself time and again, which had preserved Europe from Eastern invasion for a millenium, at whose capital art, literature and the luxury of the Caesars had continued for a thousand years after the fall of old Rome.

A part of the Byzantine world, though outside the Empire, was the medieval Kingdom of Serbia. At the end of the twelfth century the great Nemanja family began to create a realm which eventually included all Serbia, Macedonia and Albania and much of northern Greece. Its religion was Orthodoxy, its art and culture essentially Byzantine. All its rulers' luxuries – and many of their brides – came from the shores of the Bosporus. In 1345 Stephen IV Uroš proclaimed himself Tsar but died before he was able to conquer Constantinople and establish himself on the Imperial throne. His dynasty perished with his son, while much of Serbia was conquered by the Turks as a consequence of the terrible defeat at Kosovo in 1389. Nevertheless the last doomed Serbian princes remained entirely Byzantine in outlook until they were finally overwhelmed in 1458. Many of the Serbs' beautiful churches and frescoes have since been magnificently restored by the Yugoslav Government.

Only in the present century have people learnt to appreciate Byzantine civilization once more. Voltaire dismissed it as 'a worthless collection of oracles and miracles', Gibbon as 'the triumph of barbarism and superstition'. Modern historians, however, have revealed what was at once the most spiritual and the most opulent culture the world has ever known. Contemporaries were fully aware of its beauty and grandeur, to the point of obsession.

For Byzantium and its capital awed and fascinated not merely those within but those outside its mighty walls. John Beckwith gives us some idea of what it must have been like:

> The Augusti, the court, the imperial and patriarchal processions, the hymns and chants, the great diadems and robes, the high cosmetics and the heavy scents, the multiplicity of races, the great dromons breathing Greek fire, the imperial barge glittering with gold and purple, the eunuchs, secretaries, generals, admirals in the different costumes of their rank are no more than a dream on a summer's day.

Yet, if one is prepared to travel, Byzantium may still be seen, not just in Greece and Turkey but in Italy and Yugoslavia.

Both the authors of this book have been besotted with Byzantium for many years. One spent part of his childhood in Bucharest – his earliest language was Romanian – and besides hearing of the painted churches of Moldavia from his parents had acquired a lifelong interest in Orthodox Christianity. His first knowledge of the Eastern Empire had been picked up from Gibbon's *Decline and Fall of the Roman Empire*, later much altered by the works of J.B.Bury, Charles Diehl, Robert Byron and – above all – Sir Steven Runciman. The other author also dates her first interest from reading Gibbon, developing it with André Grabar's *Byzantine Painting* when it appeared in the 1950s, and with the books of Steven Runciman. She at least had seen something of Byzantium, having visited Ravenna and Moscow (where she had been enthralled by the icons in the Tretyakov). But neither had ever set foot in mainland Greece, let alone Yugoslavia.

After an Italian prologue, the search became a journey through the Balkans to Constantinople and then to the Peloponnese. Since we had only seven weeks we left out Sicily and Bulgaria, and even Mount Athos (where women are not allowed). We consulted standard works for a list of masterpieces, planning an itinerary which as far as possible took into account distances, road surfaces and hotels. A sometimes rather frenetic race against time added an element of excitement. One of us is that stock character from English fiction, a bachelor of fifty who writes historical biographies or the odd article on food and wine, living quietly in Brighton; the other, in her forties, is from the gentlest of the Yorkshire dales, where she gardens and breeds gundogs. Both of us were set in our ways, fearful of discomfort, of bad meals, grimy baths and lumpy beds; in recent years we had rarely if ever gone to bed unfed or unbathed, and never met a bedbug or a flea.

This book is essentially a narrative for armchair travellers, an account of a quest for a world which died 500 years ago. It is also intended, however, as a very simple outline guide for anyone who, like us, has fallen under the quite extraordinarily potent spell still cast by Byzantium. We have tried to write a book which will make it easy for others to follow in our footsteps.

# Prologue–Venice and Ravenna

'With our minds we all know what Byzantium was. We are aware that the Eastern continuance of the Roman Empire was a supremely beautiful civilisation . . . an art that is unique in its nobility . . . which makes all other arts seem a little naïve or gross.'

Rebecca West, *Black Lamb and Grey Falcon*

**W**E ARRIVED at Venice in the darkness of a winter's night. A few lights shone dimly from the occasional palazzo or from the end of a deserted alley, but it was too cold to remain on the water bus's deck and peer through the gloom. As we landed it began to rain again, the rain which had brought the highest floods for years and, only two days earlier, had forced the waiters in our hotel to serve breakfast in gumboots. But next morning the sun was shining, the air crisp if bitterly cold, and we could walk round the city unencumbered by the customary hordes of fellow tourists.

Venice is best seen on foot, not by vaporetto or gondola. We often lost our way in the maze of tiny streets, some so narrow that two fat men cannot pass one another, only to emerge in some secret, unsuspected square with something new and pleasing in it. Because it was winter we saw more garbage boats and water hearses than gondolas, the level of the water making it difficult for the latter's high prows to clear the bridges. There were glorious exceptions. One afternoon we were up by the Ghetto when two magnificent oared barges, one blue and silver, the other red and gold, with oarsmen in liveries of the same colours, came sweeping along the Cannaregio in a rehearsal for the regatta. For this was just before Lent and during the Carnival of Venice. Many people wore costume all day long, dressing as Moors, minstrels, popes, cardinals, dragons, three-headed monsters or silver Martians, though mostly in the three-cornered hats and traditional white masks from the days when Venice was still the Most Serene Republic. As in the eighteenth century, many were tourists. Thirty years ago Carnivale was forgotten by all save the children, but now it is big business. Whole shops are devoted to the sale of fantastic clothes and masks, the latter often very beautiful. We wondered what they sold for the rest of the year – perhaps models of gondolas and St Mark's.

For the vast majority of visitors Venice is the Doges' Palace, Santa Maria della Salute, Tiepolo and Guardi, Titian and Tintoretto, and of course St Mark's. Not very many realize that, behind its much altered façade, the latter is a Byzantine church copied from the church of the Holy Apostles at Constantinople. The links between the Serenissima and the Golden Horn were very strong indeed.

Venice was a Byzantine satellite for centuries, nominally subject to the Emperor at Constantinople. When the Byzantines lost Ravenna in 752, she became the Empire's principal city in Italy, the centre of cultural contact between the West and the East. Even after the re-appearance of an Emperor in the West Venetians continued to look to Constantinople. As late as the eleventh century the Doge was considered to be the Eastern Emperor's exarch (governor) in Italy. In the same century Doge Domenico Selvo married an Emperor's sister who shocked the Venetians by her luxurious ways, in particular by using 'a two-pronged instrument of gold to convey food to her mouth.' (To this day the Venetian for fork is not the Italian *forchetta* but the Greek word *piron*, an unconscious echo of Byzantine table manners.) The very title 'Doge' (*Dux Venetiae*) was a Byzantine one, while the state barge, the *Buccintoro*, was painted red in imitation of the Imperial barge. Even the gondola bears an unmistakable resemblance to the caïque or Bosporus wherry. By the second half of the twelfth century there were at least 20,000 Venetians living at Constantinople, an enormous number when one realizes that the total population of Venice in 1170 was 64,000.

We decided to begin our search for Byzantium with a visit to the Accademia on the other side of the Grand Canal to St Mark's. Our hotel, the Luna, was conveniently situated just off the Piazza and near a water-bus stop, but rather than cross the Canal by bus we preferred to walk.

Climbing the steep wooden bridge of the Accademia we found

ourselves in front of the Gallerie. We hoped to find examples of the influence of Byzantine art on that of Venice but, apart from a very beautiful polyptych by Paolo Veneziano with a typically Byzantine Baptism of Christ, we found nothing. We sped past acres of bare flesh and contorted limbs – nothing remotely Byzantine here. Then, in the very last room, we found what has been called Byzantium's last official gift to the Venetian Republic. It is the reliquary containing a fragment of the True Cross which Cardinal Bessarion presented to the Scuola della Caritá in 1463. The fragment is housed in a silver gilt cross with Christ flanked by the figures of the Emperor Constantine and his mother the Empress Helena, the archaeologist reputed to have discovered the True Cross. The reliquary was made in the early fourteenth century for Irene, niece of Michael IX Palaeologus, and later belonged to Gregory the Confessor, the last Byzantine Patriarch of Constantinople. The cover, which is about fifty years later than the reliquary, is painted with scenes from the life of Christ. Ioannes Bessarion (1403–72) was born at Trebizond but educated at Constantinople, after which he spent some years in a monastery near Mistra. He became Metropolitan of Nicaea and was one of the Byzantine delegates to the Council of Florence which met in 1438–9 to re-unite Catholics and Orthodox. There he became convinced that the Catholic claims were justified. In 1440 he settled in Italy, later being made a Cardinal. When Constantinople fell he was unstinting in his generous welcome to refugees, especially scholars, and he did his best to persuade the West to mount a Crusade against the Turks. He also collected and copied every Greek manuscript he could lay his hands on, bequeathing some 800 to the Venetians. In 1515 the Venetian Senate ordered the building of a library to house them. The collection is now in the Marciana Library near St Mark's. Sadly for us, it was closed in the winter.

It was to St Mark's that our steps led us next. It is impossible to keep away from it for long. The first church here, designed by a Byzantine architect, was consecrated in 832. Its purpose was to house the body of St Mark, which had been recently stolen from Alexandria and shipped to Venice hidden under a consignment of pork so as to deter Muslim customs officers. In the following century it was severely damaged by fire during riots in a rebellion against Doge Pietro IV Candiano; he fled with his son from the burning palace to the church where he was captured and then murdered. A new church was quickly built, incorporating what was left of the old one. The present building, which became a cathedral only in the nineteenth century, was begun in 1063 by Doge Domenico Contarini who again employed a Byzantine architect. It was modelled on the since destroyed church of the Holy Apostles at Constantinople. Here at least the influence of Byzantium was apparent.

Ruskin describes the interior of St Mark's as an illuminated manuscript in mosaic. The mosaics are an extraordinary mixture of no great merit but overwhelming effect. The earliest date from the twelfth century, inspired by illustrations in a sixth-century Bible. As in churches of that period at Constantinople, each group of mosaics has a common theme; besides the acquisition of the Evangelist's body and Man's Creation and Fall they show the careers of Cain and Abel, of Noah and his Ark, of Abraham, Joseph and Moses, while from the New Testament come Christ's Passion and Crucifixion, the Descent into Hell, the Resurrection and the Ascension. Countless other scriptural episodes are represented, the whole dominated by Christ in Majesty on the main apse. They were added to continually until the nineteenth century. Nothing could be less Byzantine than a fourteenth-century portrait of Salome in a skin-tight red dress slit up to the thigh and edged with white fur.

Some of the pillars and bas-reliefs which decorate the exterior are pieces saved from the original church. The great bronze doors were the gift of the Emperor Alexius I. But much is plunder from Byzantium.

The Venetians made their fortunes, and that of their city, at Constantinople. Here they sold their earliest commodities, salt and slaves. Here they bought – for resale at vast profit – gold, silks, Russian sables and the pepper and spices so much prized by Western Europe as the sole means of rendering food palatable. From here came every known luxury.

Eventually the Venetians came to see Byzantium as a commercial rival which had to be brought to heel, while they cast increasingly greedy eyes on its riches. For their part the Byzantines began to fear these piratical, slave-trading, merchant venturers who had commercial privileges far in excess of anything the native traders of Constantinople enjoyed themselves. In 1171 Emperor Manuel I confiscated their property at Constantinople. Venice responded swiftly by sacking the islands of Chios and Lesbos. Relations were broken off for a period of ten years. Manuel died in 1180 and the Empire was ruled by his Latin widow, Mary of Antioch, and her favourite, the unpopular Alexius Comnenus, nephew of the late Emperor. Hatred of the pair grew to such an extent that in 1182 revolt broke out in the capital. Alexius was thrown into prison and blinded and all foreigners living in Constantinople were massacred. The Republic bided its time. In 1202 Doge Enrico Dandolo, a blind octogenarian of truly diabolical cunning, persuaded an army of Crusaders en route for the Holy Land in Venetian ships to stop off at Constantinople and 'restore' a Byzantine pretender; two years later Dandolo had them storm, sack and occupy the city. Venice's share of the loot was summed up in the Doge's new title 'Lord of One Quarter and a Half (quarter) of the Roman Empire'. She amassed vast quantities of plunder, compelling her merchants to bring back a proportion of the value of their cargo in looted works of art for the adornment of the Serenissima. Much of the Byzantine stonework one sees decorating the churches and palaces of Venice was shipped home as ballast.

The most famous plunder from Constantinople is surely the four bronze horses which formerly embellished the west facade of St Mark's. Reproductions now face the elements and the pollution from Mestre, the originals being stabled in a room off that Byzantine institution, the church's gallery for women. These fourth-century BC Greek equine masterpieces somehow escaped being melted down in Constantinople to pay the Crusaders' wages – the fate of the Hippodrome's other bronze statues. Perhaps their incredible beauty saved them. They were erected on the west facade some time before 1270, as is proved by the only remaining thirteenth-century mosaic on the exterior, which shows the church with the horses in situ. Apart from a spell in Paris, where Napoleon had them displayed at the Tuilleries, they have been at St Mark's ever since the Fourth Crusade. A long time; yet they had already adorned the Hippodrome at Constantinople for even longer. Originating at Delphi, Nero took them to Rome from whence Constantine removed them to enrich his new capital on the Bosporus.

Much of the loot of 1204 perished in a disastrous fire at the Treasury of St Mark's not long after. A survivor was the Madonna Nicopeia. Saved from tourist hordes in an area of the church roped off for prayer, she exudes ineffable peace and holiness, for once she was the 'Victory Bringer', carried into battle before the Emperors; no icon is more venerated by Venetians. It has been repainted too often to be dated accurately. The fourteenth-century frame, set with jewels, is Venetian work, but the enamels are Byzantine from the twelfth century. On special occasions the icon is hung with pearls which only detract from her beauty. In the same chapel is a Byzantine marble relief, of great sensitivity, of the Madonna dello Schioppo.

Our attention was drawn – by an accident – to St Mark's handsome floor, part of which also dates from the twelfth century. A smartly dressed American woman standing beside us clutched at her throat and we saw a shower of pearls pouring down onto the mosaic pavement. We hunted for pearls among peacocks strutting between vines and hawks sporting brown- and white-checked trousers that swooped on black and white hares. All were immediately recognizable as Byzantine. The beads rolled toward the altar at great speed and we realized that the floor, which only fifty years earlier had been flat, was now at an alarming tilt. Nothing brought home to us better just how fast Venice is sinking.

The most fabulous of all Venetian treasurers, the gold altar-piece known as the Pala d'Oro, also incorporates loot. The first Pala was commissioned in 976 by Doge Pietro Orseolo and made in Constantinople by Byzantine craftsmen. In 1105 Doge Ordelafo Falier ordered a new one, but this was completely remade in 1209 to incorporate plunder from Constantinople. It was at this stage that what had been an enamel of the Sebastocrator Isaac Comnenus lost its head and was given that of a doge instead, the new head being smaller than those on other enamels and slightly askew. It is significant that the doge appears in a Sebastocrator's robes and that the enamel of Isaac's brother, Emperor Alexius, which must have adorned the Pala of 1105, was discarded. The Empress Irene was allowed to survive, however, doing double duty as a saint and as a companion for the doge. Finally in 1345 Doge Andrea Dandolo employed a famous Siennese goldsmith, Gian Paolo Boninsegna, to create a frame to contain the Pala's enamels together with as many more either brought from Constantinople by fleeing Venetians in 1261 or made in Venetian workshops. Now the Pala and its 137 enamels were set with literally thousands of jewels. The stones seemed so incredible to the French invaders of 1797 that, unable to believe they were real, they left them in situ.

As the Pala faces the wall behind the altar is it not visible from the body of the church. We had to buy a ticket for the Treasury to be able to go behind to see it. In fact it was only ever on view on special occasions. In 1345 a cover was made for it by Paolo Veneziano and his sons, painted with episodes from the life of St Mark. It is this cover one sees from the front. Less startling but equally interesting is the sixth-century ciborium in front of the Pala. The pillars are carved with scenes from the life of Christ, His Passion (represented by a lamb in a medallion on the Cross) and the first known depiction of the Harrowing of Hell. The pillars are quite remarkable for the quality of the carving.

Our visit to the Treasury itself was a disaster since most of its contents were absent, on exhibition in America. Fortunately we had seen them at the same exhibition in London and could remember marvellous gold and enamel reliquaries containing fragments of the True Cross, chalices and patens of onyx, alabaster or sardonyx, and cups of carved rock-crystal from Roman Egypt which had been set with gold and jewels in the workshops of Constantinople. Much of this was probably loot though it would be unfair to place everything made before 1204 into that category – the Venetians must have bought church plate or received it as a gift before they sacked the city. Some of the Treasury's most prized possessions once belonged to the then eleven-year-old Emperor John V Palaeologus; in 1342 his mother the Empress Anna pledged them to the Republic as security for a loan of 30,000 ducats. Although the Venetians reminded successive Emperors of this loan, the Empire was in such dire financial straits until the bitter end that she was never able to redeem them. In 1370 John, during a lengthy absence from Constantinople seeking aid from the West, stayed for a year at Venice. Unable to repay a loan of 4000 ducats and with no money or credit with which to equip himself for travel he was a virtual prisoner of the Serenissima until rescued by his son Manuel. One of the most interesting of all the Treasury's marvels is a votive crown given by Leo VI to a church – probably the Holy Apostles – at Constantinople; on a gold circlet and surrounded by pearls are enamel medallions of Leo and the Apostles. From the reign of Constantine the Emperors were considered equal in rank with the Apostles – iso-apostolos – a breath-taking claim exquisitely expressed in this ninth-century crown.

We came out into the Piazza to find it full of brightly dressed revellers, and workmen erecting stands in front of Florian's and

Quadri's for the weekend's entertainments. The two cafés' orchestras used to compete during Carnivale, the sentimental music of one vying with the strident tones of the other on opposite sides of the Piazza; now a truce has been negotiated, the municipality providing piped music for much of the day. A television crew had discovered what must have been an old actor or perhaps a male model, who looked at least eighty. He posed for ages after the filming had finished, drawing everyone with a camera. Dressed in white, from the neck down he was the perfect eighteenth-century Beau, though his heavily rouged and painted wreck of a face was that of an old queen. On his head he wore a huge cartwheel of a hat from which sprouted a large pair of brown felt antlers. We were not sure whether he was trying to represent a cuckold or some appalling figure from Italian literature.

On our way to the tiny bar opposite the Doges' Palace for a restorative Punt e Mes we passed further fragments of Byzantium and the Roman Empire. Two square columns outside the south door of St Mark's came from Constantinople, as did several bas-reliefs set into the wall of the Treasury. The porphyry sculpture of the Four Tetrarchs at the corner of the building was carved in Syria about the year 300. The four co-rulers of the Empire – grim-faced Roman officers armed with eagle-hilted swords reminiscent of duck-handled umbrellas – are embracing one another.

Before lunch at the Città di Vittorio we strolled through the Correr Museum where we found numerous Byzantine and Post-Byzantine icons, mostly from Crete. In another room a small rectangular Last Supper which caught our eye turned out to have been painted by the most famous of all Cretan artists. Domenico Theotocopoulos – El Greco – became a pupil of Titian at Venice before going to Rome and thence to Spain.

The Città di Vittorio was promisingly full of Venetians. Although the cooking was not of the highest we tucked into tripe soup and chicken with white polenta. Most of our companions appeared to be business men or shopkeepers and were in dark suits. One tall middle-aged man wore red velvet; however, his knee-breeches were fastened with velcro, a most practical anachronism. We kept on meeting him all over Venice, as we did a group of three masked couples, also in eighteenth-century dress, whose tricornes were trimmed with red white or blue maribou. We were never able to catch a glimpse of their faces; but somehow it was reassuring to see familiar shapes in a sea of anonymous human beings.

After lunch we walked to the Rialto, the ancient market and banking centre of Venice, to look for Byzantine palaces since the city's oldest palazzi – dating from the thirteenth century – are based on those of Constantinople. They were never more than two stories high, with a low tower at each end. Between these towers an arcade called a curia ran the length of each floor. The best example is a nineteenth-century restoration, the Fondaco dei Turchi, which although it has lost much of its character in the process, is believed to be a faithful reconstruction of the original. The Veneto-Byzantine palaces are of enormous importance since virtually all Byzantium's secular buildings have been destroyed, and these tell us something of domestic life under the Empire. Even the beautiful Gothic palazzi of Venice, with their delicate tracery and pointed arches, developed from them, and there is no major change in design until the fifteenth century. Some, such as the Ca' d'Oro, are Byzantine at ground level and Gothic above, fire having swept the quarter in the fourteenth century. The Ca' da Mosto is a sad crumbling building which still retains very beautiful Byzantine carvings above its watergate. Having been a private house for centuries it became one of the city's most fashionable hotels, 'The White Lion', patronized by among others the Emperor Franz-Josef. Now it is in a sorry state, urgently in need of restoration. Much better preserved, at least as a facade, is another erstwhile hotel, Palazzo Loredan (the building behind having been gutted and turned into municipal offices). The land entrance to the Ca' da Mosto is approached through the sottoportega of Palazzo Falier, which shares the same small island; this sottoportega is one of the earliest in Venice and, as the name suggests, is an alley going through the lowest arcade of the palace and under the portega or main hall above. We walked down it and found ourselves in a courtyard full of junk. The ground floor of 'The White Lion' is now filled with rubbish washed in from the Grand Canal. King Henry IV of England must have stayed in a palace like this when he visited Venice in 1393, before he became king, on his way back from his pilgrimage to Jerusalem. He had eight shields, painted with his arms and those of his knights, hung up in St Mark's.

Our wanderings back to our hotel took us to Campo Santo Stefano. We sat in the sun, drinking minute cups of very strong espresso and eating fritelli carnivali. These are a type of doughnut containing currants and chopped peel, filled with crème patissière or zabaglione. They are eaten only during the Carnival. The eighteenth-century painter Pietro Longhi shows a woman crouching in the street cooking them on a small brazier for passers-by. At their best they are delicious but, like all doughnuts, they can be stodgy and indigestible.

On a miserably cold morning, shivering in the dank mist which swept in from the Lagoon, we walked to the Fondamenta Nuove to catch the boat for Torcello. As we waited for it we could just see the cemetery island of San Michele, where Stravinsky was buried among the cypresses. Tenancies are short here – after twelve years the bones are dug up and thrown into a common grave, a wretched end for the mortal remains of a genius.

Torcello, not Venice, was the island where fugitives from the Lombards first found refuge in the Lagoon. Its cathedral dates from the seventh century when there were close links with the Byzantine Exarch at Ravenna, as an inscription of 639 testifies. It was a water city like Venice, rich and populous. In the tenth century that very well-informed Emperor, Constantine VII Porphyrogenitus, refers to 'the great trading station' of Torcello. Now it is pitifully desolate, a bleak and haunted place, inhabited by a few small-holders and wild-fowlers. Apart from a handful of cottages, the sole buildings are the cathedral itself, the adjoining church of Santa Fosca, a converted farmhouse containing a tiny museo archeologico, and one of the best restaurants in the Veneto – shut during the winter. The jacaranda trees with their rattling black pods give the neglected canal which leads to the cathedral a peculiarly dismal air.

There was still water on the cathedral's floor, from the recent flood. One scarcely noticed it, so wonderful are the mosaics. They date from the beginning of the twelfth century and unlike those in St Mark's are unquestionably the work of Greek artists. On the apse is a strangely elongated Virgin with an extraordinarily tender and compassionate young face, very tall and slender, very feminine. Holding the Child on her left arm she stands alone on her golden background, in striking contrast to the cluttered scenes in St Mark's. Below her are the Twelve Apostles. It has been suggested that she is later than the Apostles and dates from about 1190, replacing a figure of Christ.

The Last Judgment on the wall opposite is more Western in feeling. Although drastically restored in the nineteenth century, so that the top two rows are almost complete replacements, enough remains in the bottom three rows to tell us what was required to bring the reality of Hell to twelfth-century man. On the left fabulous beasts are devouring lost souls; the beasts look rather like birds with beakfuls of worms, only in this case the worms are hands and feet. Angels blow the Horrid Horn and on the right a siren sits on a rock with the Damned swimming in the sea around her. In another row the Good are on the left while on the right two angels with long poles are forcing the Damned – including a Byzantine Emperor and Empress – into the flames as playthings for little blue devils. Below are grinning skulls with worms writhing in the eye sockets, a subject beloved in the West for centuries to come.

In August 1986 experts began work on removing the recently discovered twelfth-century mosaic head of a saint from a church in Wales at Talygarn. Its nineteenth-century founder brought the mosaic back from Torcello when the Last Judgment was undergoing restoration and had it set up high above his family pew. At Torcello the second row of the Last Judgment shows Christ flanked by the Apostles and saints.

The church of Santa Fosca also dates from the twelfth century. It is an octagonal church with a beautiful ambulatory on five sides and unmistakably Greek pillars and capitals. Its most Byzantine quality is the brick ornamentation and blind arcades on the outside of the main apse – something one would expect to see in Greece but not in Italy. Sadly it contains no mosaics or frescoes.

On the way back we passed by Murano, where unwary visitors are dragooned into touring the very commercial glass works and then pressed to buy expensive and, on the whole, hideous products. The island's reputation dates from 1291 when the factories were transferred here from Venice because of the risk of fire. With the factories came Byzantine methods – and almost certainly Byzantine craftsmen – from Constantinople, where exquisite cups, lamps and vases had been produced at large factories. During the later Middle Ages Murano glass was on sale throughout Italy. The coloured glass which we generally think of as Venetian dates only from 1605, however, when Girolamo Magnati, a native of Murano, discovered the secret of colouring glass without dimming its transparency or lustre. In 1621 James Howell wrote home to England 'I was, since I came hither, in Murano, a little island about the distance of Lambeth from London, where Crystal-Glass is made; and 'tis a rare sight to see a whole Street, where on the one side there are twenty Furnaces together at work'. He adds that even in Venice 'they cannot make Crystal-Glass in that perfection, for beauty and lustre, as in Murano'.

For us the most precious things on Murano are in its cathedral of Santi Maria e Donato, rebuilt in 1125 to celebrate the acquisition of a prized relic – the body of St Donatus together with the bones of a dragon he had killed. It is a brick basilica in the form of a Greek cross, with two arcaded loggias outside the apse. Its great glory is the mosaic of the virgin in the apse, deep blue against the gold background, even taller and more elongated than the Lady of Torcello. Like her, she is the creation of Byzantine artists but of a lesser period, that of the Palaeologean renaissance in the fourteenth century. The fine mosaic pavement is much earlier, from about 1140.

As we left Murano the mist began to clear and a wintry sun broke through, shining on the plumes of smoke from the furnaces at Mestre. It brought the people in carnival clothes out into the squares and markets of Venice. In Campo San Lorenzo, not far from the Hellenic Institute – we went there to see the two very beautiful fourteenth-century icons from Constantinople – we met an enchanting four-year-old dressed in a black cloak and tricorne of the sort Casanova must have worn, with red breeches and a silver-topped cane. As we approached he was having trouble with his breeches and his mother was adjusting his dress. Plainly embarrassed at being caught with his trousers down, he drew himself up to his full height and gave us the most disdainful and withering glare imaginable. Our compliment of 'Molto elegante!' was received with a stiff bow and a haughty 'Grazie'. Chastened, we went off to look for a restaurant and lunch.

Food in Venice is expensive and usually disappointing. The markets are full of marvellous looking vegetables which never seem to find their way into restaurants. Mountains of tomatoes, peppers and aubergines, sprays of artichokes hung up with their leaves, mounds of corn salad or gallinelle, radicchio trevigiano and spinach decorate the stalls, but for the tourist on a strict budget are no more than a mouth-watering spectacle.

After lunch we decided to go to Santa Maria della Salute. The most popular of their churches among the Venetians themselves, it is not remotely Byzantine. Built in thanksgiving for deliverance from a terrible visitation of the plague, it stands in Baroque splendour on the opposite bank of the Grand Canal from St Mark's. Reaching it entails a particularly pretty walk through the streets of Venice, across the wooden bridge of the Accademia, down lanes filled with fish-stalls and little shops selling household goods, dried funghi and coffee beans. There are tiny gardens tucked away behind Palazzo Contarini del Zaffo, and wide tree-lined streets take one to the enormous expanse of the Giudecca Canal. From the broad shallow steps of Santa Maria one can look across to the Gritti Hotel and the enchanting Gothic House of Desdemona; Palazzo Contarini Fasan, with only one room on each floor, must be the smallest of all Venetian palaces.

The interior of Santa Maria della Salute is simple, dignified and satisfying, the calm before the Rococo. On the altar is the icon brought from Crete in 1670, just after the island fell to the Turks, the Virgin Mesopanditissa. Although a late work, with its haunting melancholy and infinite sadness it has all the depth of feeling of the best Byzantine icons.

On a rather circuitous route back to the hotel we found ourselves in the Campo San Polo. Although we had not been there before it somehow seemed familiar, but with something missing. Then we realized that the deep red building opposite was the Palazzo Soranzo and that we had seen it in a painting in the Correr by the seventeenth-century artist Giuseppe Heinz. In the painting Campo San Polo is filled with men and bulls rushing in all directions, dogs snarling at a bear and elegant ladies in white cloaks and carnival masks picking their way fastidiously through the throng. Until 1802 there was still bull bating in the squares during Carnivale, but now there were only a few children in carnival dress playing very carefully so as not to spoil their finery, and two youths testing the amplifiers for a rock concert due to take place that evening.

In the next square two girls were making up the faces of passers-by for the evening passegiata. Under their expert hands clowns, butterflies and cats emerged to join the gathering throng, moving as though by common consent to the Piazza. We were swept along with them, unable in the narrow alleys to go against the tide of people. Then we were disgorged in the dusk in front of St Mark's. Here light and the music of Vivaldi – after all a Venetian born and bred – reigned supreme.

The Michelin guide allows four hours for seeing the main sights of Ravenna. In winter, when everything shuts at 5.00 p.m., it is best to spend a night there. Our train from Venice arrived, so we thought, in time for lunch. A fine drizzle had already made the day gloomy enough when we reached our chosen restaurant, 'La Gardela', to find it *in restauro* – 'Closed for Restoration'. This was a phrase we were to learn to dread in many languages before completing our journey, though usually it applied only to churches. We trudged sullenly through the rain looking for somewhere, anywhere, to eat; unlike the sensible French, who take the whole family out to a meal, it seems that on Sundays the Ravennese lunch at home.

By the end of the fourth century the Goths had hacked their way down to the Danube, the north-eastern frontier of the Roman Empire. When employed as mercenaries, they posed a constant threat. In 401, under the leadership of Alaric, Visigoths (Western Goths) poured into Italy. Although defeated, it was terrifyingly clear that they were going to return. Honorius moved his capital from Milan to Ravenna, a water city which anticipated Venice, protected by the sea and by marshes. Its port of Classis, three miles away, was the naval base for the Empire's East Mediterranean fleet.

Son of the mighty Theodosius, last Emperor to rule both East and West, Honorius had succeeded to the throne of the West in 395 when he was eleven. His consuming passion was poultry, and he named his favourite hen 'Roma'. Procopius tells us how this led to a serious misunderstanding in 410, when a courtier burst into the Imperial presence with the news 'Roma has perished!' Horrified, Honorius protested 'But she was feeding out of my hand only an hour ago.' When it was explained that 'Roma' in this case meant the Eternal City, which had just fallen to the Visigoths, the Emperor angrily rebuked the courtier for leading him to believe his bird was dead.

The only building in Ravenna from Honorius's reign is the Orthodox Baptistery, which is not open on Sunday afternoons. So we made our way to the one remaining basilica built by his half-sister Galla Placidia, that of S.Giovanni Evangelista. Few princesses have led a more eventful life. During the sack of Rome she was captured and apparently raped before being dragged off as a hostage to Aquitaine. There she was married to the Visigoth King Adolf, with whom she fell in love. When he was murdered in 414 she was thrown into prison. Ransomed (for 600,000 sacks of wheat) by Honorius, she was then forced by him to marry his commander-in-chief Constantius, who became her co-Emperor. After the death of Constantius she quarrelled violently with her half-brother, who is said to have had incestuous designs on her, and in 425 fled to Constantinople. Honorious died from dropsy only a few months later, whereupon the Augusta Galla Placidia returned to Italy with Valentinian III, her six-year-old son by Constantius, to be the real ruler of the Western world under her death in 450.

She built S.Giovanni Evangelista as a thanks-offering for her deliverance from a storm on the way back from Constantinople. Already much altered, this was badly bombed during the last War, and what we saw is only a modern reconstruction of her original church, using ancient materials as much as possible. Beautiful enough in its own right, with a sense of space and light, it nonetheless gives a false impression of what it must have been like in her day. None of the mosaics showing the family of Theodosius, which once filled the walls above the nave, has survived, nor those in the apse. Fragments from the mosaic floor have been mounted on boards and hung around the walls of the two aisles, but they make the building look like a museum rather than the place of worship it still is. We needed a bit of colour to cheer us up.

One of the most colourful interiors in Ravenna is also a foundation of Galla Placidia. We walked through streets containing a number of attractive houses, some clearly from the sixteenth century when the city was Venetian territory. (One dates from the eleventh, the former Palazzo Guiccioli, the family home of the husband of Byron's mistress.) The drizzle had stopped and a few people had ventured out on foot or on bicycles of lurid but cheerful hues: fuchsia, lime-green or yellow. Whenever we had to ask directions we were helped with a smile and an offer to show us the way. Charming and hospitable, the people of Ravenna always seem to have time for strangers, very unlike Venetians. We began to warm to this rather plain city.

The Mausoleum of Galla Placidia was built by her as part of her church of Santa Croce, long since destroyed. If intended as a mausoleum (and also as a *martyrium* dedicated to St Lawrence), it is unlikely that it ever contained the Augusta's remains. She died in Rome and was probably buried in the Theodosian tomb near St Peter's. Due to subsidence the building, a brick Latin cross in the Milanese style, appears rather squat. In addition it is overshadowed by the magnificent bulk of San Vitale, its neighbour in the same small park, and can easily be missed. On entering one finds oneself in a different world. Clearly Galla Placidia was influenced by religious art in Constantinople, but the art historians cannot agree whether the mosaicists reponsible here came from Constantinople, Syria or Rome. However one does not need a specialized knowledge of early Christian art to enjoy the little building's incredible beauty.

Roman and Byzantine mosaicists used the same methods. Coloured glass was poured into tins and then marked out in small squares, producing cubes ('*tesserae*') with rough and smooth surfaces. Gold leaf was sandwiched between two layers of clear glass of unequal thickness; for a dazzling effect it was used with the finer, smoother layer uppermost, but for a more subdued rich glow it was turned over so that the gold was further from the surface and slightly veiled by irregularities in the glass. As well as glass, marble tesserae were employed (especially on faces and hands), mother of pearl, enamel, and very occasionally, precious stones. They were set on the wall at an angle calculated so that they could best be seen by people (generally assumed to be five feet six inches tall) standing in the middle of the church, in the dim light of oil lamps or candles. They were rarely signed since their true creator was considered the patron who had commissioned them.

The dome in the Mausoleum is dark blue, studded with golden stars symbolizing the Faithful in Heaven, dominated by a gold cross. Christ is represented on a tympanum as the Good Shepherd: he sits in a rocky landscape surrounded by six sheep, one of which raises its head for His caress. The entire vault is full of symbols of the New Testament. Stags and doves drink from the Waters of Eternal Life and True Faith. Vines clamber up the walls, a reference to the Gospel of St John – 'I am the vine, ye are the branches: he that abideth in Me and I in him, the same bringeth forth much fruit'. On the lunette opposite Christ is St Lawrence literally running toward the gridiron on which he was roasted, bearing the church plate and a book of Scripture whose hiding place he refused to reveal; at the side of the menacing gridiron there is a cupboard containing the Gospels, a fascinating glimpse of ancient library furniture. The intrados of the arch above has a marvellous geometric pattern whose startling colours complement admirably the raging flames below – cobalt and indigo, emerald and pea-green, crimson, orange, gold and white.

They would not be out of place in a gallery of twentieth-century art.

These were the oldest Christian mosaics either of us had ever seen and we were amazed by their state of preservation as well as by their vitality. We were fortunate in being able to compare them with indisputably Byzantine mosaics, those at San Vitale next door. Ravenna was still in Ostrogoth (Eastern Goth) hands at this church's foundation in 525; but King Theodoric, who then ruled Italy regarded, in theory at least, the Emperor of Constantinople as his overlord, while the Emperors saw him as their viceroy. The building was begun by Bishop Ecclesius, after a visit to the Golden Horn with Pope John I. The unknown architect must certainly have visited Constantinople, since San Vitale is very similar to the church there of SS. Sergius and Bacchus, and unlike any other building of that period in Italy. A Greek banker, Julian Argentarius, a resident of Ravenna, gave 26,000 gold solidi towards its construction, and it was consectrated on 19 April 548 by Bishop Maximian. A brick edifice, it is octagonal in shape with a central core surmounted by a dome resting on a circle of columns and piers. Between the columns and the external walls are two ambulatories, one above the other, the upper being a gallery reserved for women. There are three apsidal chapels, one of which – longer than the other two, which flank it – is the sanctuary and choir. The church's harmony, interplay of light and shadow within and sheer majesty are truly awe-inspiring. Originally all the walls save those of the choir were covered with marble, of which very little remains. All the curved surfaces – vaulted ceilings, domes, apses – and the walls of the gallery and choir were covered with mosaics. Only those of the choir and sanctuary survive, but San Vitale has been called 'The most glorious example of Byzantine art in the West', and with good reason.

The mosaics are in two distinct styles. The scenes from the Old Testament, which all symbolize Christ's sacrifice and the Eucharist, are drawn with great naturalism. The three angels at Mamre sit at a table under a tree while Abraham brings them what appears to be a complete ox on a dish. In another scene on the same lunette Abraham is shown about to sacrifice his son Isaac. Opposite, Abel and Melchizedek makes sacrifices at an altar. Above the two lunettes are seated the Four Evangelists, each in a rocky landscape with a stream at his feet, in which swim storks, ducks, herons and coot; in the act of composing the Gospels, they have desks with inkwells and quills, and lidded leather buckets with locks to hold their scrolls. (We found these particularly fascinating, exactly like the leather cases in which our grandfathers kept their silk top hats.) With each evangelist is his symbol: the Lion of St Mark (a most ferocious beast); the Bull of St Luke; the Eagle of St John; and the Angel of St Matthew. All these, together with the vines and acanthus leaves holding every sort of bird, the animals, the garlands of fruit and flowers stretching up into the dome – where, in a garlanded medallion, Christ is depicted as the Lamb – are direct descendants of the Classical past which have been Christianized; the pairs of flying angels bearing a medallion of the Cross might have come off a Roman tomb of the Golden Age.

It is fascinating to compare these with the other mosaics in the conch of the apse and on the lower walls of the sanctuary, which portray the Emperor Justinian and the Empress Theodora with their retinues. These are all very formal and stiff, undoubtedly the work of mosaicists sent from Constantinople. We began to realize that Galla Placidia's mausoleum is not truly Byzantine. From a common ancestry the two branches of the family had developed in different directions. In the East the Emperor was considered to be God's representative on earth and the 'Thirteenth Apostle'. While art in the West continued to consist of natural representations of the outside world, Byzantine art reflected the stiff formality of court ritual.

Yet this formality is not detrimental. The figures' slight stiffness adds a tremendous sense of majesty, of beings above the reach of common man. In the apse, against a golden sky, Christ is seated on a blue orb and attended by two angels who are presenting San Vitale (elegantly dressed in flowery blue hose) and Bishop Ecclesius holding a model of his church. The mosaics of the Emperor and Empress are possibly the most famous in the world. The son of a Macedonian peasant and the daughter of a Cypriot bear trainer at the Hippodrome are shown in all the splendour of the Imperial court. Theodora, besides being a prostitute, had been an actress who appeared on the stage naked. Perhaps realizing that as she grew older her profession would become insecure she decided to lead a new life. She met Justinian who, completely infatuated, determined to make her his wife. The fact that she had been a prostitute was no barrier in itself to marriage with a Senator who was the heir to the Imperial throne; but it was illegal for a Senator to marry a woman who had been on the stage. Justinian persuaded his uncle, the Emperor Justin, to abolish this law. Not only did he marry Theodora but, on becoming Emperor, insisted on her sharing the throne with him. Perhaps in consequence of precautions taken against conceiving during her working life, however, she was unable to give him an heir.

Accompanied by her ladies and two eunuchs, Theodora holds a chalice to be used at Mass. She wears the Imperial crown (whose pearls are made of mother-of-pearl), a jewelled cloak the hem of which is embroidered with the three Magi bearing their gifts to Christ, and – a little surprisingly in view of her past – a halo. On the wall opposite, her husband – also with a halo, as God's representative on earth – wears a purple cloak trimmed with gold silk woven with a design of birds and held in place by a great jewelled clasp. (The silk trimming is most interesting since it was during Justinian's reign that Byzantine agents first secured the secret of silk manufacture by smuggling silkworms out of China; this portrait of the Emperor probably shows some of the earliest silk produced in the Empire.) With him are soldiers and prelates bearing the cross, a jewel encrusted book and a censer for the Mass. Justinian himself carries the paten.

Dusk was falling and soon everything would be closed. Yet even had we been able to visit another church that day we would not have done so. San Vitale is very hard to follow; there is so much to absorb, and one can so easily be stricken with mental indigestion. There would be time enough next day to see the rest of Ravenna.

We were staying at an hotel near San Vitale. Our lost lunch was rewarded by a really excellent dinner at the Tre Spade not far away. Crudités and rillettes came while we waited and drank some modest but very agreeable red wine, Sangiovese di Romagna, which went down very easily indeed. Then came *pasticcio di crespelle al radicchio trevigiano* – layers of pancakes in a creamy sauce, with slivers of the narrow-leaved radicchio from Treviso – bubbling and golden from the oven. Then, firmly dismissing myxomatosis from our minds, we had excellent rabbit with fennel. We were to look back on this meal as the best of our travels, especially when in Greece.

The next morning was as cold and damp as the previous day. At least it meant that we were still probably the only tourists in Ravenna. We set out in good spirits to look for the Orthodox Baptistery; but Ravenna, although small, is unaccountably confusing. Having lost all sense of direction we were forced to ask for help. An extremely stout old lady, pushing a bicycle of the same vintage as herself, accompanied us to the cathedral. She chattered non-stop about her two talented but ungrateful sons, a doctor and an engineer, who never visited her – of course their wives were to blame.

The Orthodox Baptistery was converted from a bath-house by Bishop Ursus early in the fifth century during Honorius's reign, but not completed until sometime after 452 during Valentinian III's, when Bishop Neon built the dome and decorated the interior. The dome is constructed out of terracotta pipes and pumice to lighten the load on the marshy ground beneath. Inside, the mosaics in the dome are of the highest quality. A central disc depicts the Baptism of Christ. Unfortunately the section showing His head, the head and right arm of St John the Baptist and the dove representing the Holy Ghost are nineteenth-century restorations, and nineteenth-century restorers were notorious for preferring their own interpretations. (We were to notice this at Sant 'Apollinare Nuovo, where the wine-jars at Cana have turned into baskets.) What is unusual about the baptism is that St John is pouring a dish of water over Christ's head, whereas normally in early Christian art he would be shown laying his hand on it. The face of Christ is remarkably insipid and sentimental, totally out of keeping with the strong faces of the Twelve Apostles who, radiating from the disc, are golden princes bringing their crowns in veiled hands. Full of vitality, they almost dance around the dome amid gold acanthus plants. There is an outer ring of eight temples, four containing altars (each with a Gospel open on it) alternating with four thrones – two bearing crosses and two bearing the Etimasia (symbolic preparation of the throne of God for the Last Judgment).

A notice on the door of the cathedral forbids anyone to bring a bicycle inside, as though to stop the aisles being used for races. The brightly coloured machines we had seen in the streets might have cheered up the gloomy interior. They would have been less of an outrage than the destruction in the eighteenth century of the church built by Bishop Ursus at the same time as the Baptistery next door. All that remains from his edifice are a beautiful ambo shaped like a tower and, in a side chapel, two magnificent fifth-century sarcophagi in white marble decorated with figures of Christ and the Apostles Peter and Paul. Ursus's cathedral was famous for its beauty and it is impossible to comprehend how anyone could have thought the present sub-baroque horror an improvement.

Luckily the adjoining Bishop's palace was spared. The first floor, which includes the Bishop's private chapel, the fifth-century oratory of Sant' Andrea, is now a museum. The curator is a splendid motherly creature, invincibly cheerful, who let us in, then disappeared into the bowels of the palace singing lustily. As we were leaving she pressed postcards on us since we were the first customers of the day. Her most precious treasure is the wonderful throne of carved ivory which was Justinian's gift to Bishop Maximian. It was made in the Imperial workshops, four masters being employed to create the series of carvings which adorn it. In addition to Constantinople they came from Alexandria and Syria, then still part of the Byzantine Empire. The best panels depict scenes from the Old Testament and the Four Evangelists with John the Baptist. The markedly inferior panels on the upper part of the seat and on the back are of scenes from the New Testament. Some have been found comparatively recently and replaced – they can be identified by their darker colour, the throne having been cleaned during the last century. We particularly admired the frieze which unites all the panels. Carved by a fourth artist, its recurrent theme is the vine, a common enough one but enlivened here by the beautifully executed birds and animals which are tucked into its tendrils. Tiny yet immensely fierce lions spring forward with snarling jaws, stags browse among the grapes, and in the front are two notably handsome peacocks, symbols of incorruption. There are many more – hounds and ducks, leopards and storks, a veritable zoo – all carved with great delicacy and a cunning use of light and shade. Other exhibits in the museum which caught our attention were a massive, headless, porphyry statue of Theodosius, fragments of mosaics taken from the old cathedral, and a twelfth-century chasuble woven with Byzantine eagles.

The mosaic in the oratory's atrium, with its charming white lilies and brightly coloured birds, is certainly original, as is a group of four angels supporting the monogram of Christ in the dome of the chapel. Sadly, the other mosaics have been restored again and again. Another of Bishop Neon's foundations is the church now called San Francesco. All that remains of an earlier church of SS. Peter and Paul is a fifth-century mosaic floor in the crypt and some sarcophagi of the same date – Bishop Liberius's serves as the high altar. The crypt is visible from steps below the altar and when we visited it was half filled with water in which swam two goldfish. We could see inscriptions in Greek and Latin, their submersion giving them an undeniably eerie look in the semi-darkness; one refers to the burial of Neon, Bishop of Ravenna in Valentinian III's reign.

Galla Placidia's dissolute son Valentinian preferred to live at Rome. Last of the Theodosian dynasty, he was murdered there by the servants of a senator whose wife he had raped. He has been described as a 'contemptible creature, cowardly, self-indulgent, without spirit, and without ability'. He was followed by a succession of even feebler Western Emperors until 476 when the last of them was deposed by the Ostrogoth Odoacer, who came from the Baltic. Odoacer made himself master of all Italy.

By now frozen, we needed coffee and shelter from the wind. We found a café in the pretty little Piazzo del Popolo and sat in the window. In the square we could see the Palazzo Veneziano, built in the fifteenth century under Venetian rule. What interested us most about this small and elegant palace were the granite columns which support its arcaded façade – they come from a long vanished church, St Andrew of the Goths, and bear Theodoric's monogram.

Theodoric, the Ostrogoth king who reigned at Ravenna from 493 to 526, belonged to the royal house of Amal and spent his boyhood as a hostage at the East Roman court in Constantinople. Although nominally acknowledging its overlordship, Odoacer fell out with Byzantium at a time when Theodoric, by now Prefect of Illyricum, had grown alarmingly powerful. To remove Theodoric from the Eastern Empire the Emperor Zeno sent him to drive Odoacer out of Italy. After five years, three of them spent besieging Ravenna, he succeeded, and murdered Odoacer with his own hands at a banquet in the city. Having spent his youth at the Imperial court he was a civilized and indeed educated man, admired for his wisdom, courtesy and fighting qualities. He visited Rome in 501, being so impressed that he set aside money to restore its monuments and appointed a custodian. He chose gifted Romans, such as Boethius and Symmachus, as his ministers and made Ravenna even more splendid a cultural metropolis, where Gothic warriors dabbled in classical literature. It was his favourite residence, and during the long periods of peace he brought to his new country he spent all his time there, creating an orchard with his own hands and building churches and palaces.

Yet despite his undoubted good qualities, and although his reign was in many ways a golden age for Italy, Theodoric was not popular with his Italian subjects. He had a suspicious streak, which could turn murderous – at the end of his reign he had both Boethius and Symmachus clubbed to death. He also rewarded his Ostrogoth followers with a third of all landed property and prohibited inter-marriage between Romans and Goths. The strongest cause of his unpopularity was the fact that like most Goths he was an Arian, one of those Christians who denied the divinity of Christ (rather like today's Unitarians).

Theodoric built the Arian Baptistery, a small brick building whose mosaics are a simplified version of those in the older Orthodox Baptistery. They lack the movement and grace of the earlier mosaics. Yet although at the time we found them slightly disappointing, had we seen them anywhere else they would have delighted us.

By now we were in the heart of Theodoric's Ravenna and a stone's throw from his church of Sant' Apollinare Nuovo, originally dedi-cated to Christ the Redeemer. When Belisarius re-conquered Italy it was taken over by the Catholics and re-dedicated to St Martin, a staunch opponent of heresy. Finally, in the ninth century it received its present name. The nave is divided from the aisles by grey marble pillars brought from Constantinople. Above the nave's windows are thirteen panels of the miracles of Christ on the left-hand side and thirteen of the Passion on the right. They date from Theodoric's reign, as do the white-robed saints between the windows. In the miracles Christ is fair-haired and clean-shaven; the scenes are simple and uncluttered. The scenes from the Passion are very different and obviously the work of another artist. In these Our Lord is darkly bearded and stern, the crowded panels full of movement and life. The Crucifixion is omitted (as was usual at that time) and the Last Judgment is symbolized by Christ separating the sheep from the goats. Below the panels, one on each side of the nave, are two long lines of saints processing through palm trees; at the right martyrs in togas (apart from St Lawrence, who wears a gold tunic to indicate that he is a deacon) march from the royal palace towards the enthroned Christ; at the left virgins in golden robes, led by the three Magi, march from the port of Classis towards the Virgin and Child. It is likely that Theodoric, his queen and his courtiers were once included in the processions – which is why the palace and the port are shown – but were replaced when the Byzantines recaptured the city. The tesserae catch the light in such a way that the rather stiffly drawn processions seem to move. The shimmering greens and golds of Paradise are magnificent.

We wandered through the streets of Ravenna, looking for La Bella Venezia where we hoped to have our lunch, trying to imagine the city's appearance when there were canals like those of Venice. The only secular building of any great age, the so-called Palace of Theodoric, is next to Sant' Apollinare Nuovo. In reality it dates from the eighth century and, far less imposing than his palaces must have been, was probably the offices of the Exarch.

Theodoric died in 526 and was buried in a monstrous mausoleum roofed with a single slab of granite thirty-six feet across, just outside the city. His daughter Amalasuntha succeeded to the throne. Her murder in 534 by her husband, King Theodahad, gave the Emperor Justinian the pretext he sought for invading Italy. His general Belisarius occupied Rome in 536 and captured Ravenna four years later. By 552 all Gothic resistance had come to an end. Italy was once more part of the Roman Empire.

For 200 years Ravenna was the centre of Byzantine Imperial authority in Italy and, in theory at least, the peninsula's capital. Beautiful gold solidi issued from its mint. Even after a fresh wave of German invaders, the Lombards, seized large areas of Italy the Byzantine Exarch of Ravenna continued to hold a string of towns on the Adriatic coast as far south as Ancona. To the north his suzerainty was acknowledged by Venice, while a thin strip of territory linked the Exarchate to Rome, so that the Popes had to tread warily in their dealings with the Emperors.

But this period of prosperity was not without incident. In 691 the inhabitants revolted against the pronouncements of the Council in Trullo called by Justinian II at Constantinople which, among other things, allowed priests to marry and forbade fasting on Saturday. The situation was exacerbated by the Emperor's attempting to arrest the Pope. Justinian was soon dethroned – his nose cut off – and exiled to Cherson in the Crimea. Mutilation rendered the victim ineligible for the throne (as Christ's representative on earth the Emperor must be physically perfect) but after ten years of adventures during which he married a Bulgar princess, Justinian in fact regained the throne. He took his revenge on Ravenna. The leading citizens were brought to

Constantinople in chains and executed. Their bishop was blinded and the city sacked and pillaged. Two years later Justinian was assassinated by one of his officers and his noseless head was brought to Italy to be displayed on the gates of Rome and Ravenna.

After an unmemorable lunch we caught a number 4 bus to Classis. We met an amiable man who told us he had been a prisoner-of-war in England; he had acted as interpreter between those working on the farms and the English farmers, who were frequently enraged by the use of the word '*Basta*'! ('Enough') which they thought meant something very different. He kept us amused for most of the journey which, as a result of the fog swirling in from the sea, was dreary and dull. Normally the tenth-century campanile of Sant' Apollinare in Classe can be seen for miles – 'like the tower of some great Fenland church' – but on that wintry day it loomed through the mist only at the last moment. We scrambled off the bus, just in time. A biting wind blew the fog round us in whispy eddies and we were glad to reach the comparative warmth of the narthex.

Sant' Apollinare in Classe is all that remains of the once bustling port of Classis. Destroyed by the Lombards in 728 it was never rebuilt; because of the Po's silting up and damaging the canals the sea had receded, stranding the port several miles inland. The last of Ravenna's great churches, Sant' Apollinare was consecrated in 549, a year after San Vitale: the funds for its construction had been provided by the same benefactor, Julius Argentarius. Unlike San Vitale, it retains the classical basilical form. The nave is divided from the aisles by twenty-four columns of striped grey marble, on massive pedestals with Byzantine capitals, which came from the Imperial workshops of Proconnesus, an island near Constantinople. They lead the eye to the triumphal arch where twelve sheep (the Twelve Apostles) march from Bethlehem and Jerusalem up a hill towards a medallion of Christ at the top of the arch. These mosaics date from the seventh century, a period of decline at Ravenna, as do the definitely crude examples at either end of the lower part of the apse which show the sacrifices of Abraham and Melchizedek, and the Emperor Constantine IV giving the Privilegia to Bishop Reparatus.

But it is the conch of the apse which dazzles one. Here is a sixth-century mosaic of the Transfiguration; against a golden sky a jewelled cross on a great starry blue orb bears Christ's head in a medallion while far below, on a green hillside amid birds, trees and flowers, are three sheep representing the three witnesses – Peter, James and John. Near them, white bearded and vested in purple, stands St Apollinaris, founder of the diocese, who raises his hands in prayer. No less dazzling are the Archangels Gabriel and Michael in Byzantine court dress, who flank the triumphal arch. Against the church's walls are some truly magnificent sarcophagi, many of them dating from the fifth century and some of which were re-used during Ravenna's decline. That of the saint was removed to Sant' Apollinare Nuovo in the ninth century when his relics were threatened by the raids of Arab pirates.

In the fifteenth century Sigismondo Malatesta, Tyrant of Rimini, stripped the church of its marble to adorn the tomb of his mistress Isotta – the Tempio Malatestiano. (He was quite as violent as any Goth, poisoning one wife and strangling another.) In the eighteenth century the addition of a wide flight of steps spoiled the proportions of the apse. Yet the overall effect is still awesome, and the church keeps its beauty and its spirituality.

Ravenna finally fell to the Lombards in 752. The former capital of the Western world became an obscure little backwater. Eastern Emperors could no longer threaten the Papacy, and within fifty years a Pope would crown Charlemagne Emperor of a new Western Empire.

The salvation of Ravenna's treasures began under the Holy Roman Emperor Frederick II of Hohenstaufen. He visited the city in 1231 and ordered the first systematic excavation, discovering Galla Placidia's mausoleum which had been hidden by rubble.

# Royal Serbia

'Now we will climb up like eagles!' cried Dragutin.
Rebecca West, *Black Lamb and Grey Falcon*

'Remember, Lord, them that voyage and travel.'
*The Orthodox Liturgy*

W E FLEW into Belgrade at night to find ourselves in a heat wave, even though it was only the first week in April. Everything was green or in blossom. We were a little nervous. One of us had been on a short, closely shepherded tour of Moscow and Leningrad, but otherwise we had never set foot on Socialist soil before. We expected to see plenty of secret policemen and very few luxury goods. In the event we hardly saw a policeman – those we did were invariably friendly and helpful – while people were well dressed, and the Belgrade shops full of good things. We found plates for sale bearing not only the ornate coat-of-arms of the Serbian Patriarch but portraits of Karadjordje – 'Black George', the pig dealer who founded the royal family ousted in 1941.

With a very few exceptions Byzantium in Yugoslavia means the churches, frescoes and icons of Serbia and Macedonia. Although their spoken language is virtually the same, the Serbs are Orthodox, unlike the Catholic Croats of the north. They were converted to Christianity in the ninth century by SS. Cyril and Methodius, who gave them their Cyrillic script. For a time they accepted Byzantine overlordship. In the twelfth century Stephen Nemanja, Grand Župan of Ras, fought fiercely for independence; but in 1172 he was defeated and humiliated by being led barefoot with a rope round his neck before the Emperor Manuel II, then made to walk beside Manuel's

horse at the triumphal return to Constantinople. Eventually Stephen
succeeded. His son Stephen was crowned King of the Serbs, his
great-great grandson Dušan Emperor. The Nemanja dynasty came to
an end with Dušan's son while the medieval Serbs' last truly
independent ruler was Lazar Grebeljanovic (1374–89), who styled
himself only Prince. After Lazar was defeated and killed at Kosovo,
Serbia became a vassal state of the Turks, who overran what was left
of it in 1459.

Although a bit dour, sometimes a trifle haughty, Serbian manners
are polished, especially those of the peasants in the fields, who seem
to have handed them on to the new urban proletariat. The only
unpleasantness we met was from hotel clerks. On the whole we liked
the Serbs very much indeed. They invariably became still more
likeable over a glass of šlivovica, distilled from plums. We enjoyed
most a 25 per cent proof variety, but it is normally 40 per cent; there is
a double strength version – *prepenica* – which is better left alone.
Some šlivovica is flavoured with berries, and much is distilled at
home (illegally). The strength of all alcoholic beverages has to be
stated on Yugoslav menus; very helpful for anyone who is driving.

Most of Belgrade's buildings date from after the Second World
War and, if pleasant enough on its superb site at the junction of the
rivers Sava and Danube, it contains little which is Byzantine. We
stupidly missed the Museum of the Orthodox Church, which has one
of the earliest epitaphioi (bier veils) to survive, the gift of King Milutin
to an unknown church. The National Museum possesses an impressive bronze – once gilt – bust of the Emperor Constantine the Great,
found at Niš, his birthplace. We saw two rings with dramatic
histories. One bears the inscription 'The betrothal ring of Stephen,
descendant of the Dukas Dynasty, received on the hand by Anna of
the genus Comnenus.' (Stephen was Stephen Radoslav, King of the
Serbs, dethroned in 1234, while Anna was the daughter of the
Emperor of Thessalonica, captured and blinded by the Bulgarians.)
The other ring, made at Constantinople in the early fourteenth
century, belonged to Queen Theodora, great-niece of the Byzantine
Emperor Andronicus II and mother of Dušan, Emperor of the Serbs;
it is inscribed 'God help the one who wears this.' There is also the
Fresco Gallery in the Cara Uroša, with replicas of the nation's most
famous frescoes.

Frescoes were the poor man's mosaics. Often it was too expensive to buy and transport the glass cubes, several million being needed to decorate even a small church. For, as the Byzantine mystic St Simeon the New Theologian wrote a thousand years ago, an Orthodox church is 'an image of the Divine Church, representing what is on earth, in the heavens and beyond the heavens . . . The narthex corresponds to earth, the church to heaven and the Holy Sanctuary to what is above heaven.' The iconostasis – until the seventeenth century low enough for the apse to be seen – is the veil separating the two worlds. Frescoes were intended to portray aspects of divine reality, especially Christ, His mother and the saints, churches being decorated with them in order to provide a background against which men might more easily seek union with God and the next world. The artists usually worked in pairs, one painting, the other mixing the colours. A base of white lime and chopped straw was first applied, then as many as three coats of plaster, a cartoon being incised on the second coat; the top coat was applied in amounts small enough to be painted while wet, so that the plaster could absorb the pigments – including cobalt, ochre, haematite, terre-verte, carbon, chalk, lapis lazuli and gold dust.

Throughout the Middle Ages the Serbs were almost completely Byzantine in culture, many of their most famous frescoes being painted by Greek artists. The first frescoes, a purely Byzantine group in Macedonia, date from before the rise of the Nemanja in the twelfth century. Under the Nemanja there were two groups, the Raška school and the later Serbo-Byzantine school which flourished from the end of the thirteenth century until the collapse of the Nemanja monarchy in the last quarter of the fourteenth. A fourth group, the Morava school, comes from the terrible years when the Serbs were at bay, before their enslavement by the Turks.

We had small inducement to linger in Belgrade, hastened on our way by memories of a breakfast of *burek* – a huge wad of greasy pastry stuffed with lumpy cream-cheese – washed down by a carton of watery yoghurt. We realized why the man opposite was breakfasting more simply, on a glass of plum brandy. We collected our hired car, the cheapest model available, from the Hertz office on the outskirts of Belgrade. It was a Renault 4 with a left hand drive and a dauntingly stiff gear-lever which needed an iron wrist. A slow, simple little car, a bit cramped, absolutely functional and without any frills, it nonetheless served us nobly throughout our journey in Yugoslavia.

As in Italy, for our essential reading we took Sir Steven Runciman's *Byzantine Style and Civilisation*. We could not bring the monumental tomes of Grabar or Beckwith because they are much too bulky to pack. Steven Runciman's marvellous little book – which in any case had largely inspired us to set out on our journey – was our Bible throughout, and not merely because we know the author. A comparatively slim paperback, what it lacks in detail it more than make up for in discernment and sheer readability.

We would have liked to drive beside the Danube to Smederevo, whose ruined walls follows the design of those of Constantinople and represent the Christian Serbs' last desperate struggle against the infidel Turks. We were dissuaded from doing so by the Tourist Office who said the road would be very bad after the winter floods. Instead we took the main road south out of Belgrade – the route taken by Frederick I Barbarossa and his armies of the Second Crusade on their way to Jerusalem. They continued to Niš where they were received with great ceremony by Stephen Nemanja. The crusaders travelled in June, and must have missed the white blossom of bird cherry and wild pear and the dazzling green of early spring which surrounded us on all sides. We could well understand why green and white were, with purple and gold, the most admired colours of the Byzantines.

The English find the landscape of Yugoslavia oddly familiar in certain regions. Crossing Serbia in 1834, Kinglake and his friend Lord Pollington (one from Somerset, the other a Yorkshireman) were astonished by its similarity. In *Eothen* Kinglake writes 'our road lay through scenes like those of an English park' and that 'In one or two spots the hanging copses look down upon a lawn below with such a sheltering mien that seeing the like in England, you would have been tempted almost to ask the name of the spendthrift or the madman who had dared to pull down "the old hall" '. One has to admit that such spots are comparatively rare, however, and that on the whole the landscape alternates between wide fertile plains and rugged mountains.

We left the main road and took to the country lanes, through Svilajvac and Despotovac, the country growing even prettier as we climbed into the hills to Manasija. The monastery is on a small mound amid orchards just above the little river Resava. Its monks may have wanted seclusion but were clearly not averse to a charming setting. Eleven mighty towers with high curtain walls put one in mind of the ramparts of Constantinople; nor had their builders any reason to suppose that the latter were not the finest in the world, since they were still capable of withstanding Turkish cannon when Manasija was erected between 1408 and 1418. The founder was the Despot Stephen Lazarević, son of the hero Knez Lazar who had fallen before the turks at Kosovo in 1389. Kosovo meant the loss of Macedonia and southern Serbia, and henceforth the doomed Serbian princes were confined to the mountains of the north, to wait in remote valleys for the inevitable Turkish onslaught. Manasija's function was to provide not only its monks with a home but the Despot and his family with a mausoleum and a country retreat.

The church behind the massive walls has been beautifully restored. It has a strikingly high cupola, the founder having told the builder to 'make the church so high that nothing can surpass it'. The exterior is noticeably plain, constructed of smooth blocks of marble.

Inside are some very fine Morava frescoes. Although a mere third remain, many horribly defaced, a Last Supper, St Peter of Alexandria's Vision of Christ, an Archangel Michael – and, a grim reminder of the times in which they were painted – some warrior saints with elegant patrician faces are well worth seeing. Less Byzantine (we were to see it nowhere else) is the story of Dives and Lazarus: Dives and his household are however dressed as Byzantine nobles, while Lazarus stands in the foreground, naked and covered with the spots of leprosy, his sores licked by a brown cur and a graceful Saluki-like hound. All were painted by a master who came either from Thessalonica or Mount Athos and who made his assistants follow his style exactly.

There is also a badly damaged portrait of the founder, the Despot Stephen Lazarević Visoki (the Tall). He wears robes embroidered with the double-headed eagle of Imperial Byzantium. Subtler than his martyred father Lazar, he also was a diplomatist but, unlike Lazar, who lost his life on the Field of Blackbirds, he was a survivor who managed to die in his bed. Moreover he was a patron of letters who liked to have scholars around him at a court which was noted for its learning as well as its elegance; there was a famous scriptorium at Manasija supposedly established by him. Although Kruševac was his capital he spent much time here in a tower which he kept for his residence, still called 'The Despot's Tower'. A deeply religious man, who enjoyed the company of hermits, he sought comfort in mysticism from the spectre of his country's forthcoming destruction, which he knew might occur at any moment. Before his death in 1427 he was forced to hand over his beloved Manasija to the Turks, who coveted it as a fortress. What saved him from an even worse fate was the temporary check to the Turkish advance in 1402, when Tamberlane defeated the Ottoman Sultan Bayezid at Ankara.

Manasija is cared for by a flourishing community of twenty-one nuns, many of them young, who inhabit a most attractive convent inside the walls and overlooking the river Resava far below. They support themselves by farming. The nun who showed us the church told us that they were very worried by the lack of rain and were praying for the weather to break.

In the late afternoon, still under a blazing sun, we drove to Ravanica, not far from Ćuprija. Set, like Manasija, in the hills beside a fast flowing stream, all that remains of its once formidable defences is a long whitewashed wall. Behind this is a pretty eighteenth-century monastery whose low buildings are grouped round a covered well beneath a vast cherry tree, in full bloom for our visit. It has a community of twenty-five nuns and one or two monks who act as chaplains.

A young sister showed us the adjoining church of cream stone striped with intricate patterns of brick, beautifully restored like Manasija. It has five cupolas but its three apses form a trefoil, while its nave is unusually wide. This is a plan typical of the Morava school and derived from Mount Athos, where it had evolved, by way of Macedonia.

The first of the Morava school, Ravanica was begun by Knez Lazar in about 1370. He and his army took Communion here during their march to the fatal field of Kosovo. There are many strange legends about the recovery of his body and its miraculous reunion with his head but his remains certainly rested at Ravanica for two centuries until 1683 when, fleeing from the Turks, the monks took them with them to a monastery north of the Danube. Here too rested the bones of his friend St Romil, a hermit who inhabited a cave nearby.

The frescoes are more complete than those at Manasija, though badly faded. It is surprising that they have survived. According to the sixteenth-century chronicle of Sečenićski Letopis the church, completed in 1389, was burnt in 1398 and destroyed by Sultan Murad II in 1436. This cannot be true literally, but a great deal of damage was undoubtedly done, and the narthex was only a heap of rubble when the monks returned in the eighteenth century. The frescoes are of Christ's miracles and of the saints and, badly mutilated, of the founder and his wife Milica with their sons, the Despot Stephen and Prince Vuk (or 'Wolf'). We know the name of the artist, Constantine, from an inscription in one of the apses. (The frescoes in the narthex date only from the rebuilding in the eighteenth century.) The warrior saints seem much gentler than those at Manasija, perhaps because there was less to fear when they were painted thirty years earlier. Softer, if also beautiful, the general effect is not so impressive as at the later monastery. Nevertheless Ravanica has its own charm, and its interior did not belie that lovely exterior glowing pink in the evening sun.

Although once the capital of Serbia, Kruševac, like so many Yugoslav towns which suffered during the War, is modern, dull and lacking in character. It nonetheless boasts an excellent (by Serbian standards) new hotel, the Rubin, which is a good base from which to explore the Morava monasteries. For some reason we inspired distrust in the grim-faced receptionist, who told us sternly after handing us our keys, 'You may go now'. Eating out that night we could find nothing better than beer and sausages.

At Kruševac are the ruins of the fortress-palace from which Knez Lazar rode out to his last battle, and a church which he built at about the same time as Ravanica. We walked to them through a street market where hens, resigned to their fate, lay on the pavement with their legs tied. We marvelled at how little some people had brought to sell – spring onions, a few eggs, some bunches of tulips.

The fortress palace of Prince Lazar is no more than a heap of stones, but his church is a different story. Covered in whitewash at the beginning of the last century, the exterior has now been stripped to reveal the elaborate brickwork decoration, which is perhaps too involved and convoluted – some have called it 'fussy' or 'decadent', though this is an exaggeration. We found it fun, enjoying the smallness, the elegance and its miraculous state of preservation. The carved stonework around the windows is cruder than at Ravanica, yet adds a naive charm; the Byzantine eagle flanked by two extremely coy peacocks looks very like a two-headed vulture. The paintings (apparently bad) noted by Andrew Archibald Paton in his memoirs published in 1844 – *Servia or a Residence in Belgrade* – have disappeared, and the interior is dark and gloomy. Perhaps further restoration will discover frescoes under the internal whitewash.

The Great Map Theft was discovered only when we left Kruševac. Bringing our bags into the hotel the previous evening, having taken everything we could out of the car, we had somehow dropped a pile of papers. Seemingly they had all been retrieved for us by an amiable Yugoslav. It was not until we had reached Trstenik that we discovered our Michelin map was not among them. We were reduced to using a tourist brochure.

The Morava valley is quietly pretty, and in April the distant hills are covered in snow. We crossed the river at Trstenik and, mapless, drove through rolling countryside – arable and grassland – enquiring for Kalenić, the third of our Morava monasteries. Between Kruševac and Kragujevac, it is not easy to find, approached by unmetalled roads. Occasionally we went through a village where we were able to ask the way. Apart from the lack of a common language, those we asked were obviously more accustomed to travelling by cart than by car. It was a miracle that we completed the journey without a puncture or a fractured oil sump.

Set in an enchanting valley and at the foot of beech-covered slopes, Kalenić is a true refuge from the world. Built between 1407 and 1413, it is contemporary with Manasija. Outside, the church has unusually sophisticated stone carvings in high relief which include the centaur Chiron playing his flute, a dog saving a man from a bear, lions and gryphons, all of them showing traces of paint. We were shown round by a courteous and diminutive nun who reminded us of an elderly sparrow. Inside the best of the many frescoes is, in David Talbot-Rice's opinion, that of the Marriage Feast at Cana. It contains a bizarre detail: the bridegroom is pricking his bride's finger in order to drink her blood with his wine in token of fidelity. Despite this somewhat barbarous Serbian flourish, it is a composition graceful enough to have been painted by a Constantinopolitan artist. Less graceful but pleasing are portraits of the founder, the noble Bogdan, and of his lord the Despot Stephen. The latter looks gloomy, as well he might. Perhaps significantly the warrior saints seem exceptionally aggressive as they lean on their lances; Serbia was in desperate need of a heavenly host when they were painted, for the Turks were coming nearer every day.

The Marriage Feast shows a table which gives otherwise unobtainable glimpses of Byzantine manners, of Byzantines at their food. The Serbs had acquired the luxury of Constantinople. Here, for example they are using forks, something almost unknown in the contemporary West outside Venice. (Even Louis XIV never used a fork.) The Serbian court had been importing Byzantine refinements for many years. During the reign of King Milutin (1282–1321) an Imperial envoy commented with approval on the elegance of his household (though his palaces were built of wood instead of stone), on the splendour of his robes, how visitors were served excellent food on gold and silver plate, how everything was conducted in the 'Roman' (Byzantine) manner. The Nemanja Kings and their successors paid for much of this out of revenues from their mines, such as the silver mines of Novo Brdo.

As we drove away from Kalenić through the valley the weather broke, making the place greener than ever. We began to notice contrasts between the old and the new, which we were later to realize are characteristic of Yugoslavia as a whole. On the one hand the standard of housing was especially high, the peasant cabins in the past having disappeared almost without trace. Yet women were hoeing in the fields with archaic implements, or spinning wool as they walked along the road, men were ploughing with primitive light ploughs drawn by oxen, and we met many ox-carts.

Near Trstenik is the monastery of Ljubostina. Another of the Morava group, it was founded in 1395 by Knez Lazar's widow Milica and her kinswoman the widowed Despina Helena, who both became nuns, along with the widows of many of the nobles slain at Kosovo. Milica, who died here in 1405, is buried in the church. This was built in 1402–4 and its few surviving frescoes have been tentatively attributed to a certain Macarius, a monk painter from one of the rock monasteries of the Meteora.

There is in the Museum of the Orthodox Church at Belgrade a piece of silk embroidered at Ljubostina by the Despina Helena. In the outside world she had been the wife of John Uglješ, Despot of Eastern Macedonia, who was killed by the Turks in 1371 at the battle of the Marica together with his brother, the self styled 'King' Vukašin. In religion she was Sister Jefimija (Euphemia). She composed and then wrote in stitches a moving lament for her protector and friend 'O new martyr, O Knez Lazar', in which she claims that he has obtained his two greatest wishes – 'to slay the Dragon and to receive from God the Martyr's crown'. She adds 'Now that thou has departed to eternal bliss thy children are plunged into pain and sorrow, for they live under the hand of the infidel and have sore need of thy help. So we beseech thee to offer up thy prayer to the Almighty Ruler of All for thy children and for everyone who serves them with love and faith, for they are in deep affliction. Those who have eaten their bread plot against them, and thy most holy deeds are forgotten, thou holy martyr. Though thou hast left this life, thou knowest the anguish and misery of thy children'.

At lunch in what appeared to be Trstenik's sole restaurant, in an upstairs room alone in solitary splendour – no-one seemed to eat downstairs or indeed anywhere else in Trstenik – we made the mistake of asking for 'something typically Serbian'. So, with the best intentions in the world, we were served with '*Srbska Plošča*', which turned out to be the biggest mixed grill either of us had ever seen – steak, veal, pork chops, lamb chops, sausages. Our digestions suffered torment.

Žiča the Seven Gated, seat of the Archbishopric of Serbia until in the reign of Dušan it was moved to Peć, stands on a low hill about three miles south-east of Kralevo. St Sava, on his return from Mount Athos where he had with his father Stephen Nemanja founded the monastery of Chilandari, created the see of Žiča and built the monastery and church. It became the coronation church for seven successive rulers, a new entrance being made in the surrounding walls for each ceremony; but it is unlikely that Sava performed a second coronation of his brother Stephen the First Crowned, who had already been crowned by Papal Legates in 1217.

In the rain which was now falling in answer to the prayers of the nun at Manasija, we found the buildings (painted blood red to resemble the monasteries of Mount Athos) dismal and unimpressive. Some of the frescoes, according to documentary evidence, were painted by artists brought from Constantinople by St Sava. David Talbot-Rice says others were the work of Michael and Eutychios and date from about 1300, but it is difficult to believe that the rather stiff Dormition of the Virgin on the West wall is from their hands.

Žiča belongs to the Raška school, the most Western. It takes its name from the long vanished city of Ras, the capital of the Nemanja rulers during the twelfth and thirteenth centuries. The monastery of

Studenica near Ušće is generally regarded as its most representative example.

Leaving Žiča for Studenica we entered the Ibar valley. Here the scenery changed dramatically. In place of gentle, fertile country we were faced with barren, rocky hillsides towering above the fast flowing Ibar. On a crag above the far bank stood the castle of Maglić, an oddly grim setting for a bishop's palace. Impressive as it was, we had no desire to ford the river on foot for a closer inspection.

The approach to Studenica is along a high, winding road with an alarmingly steep verge through a narrow pine clad valley and high mountain pastures, the little river Studenica (a tributary of the Ibar) twisting and turning far below. It is scenery which is almost Alpine. The road surface, normally fairly good, was abominable, being in the process of extensive repairs. The site of the monastery was chosen by Stephen Nemanja in the twelfth century because of its remoteness in a wilderness inhabited only by wolves and bears; he wished his bones to have a resting place like that of a hermit. He entered the monastery on his abdication in 1196 before retiring to Mount Athos.

Studenica contains three churches in a walled complex not unlike a medieval Russian kremlin. Until the eighteenth century it held another six as well. Even today it remains one of the most prosperous religious houses in Serbia, with a thriving community of monks. The first church to be built here was that of the Bogorodica (Our Lady), consecrated for Stephen Nemanja in 1191. Like all the Raška churches it is constructed of polished stone and, despite a Byzantine cupola, has some unmistakably Romanesque touches. Faced with white marble (originally painted red), its windows and doors are embellished with very Western-looking monsters and vine-leaves. Stephen Nemanja is buried here, brought back by his youngest son St Sava from Mount Athos where he had died a holy death in 1204. 'My child, do this to please me,' he told Sava. 'Put on me that habit which is to be my shroud, and prepare me, as is the holy custom, for laying in my grave. Strew rushes on the earth for me to lie upon. Then place a stone beneath my head so that I may lie there until the Lord comes to take me hence'. When his body reached Studenica, in the middle of the night, it was welcomed by his eldest son King Stephen the First Crowned and a host of chanting monks with tapers and censers. Above his simple tomb there is a fresco of him in which, accompanied by St Sava and in a monk's habit, he holds up a model of his church to Christ and the Virgin. (It was painted in 1233 by command of his grandson King Radoslav.) His relics are said to fill the church with an odour of violets.

The earliest frescoes in the Bogorodica were finished in 1209 and have undeniable grandeur. It is thought that they were painted by refugees from Constantinople who had fled from the new Latin rulers of the city. The most important is the Crucifixion. The colours, especially the blues and purples, are exquisite and although it, like all the frescoes at Studenica, is badly damaged it still has power to move.

Next to the Bogorodica – which is currently being restored – is the little Kraljeva Crvka (or King's Church) erected by another Nemanja monarch, Milutin, in 1314. This contains frescoes of less distinction though unquestioned charm; most recount the life of the Virgin and include a good Dormition, while there are portraits of King Milutin and his Byzantine queen, Simonida Palaeologina, both in Imperial robes. The story of Simonida is typical of the age. In an attempt to contain the expanding power of the Serbs the Byzantine Emperor Andronicus II offered Milutin (already married for the third time, to a Bulgarian) the hand of his sister Eudocia. Milutin was delighted by the proposal but Eudocia flatly refused to marry him. By now committed, Andronicus was forced to offer his five-year-old daughter Simonida instead. The Grand Logothete, Theodore Metochites (whose portrait we were to see later in Constantinople) travelled to the Serbian court to arrange the marriage, which took place in 1299. Court life was greatly affected and improved by Byzantine influences, but even so, when the child queen's mother, a Latin with Western feudal ideas, attempted to secure the succession of the Serbian throne for one of her sons, her plan failed, since the prince could not stand the primitive life in Serbia. Seeing this portrait of the austere Milutin one can only bemoan the fate of medieval women – pawns in a struggle for power.

The third church, St Nicholas, was built about the same time as the Bogorodica. It is tiny and contains only fragments of fresco. This is the church used at present by the monks for their services, and the soft chanting of Vespers which came from it sounded not unlike the humming of a beehive. The golden light of the evening sun casting long shadows in the monastery compound reminded us to seek accomodation before dusk.

Yugoslav nationals pay only a third of the price tourists are charged. We had hoped to stay in an hotel just past the monastery, but it was filled with the men repairing the road, nor were there rooms to be had anywhere in the valley. We tried Raška, an hour's drive south. The only hotel filled us with such horror (we would have had to share a room with several others) that we resigned ourselves to driving on to Novi Pazar.

In the dark, with its multitude of tall factory chimneys, lit up by the flames of seemingly countless-fiery furnaces, Novi Pazar appeared hellish, a menacing concrete jungle. Exhausted and dispirited, we stopped to ask if there were an hotel. A huge red-faced man with a black moustache like Joseph Stalin's jumped into the car, filling it with fumes of šlivovica. Shouting all the way in a mixture of Russian and German how much he loved the British, he directed us to the glaringly floodlit Hotel Vrbak. Desperate to be rid of our affectionate friend, and in any case too tired to drive any further, we decided to risk it. Bellowing farewells our guide folded Desmond in an ursine embrace and, to his horror, kissed him on both cheeks.

The Vrbak proved to be a monstrous piece of neo-Turkish kitsch. The reception hall was like a great domed mosque, decorated by a whole forest of ferns and Swiss Cheese plants stretching up, layer upon layer, to the glass roof. Obviously the centre of Novi Pazar's social life, on that particular night the dining room was crowded out by the local youth, and the unceasing roar of the Serbian pop group was so deafening that, fortified by our Gargantuan lunch, we made up our minds to go to bed supperless. There were other dining rooms, but these were all filled by enviably cheerful private parties. We comforted ourselves with a large slug of šlivovica – fortunately the weak, 25 per cent proof sort – though even this had to be ordered from the chef in person through the receptionist. Mercifully the rooms turned out to be clean and comfortable, with baths. They lacked one thing alone. As we were to discover as we journeyed further and further from Belgrade, the bathplug is a great rarity in Serbia and Macedonia.

Waking up to a sunny morning we changed our minds about Novi Pazar. Even if the centre of the town has too many tower blocks, the old Turkish quarter survives, with Albanian women in voluminous trousers and the occasional man in a gold-braided red fez. The smell of spices permeated the town while Koranic scrolls were displayed in some of the shops. For until Austro-Hungary occupied it in 1878 – to drive a wedge of territory between Serbia and Montenegro – this was part of 'Turkey-in-Europe', the Sandjak of Novi Pazar. (A sandjak was a sub-division of the territory ruled by a pasha.) The contrast of old and new was as strong as anywhere else in Yugoslavia. Men in fezzes were often accompanied by boys in Benetton sweat shirts, while bullock carts, and ponies laden with logs, were jostled by the most up-to-date cars and lorries. We were sorry we could not stay for the market next day, when the shepherds would come down from the hills.

Just outside Novi Pazar is Sv. Petar, the oldest church in Serbia, which dates from the tenth century. Here the Grand Župan Stephen Nemanja of Ras, Duke of the Serbs, committed his subjects to Orthodoxy – and to Byzantine civilization – by formally denouncing the Bogomils. It is built on top of a burial ground of the Illyrians, that ancient and mysterious race who inhabited the Balkans long before it became part of the Roman Empire and to whom Alexander the Great's mother belonged. In 1958 the grave of a fifth century BC Illyrian chieftain, complete with gold rings and ear-rings, was discovered beneath the church. Modern Albanians claim descent from these Illyrians and consider the Serbs to be interlopers in a country which by right belongs to them.

On the way to Sopoćani we drove past a Turkish cemetery, each pillar-like tomb crowned by a bulbous turban. The newer graves had enormous wreaths of flowers made out of coloured foil. We often came across these wreaths by the side of sharp bends on the mountain roads, commemorating some fatal car crash.

We had our lunch in the mountains which overlook Novi Pazar, in a meadow on the banks of the fast-running river Raška. We ate *ćevapčići* (small spiced sausages) liberally sprinkled with ground chillies, thick disks of bread, huge tomatoes, pears, yoghurt and heavy but clean local red wine, all bought in the Turkish back streets of Novi Pazar. Not far away were the scanty stones which are all that remain of the old Nemanjid capital of Ras, abandoned in 1314 by King Milutin.

Further up into the mountains is Sopoćani, generally acknowledged to be the best of the Raška monasteries and perhaps the most beautiful of all Serbian churches. It is on the official UNESCO list of the world's heritage of cultural treasures. It is a miracle that its frescoes should have survived, let alone in comparatively good condition. After 200 years of exposure to wind and rain the church was re-roofed in 1927–9 – the exo-narthex is still roofless – and it was used as a stable by the Nazis during the Second World War, as though to complete the destruction wrought by the Turks. The only custodian we could see was an aged and rather crabbed nun, ceaselessly sweeping the floor, who told us she could not read.

We were starting to get our eye in. We now knew that frescoes were painted to an overall plan. This plan originated in the ninth century with the Triumph of Orthodoxy after 150 years of the Iconoclast suppression of images. Christos Pantocrator always occupies the dome (the dome of Heaven) supported by the Apostles and Old Testament Prophets. In ancient Rome judgment could not be pro-nounced in the absence of a portrait of the ruler – Christ became the Ruler. The Virgin is in the apse which represents the cave at Bethlehem. The presence of the Virgin above the altar presupposes the Incarnation, without which there could be no Communion.

High on the walls or in the squinches scenes from the life of Christ were depicted. Most important of these were the Annunciation, Nativity, Presentation at the Temple, Baptism, Transfiguration, the Raising of Lazarus, Ascension and Pentecost. Scenes of the Washing of Feet, the Incredulity of Thomas, the Harrowing of Hell and the Deposition from the Cross were gradually introduced, then the Last Judgment (of which that at Torcello is one of the earliest examples) and finally the Imposition on the Cross, which did not appear until the thirteenth century. The Last Judgment was speedily banished to the narthex or to the refectory of a monastery.

Also included were scenes of the Miracles and Passion of Christ, scenes of the life of the saint to whom the church was dedicated, and sometimes a cycle of the life of the Virgin. On the west wall it was usual in any case to show the Dormition of the Virgin.

The Dormition of the Virgin is a particularly Byzantine subject, rarely met with in the Western Church. The dead or sleeping Virgin lies on a bier surrounded by angels, bishops and the Apostles (Thomas is late because he had to travel from Parthia) while Christ holds in His arms the baby which represents her soul. Sometimes the soul has tiny wings but usually it is wrapped in swaddling clothes. Occasionally the Apostles are shown in the same fresco taking the Virgin's body for burial – we were to see this at Gračanica and Mistra. She is thought to have fallen asleep in the Lord at Ephesus.

In churches near frontiers such as Manasija, warrior saints appear in great prominence, their uniforms those of contemporary regiments in Byzantium. However fantastic they may seem compared with Western armour of the same period, these kilts and elaborate helmets were those actually worn by soldiers of the Imperial army. Interestingly, in the frescoes painted by Piero della Francesca for the church of San Francesco at Arezzo, in the battle scenes of Constantine at the Milvian Bridge and Heraclius fighting Chosroes for the return of the True Cross, soldiers wear the uniform of John VIII Palaeologus's Imperial bodyguard. Piero was in Florence when the Emperor stayed in the city in 1438–9.

Sopoćani was built as a Nemanja mausoleum between the years 1245–60 by King Uroš I, a man of strong family feeling. The youngest son of Stephen the First Crowned, Uroš deposed his brother King Vladislav, who had in turn deposed their eldest brother King Radoslav; Uroš himself ended his reign by being deposed by his own son Dragutin. Uroš was responsible for the frescoes at Sopoćani, painted by Byzantine artists from the exiled Imperial court at Nicaea who may have been trained on Mount Athos. (Constantinople was still occupied by the Franks.) They are genuinely superb, with a dignified grace which has been compared to that of Classical statuary, the faces majestic and tranquil whether joyful or sad, filled with mystical devotion. They put Bernard Berenson in mind of Cavallini, Giotto or Duccio (all born after they were painted); he considered that they combine 'antique grandeur with Quattrocento light and shade'. The palette is enchanting, notable for delicate pinks and greens and ochres, subdued purples and subtle blue.

The Dormition on the west wall of the main body of the church is the largest composition in Serbian medieval painting and one of the finest things in all Byzantine art; Germain Bazin, the art historian, considers it the most beautiful fresco in the world. We also admired in particular the unforgettable Anastasis (Harrowing of Hell). There are some magnificent warrior saints dressed as Byzantine nobles in flowing robes and buckled cloaks, one with diamond-shaped sleeves, and a stunning Archangel Michael. Not so good but amusing are some naked men and women, the latter with snakes coiled around them, who are plainly destined for Hell. Unfortunately the upper part of the church – painted by another and less talented artist – was undergoing restoration and was completely hidden by scaffolding.

We were unable to see the very attractive and naturalistic Nativity.

On the back wall of the narthex there are scenes from the life of Joseph (with ox-carts of a type still to be seen in the streets of Novi Pazar), which symbolize the life of St Sava. Like Joseph, Sava was a youngest son who devoted his life to his people. He is also shown in the Sanctuary, in the Adoration of the Sacrament, accompanied by St Arsenius and Archbishop Sava II, a representation of the first three archbishops of Serbia which is unique in Serbian art; they were probably painted as an act of defiance against the Emperor Michael VIII Palaeologus in 1272, when he proposed to deprive the Serbian Church of its autonomy and place it under the Archbishop of Ohrid.

However, the most interesting fresco historically is the burial of the King's mother, portrayed on the north wall of the narthex, which might almost be mistaken for a Dormition. She is lying on a bier but in place of Christ an angel is holding the baby which represents her soul while Our Lord and the Virgin are approaching from the left. Her son Uroš leans over the bier, beside him her grandsons Dragutin and Milutin – the portrait of Uroš bears an uncanny family resemblance to that of Milutin at Studenica. One of the courtiers standing nearby holds a handkerchief to his eyes, an article barely known in the thirteenth century, which the painter may have seen at the court of Nicaea. The King's mother had been born Anna Dandolo, grand-daughter of the Doge Enrico Dandolo, the architect of the Eastern Empire's overthrow in 1204. Stephen the First Crowned had married first Eudocia, niece of the Byzantine Emperor Isaac II Angelus. On finding Rome more helpful than the enfeebled Byzantine Empire in his struggle for power with his elder brother Vukan, Stephen divorced Eudocia and married Anna Dandolo. Eudocia then married the Emperor whose reign must have been the shortest in Byzantine history, the ill-fated Alexander V, who assumed the purple for only three months before fleeing from the Crusaders camped outside Constantinople. His father-in-law, Alexius III, had also fled, taking with him all the Imperial treasure.

Our route to Mileševa took us high up into the hills towards Sjenica through beech woods to a green plateau where ponies outnumbered sheep and where most of the houses were roofed with planks or thatch. It was lovely open country, with mile upon mile of cropped grass, different from anything else we had seen.

We came down into Prijepolje on the borders of Montenegro. Here we spent the night at the Motel Mileševa, named unsuitably after the famous monastery nearby. We had an excellent dinner of *pleskavica* (a species of kebab) served with *kajmak* cream, accompanied by a strong red wine called Vranac which was very nice indeed, one of the most drinkable we encountered in Yugoslavia. There was even a floor show, an enthusiastic young band and leather-lunged girl singer roaring out the slightly Turkish-sounding but undeniably pleasant Serbian pop music. She had an admirer in a white suit and thirties co-respondent shoes, who sat alone at a table near the dais drinking in every raucous note.

In the hotel we talked to a Serb woman in her mid-sixties. A little haggard, with tired eyes, she had neat white hair and was elegantly if cheaply dressed. She possessed a true Serb's dourness but eventually thawed, speaking perfect French. She came from eastern Serbia and knew a great deal of history, especially about the Nemanja of whom she was inordinately proud – above all of 'L'Empereur Dušan'. We suspected she was still a monarchist. She despised all Albanians, judging by her expression when speaking of them, and probably all non-Serbian Yugoslavs as well. We both had a distinct impression that she was what the Russians used to call amiably *byvshie ludi* – a 'former person' or *ci-devant* – from the old pre-war monied class, though she seemed to have survived well enough. It is easily forgotten that there was once a bourgeoisie in Yugoslavia which was forcibly dispossessed by the post-war Revolution.

There are still monarchists in Serbia though scarcely in a political sense. Like Jacobites in Britain they do no more than look back to the royal heroes of the past – to the legendary Nemanja, to Karadjordje and to old Peter Karadjordjević. Some years ago the police called on an unusually vociferous monarchist; when they discovered his views they apologised profusely for disturbing him, explaining that he had been mistaken for a Stalinist. However royalist sentiment survives in Serbia alone, other Yugoslavs taking small interest in Serbian heroes.

Mileševa has the wildest and the most dramatic setting of all Serbian or Macedonian monasteries, among jagged crags, one of which is surmounted by a castle – half hidden by swirling mist when we were there. This is very much a Muslim area and the monastery is poor, but during the Middle Ages it was very rich, adorned with gold outside and in, and the second in the realm of Serbia. It was built as his mausoleum about 1234 by the ill-fated King Vladislav, who had dethroned his elder brother King Radoslav the previous year but who would himself be forced to abdicate by their younger brother Uroš (the builder of Sopoćani) in 1243, living on for another forty years. Vladislav added a narthex in 1235 to contain the body of his uncle St Sava, who had died in Bulgaria while on a pilgrimage to the Holy Land. The fresco of Sava in the church is deeply venerated, since it was painted by someone who had seen him; it shows a long thin face with a high bridged nose and the large and burning eyes of a visionary. For centuries it was his resting place until the Turks grew irritated by the vast number of pilgrims visiting his shrine; in 1595 they dug up his corpse, impaled it on a stake and burnt it publicly at Belgrade.

Outside, the plain, whitewashed church is unpromising. The inside is very different, on account of the quite outstanding frescoes. Twenty years ago the names of the painters were discovered – Demetrius, George and Theodore. Some experts believe that they were Serbians though others think, on the evidence of style, that they came from Thessalonica. The paintings are naturalistic, especially a peculiarly unflattering portrait of King Vladislav, who has bulging eyes, a loose weak mouth and a woebegone expression. The white-clad Angel of the Resurrection at the empty tomb is justly famous, while the exquisite Virgin in the Annunciation is perhaps the most beautiful in all Byzantine art. There is also a very moving Deposition from the Cross with Mary Magdalene tenderly holding Christ's hand to her cheek. In the exo-narthex the rather crude Last Judgment (painted by a lesser artist) shows what appears to be the entire Orthodox hierarchy accompanied by a bevy of monarchs in Byzantine crowns being consigned to the flames by pitiless angels with spears.

Once again only a miracle can explain the survival of this second finest church of the Raška school. In 1508 a monk copyist here completed a manuscript with the words 'in harsh times under the rule of the wicked Emperor Bayezid who breaks the Law, blasphemes against the Holy Trinity and is insufferable to Christians'. In the seventeenth century the monastery was burnt down and the monks fled. Like Sopoćani it was roofless for a century. The fact that, unusually, an oil or wax-based medium was used for many of the faces in the frescoes, together with sixteenth-century over-painting, may in part explain their durability under such conditions. André Grabar points out that they illustrate developments of which we might otherwise know nothing, because so little from this date has survived elsewhere, and that the work commissioned by the Serbian kings 'is valuable to us for the light it throws on the art of the Orthodox Byzantine world as a whole'.

In Serbia we frequently saw people who looked as if they had stepped out of the frescoes. In particular there were female faces with aquiline noses, very high cheekbones, pointed chins and huge dark eyes, halfway between Russian and Italian – just as the Southern Slav languages sometimes sound like Russian spoken with an Italian accent. Serbian women have a reputation for ferocity, such as Karadjordje's beautiful but formidable wife, Princess Ljubica, who was a dead shot with her musket. More recently an Englishman in London sued his Serbian wife for non-consummation of their marriage, complaining that she rolled herself tightly in a blanket every night. She explained that in her village it was the custom for bridegroom and bride to fight on their wedding night so that the former could assert his male dominance – her husband had lost.

After a lengthy drive via Ivangrad to Andrijevica, where we lunched well, we decided to go on despite the heavy rain. This was no light decision since our destination, Peć, had to be approached by way of the Čakor Pass, which is nearly 6,000 feet up, along a narrow un-metalled road with no barriers against a brutally sheer drop. Until 1925 it was only a track, but now it has been widened to take buses and is not nearly as dangerous as the guide books imply. We gathered from these that only the foolhardy would attempt this road over the roof of Yugoslavia.

It is a place all too full of grim memories and full of ghosts, especially those from 'The Great War'. Rebecca West, who had spoken with many who had taken part in it, describes the harrowing retreat of the Serbian army at the end of 1915:

> Monks came out of the monasteries and followed the soldiers, carrying on bullock-carts, and on their shoulders where the roads were too bad, the coffined bodies of the medieval Serbian kings, the sacred Nemanyas, which must not be defiled. So was carried King Peter, whose rheumatic limbs were wholly paralysed by the cold of autumn ... It is like some fantastic detail in a Byzantine fresco ... When they came to the foot of the mountains the weeping gunners destroyed their guns with hand grenades and burning petrol. The motor-drivers drove their cars and lorries up to a corner where the

road became a horse-trail on the edge of a precipice, jumped out, and sent them spinning into space. Then all set out on foot to cross the five-thousand foot peaks that lay between them and the sea ... They trudged in mud and snow over the mountain passes, the December wind piercing their ragged uniforms. Many fell dead, some died of hunger. They were passing through one of the poorest parts of Europe, and the inhabitants had little to sell them, and in any case were instructed by the King of Montenegro who, though he was Serbia's ally and King Peter's father-in-law, had come to an understanding with Austria. The Serbians ate the raw flesh of the animals which fell dead by the tracks, they ate their boots. Some died of dysentery. Some were shot by Albanian snipers. Of the quarter of a million Serbian soldiers, one hundred thousand met such deaths. Of thirty-six thousand boys nearing military age who had joined the retreat to escape the Austrians, over twenty thousand perished on this road.

When first we saw him we were driving very slowly and nervously at about 4,000 feet and we thought he was a dog out for a walk. He was a very long way from the last cottage and it was too early in the year for him to belong to one of the shepherds who take their flocks up to the summer pastures. He came trotting unconcernedly along the road and it was not until he was fifty yards away that we realized he was in fact a wolf – the ultimate predator in European legend. He took absolutely no notice of us as he passed within a yard of the car and continued down the road.

Later we mentioned our meeting with him to the locals who were not in the least surprised, grumbling that during very bad winters the wolves were a real danger to children on their way to school and back. Sir William Deakin, who had been with the British Military Mission to Tito in the Second World War, told us that not only did wolves eat the dead and sometimes the wounded – as they had in the Čakor Pass in 1915 – but that he himself had eaten wolf. (It may not taste as ghastly as it sounds; after all, Chinese *gourmets* consider a chow-dog a delicacy.) He added that he had never had to eat bear since, although plentiful enough in those days, bears loathe battles and cleared out to more peaceful mountains at the first hint of fighting.

We drove higher still, up into the snowline, and met snow finches. At 5,600 feet we reached the razor-edge which is the Čakor Pass, crossing the border between Montenegro and the Kosmet – until

1912 the frontier of 'Turkey-in-Europe' – and descended down hairpin bends through Alpine scenery into the Rugovo Gorge, a strange dark canyon whose twisted crags all but close over one's head. It is deeply impressive and, in swirling cloud and mist, the perfect setting for a Gothick novel. It was a curious sensation to come out of the wild gorge and see before one a flat plain and the Patriarchate of Peć.

# Old Serbia

'No nation are so dreaded and detested by their neighbours as the
Albanese.'

Lord Byron

'We will stop at Grachanitsa, the church I told you of on the edge of
Kossovo Plain, but I do not think you will understand it, because it is
very personal to us Serbs, and that is something you foreigners can
never grasp.'

Rebecca West, *Black Lamb and Grey Falcon*

THE LAND into which we descended from the Čakor Pass
was Kosovo. 'The Kosmet' – an abbreviation for the autonomous state
of Kosovo Metohija. Historically it is southern Serbia but though
many Serbs still live here they are increasingly outnumbered by
Albanians, of whom there are now more here than in Albania itself.
There are also Macedonians and Gypsies. The television station at
the state capital, Priština, broadcasts in four languages – Serbo-
Croatian, Albanian, Macedonian and Romany. Mainly Muslim, the
Albanians were originally encouraged to settle by the Turks, after
much of the land had been abandoned by Serbs fleeing north from
Ottoman oppression. They constitute one of Yugoslavia's most turbu-
lent minorities and want the Kosmet to become an Albanian republic
with the same status as the country's other republics. Serbs dislike the
idea intensely, being very conscious that the region (which they
prefer to call 'Stara Srbija', Old Serbia) has played a vital role in their
own history as a nation, especially during the Middle Ages when it
was the heart of their empire. It contains many churches and castles,
much Byzantine art, and some unexpected links with Imperial
Byzantium.

Over 80 per cent of the Kosmet's population is Albanian. (In
Yugoslavia as a whole, because of their high birthrate, they will soon
number a third of its people.) They look different from Slavs – lean

and hawk-faced, often brown skinned. The poorest, least literate of Yugoslavs, they farm with primitive implements or work as seasonal labour, though this is beginning to change in the Kosmet. The Serbs regard them with an attitude which can only be described as racist, rather like that of so many Western Europeans towards coloured immigrants, a dislike returned with interest by this proud people; often there is rioting and vicious fighting between the two communities. The 'Sons of the Eagle', as all Albanians call themselves – very suitably too, with such faces – insist that they are the ancient Illyrians, who are merely re-occupying lands stolen from them by the Serbs during the Dark Ages. Personally, we found the Kosmet Albanians extremely pleasant, friendly yet dignified, hospitable to strangers.

The most dreadful tidings in Serbian history, those of the defeat and death of Knez Lazar at Kosovo Polje – 'The Field of Blackbirds' – are said to have been brought to his widow, Princess Milica, by blackbirds. Sultan Murad I had already conquered the Bulgarians and had planned his invasion with the utmost care. As it was, Lazar's position was already difficult enough. He ruled only Serbia, since the great Serbian Empire of Dušan had fallen to pieces during the 1360s. On the death of the last Nemanja, Tsar Stephen Uroš, Lazar through his many fine qualities and genuine nobility of character managed to unite the Serbian nobles under his rule; moreover, he had a powerful ally in the Bosnian King Tvrtko, a descendant of a side branch of the family of Nemanja.

Lazar contrived with great difficulty to assemble an army of 30,000 Serbs and Bosnians to confront the Turkish invaders, who may or may not have been as many as 70,000 but who certainly outnumbered the Christian troops. They met on the plain of Kosovo not far from Priština. The assassination of Sultan Murad during the height of the battle by Milos Obilić, a Serbian noble who, taken prisoner and brought before Murad managed to break free and stab the Sultan, merely infuriated the Turks. Murad's bloodthirsty son Bayezid took command, pausing only to order that his brother and rival to the succession, Yakub, be put to death. At one moment a desperate charge by the Serbian right wing seemed as though it would win the battle for the Christians but Bayezid counter-attacked in the centre and then turned the Serbians' right. Lazar's army disintegrated. The ground for miles around is said to have been crimson with blood, while the red peonies which grow on the battlefield are still popularly believed to have derived their colour from the blood of the dead Serbian knights. Knez Lazar together with many of his nobles was captured. They were taken before Bayezid who commanded that they be beheaded instantly. Milica, on retiring to her monastery of Ljubostina, had lost not only her husband but her father and nine brothers as well. The day on which this battle was fought was 15 June 1389.

The southern Serbs had lost their freedom, and within less than a century the northern Serbs would lose theirs too. The Turks imposed their own sectarian version of feudalism, fiefs being given to Muslims in return for obligatory military service. Serbs who would not convert to Islam were enslaved, all Christians became *rayah* or serfs (often translated as cattle), forbidden to bear arms, ride a horse or wear green – the holy colour of Islam. Their male children were dragged off to be Janissaries in the Sultan's army. For centuries they were to suffer savage taxation and religious persecution, enforced by punitive massacres and impalement.

The latter was a traditional Turkish punishment in use throughout the entire Ottoman Empire. Peter Mundy, a Cornish merchant travelling to Constantinople in May 1621 gives this description. 'Hard by us wee discovered the carcasses of Two men eaten with the Doggs, there remaineinge nothinge but their bones. They were taken some six dayes past in the Mountaines adjoyninge, robbinge and killinge, soe were staked alive, after throwne downe to bee eaten by Doggs.

'This punishment of Stakeinge is ordinarily inflicted on such kinde of Offenders, which is by driveinge with a great Sledge a bigge, longe, sharpe, poynted pole in att their Fundament quite through their Body, until it come forth betwene head and shoulders. The Malefactor is first laid on the Ground flatt on his Belly with ropes tied to his feete, where divers hold on and pull, one or two kneeling on his backe to keepe him from strugglinge; while another, att the farther end, with a Mall or sledge beateth it into his body. Then they sett the Pole an end, where the body is to remaine three dayes, and continueth alive ordinarily Eight or nine howres, sometymes more. Myself was present att one of theis Executions att Constantinople, where I heard the blows of the Mall, and the most horrible and fearefull Crye of the Tortured wretch; but hee sodainely left off, even as the Stake was through his Body, all though hee lived and spake many howres after.

I could not well come neere to see him for the presse of people till hee was sett upp.' Alexander Kinglake, in Eothen, describes seeing the corpses of some brigands on his journey through Serbia in 1834 – 'the poor fellows had been impaled upon high poles, and so propped up by the transverse spokes beneath them that their skeletons, clothed with some white, waxlike remains of flesh, still sat up lolling in the sunshine, and listlessly stared without eyes.' At Bucharest in the 1920s the father of one of us met two very old men who had been spectators at a Turkish impalement.

After the Čakor Pass and the Rugovo Gorge, Peć cannot help being something of an anti-climax. We had the impression that it has never quite got over losing its role as a Turkish frontier town in 1912; after all, for over 500 years 'Ipek' had been menaced by its untameable Montenegrin neighbours, sending punitive raiding parties against them up into the colossal 'Black Mountains' which tower over the old city. The centre has suffered brutal modernization and the side streets have an undeniably seedy look. Yet one is still aware of the 'tottering and dilapidated charm of Petch' which Rebecca West discerned fifty years ago. There are several quaint little mosques together with curious fortified houses like towers, while many streets have streams running down them in the traditional Turkish fashion to wash away the rubbish. There are Albanians everywhere, the men in skull-caps, sometimes in turbans and felt breeches, the women semi-veiled and wearing Turkish trousers. And the Patriarchate of Peć, with its impressive backdrop of mountains at the entrance to the Rugovo gorge, has genuine splendour.

The Patriarchate is no longer the seat of a Patriarch but a group of four churches. Three of these are set side by side and joined by a common narthex. Scaffolding made it impossible to see much of the narthex, an obstacle which we had encountered at Studenica, though at least it means that restoration is under way.

The earliest church is that of the Holy Apostles, the centre of the three. Reputedly it was founded by St Sava the genius who created the Serbian Church and, to a large extent, the Serbian monarchy. He is believed to have planned that it should resemble the church of Sion at Jerusalem which he had visited personally; this was said to be on the site of the house of the Apostle James, in the upper room of which the Holy Ghost had come down on the Apostles. The building and decoration of Sava's new church was carried out by his pupil,

Archbishop Arsenius, who moved the Serbian Church's headquarters from Žiča to Peć to escape from the menace of Hungarian raids. Among the earliest frescoes, in fulfilment of Sava's plan, are the Descent of the Holy Ghost, the Last Supper and, in the dome (an innovation imported from Constantinople), a magnificent Ascension. (An angel in the latter has a markedly feminine face; while in no way dissenting from the Western definition of an angel – a supernatural being consisting purely of intelligence – Byzantine piety gave angels the features of beautiful women.) Every scene in the early frescoes is of some incident in the Apostle James's house. These paintings all belong to the Raška school and it has been suggested that they are by artists who also worked at Studenica. More frescoes were added at later dates. Those from the fourteenth century were probably commissioned by Milutin; they include portraits of Stephen the First Crowned and Uroš, together with a Washing of the Apostles' Feet in which Our Lord wears an apron and has rolled his sleeves up in a most business-like way. On either side of the entrance on the west wall are very fine icon frescoes – on the right St. Nicholas and on the left a rather formidable Virgin Hodegetria. These are in a very different style from the earlier frescoes and also the later ones around them, some from the end of the fourteenth century and others from the seventeenth.

The church of St Demetrius, to the north of that of the Apostles, was built in 1317–24 by Archbishop Nikodim, of whom a panegyrist wrote: 'Your love of God and the warmth of your faith is attested by the holy church ... dedicated to his beloved martyr Demetrius.' It was shut when we arrived but an excellent nun, Sister Ekaterina, produced an enormous key, explaining that it has to be kept locked because it contains the Patriarchate's Treasury. Its best fresco is an exquisite Birth of the Virgin with handmaidens of a physical type one may see in the streets outside today, if one is lucky. (Peć is famous for statuesque beauties.) A most war-like St Mercurius with a walrus moustache carries a crossbow – a deadly and justly feared weapon. The treasury has some good late icons, notably one by Radul of the two physician saints, Cosmos and Damian, and a bell cast in 1432 by Master Rodop, just before the Turks prohibited his craft.

The church of the Virgin Hodegetria to the south and its frescoes date from about 1330. There are a Harrowing of Hell with rose-coloured crags surely inspired by the Rugovo Gorge; a Nativity set in a rocky landscape in which shepherds look down from a cliff and goats fight at the bottom; and a Raising of Lazarus in which the men removing his grave bands hold their noses while even Christ backs away – a detail common enough but here one can actually see the expressions of intense disgust. There is also a noble Virgin, under whom is the signature of a certain John who was one of the artists who worked in the church next door and came from Thessalonica.

The narthex, added behind all three churches in the fourteenth century, has been ruined by rebuilding in the sixteenth. Originally it was open on three sides with elegant arches and pillars, but these were filled in with solid walls and painted with frescoes in about 1560. The family tree of the Nemanja dynasty dates from the original narthex and is enough to refresh the weariest genealogist.

The tiny church of St Nicholas is joined to the south wall of the church of the Virgin. Built before 1337, it was decorated in 1673–4 by Radul, a popular Serbian artist. If his paintings of the Legend are inferior to the art of earlier centuries they nonetheless possess considerable charm and are still Byzantine in feeling. Nicholas, the original of Santa Claus, was a fourth-century Bishop of Myra in Lycia and is the patron of children, sailors and pawnbrokers; he is famed for such miracles as bringing to life three murdered children hidden in a tub by the Sweeney Todd of the day, saving sailors from shipwreck and persuading a Jew to be baptized by recovering his money. He was buried at Myra but in 1087 his relics were removed from his shrine and taken to Bari, where they are still greatly venerated.

In 1346 Peć had the honour of becoming the seat of the new Patriarchate of Serbia, which it remained intermittently until 1766. Even today Serbian Patriarchs are always enthroned at Peć.

We stayed at the Hotel Metohija for two nights, grateful for the luxury of at least one morning without packing. It was still raining, as it had been ever since our arrival, when we set out for Dečani nine miles away. The country was gentle and flat, not unlike the Somerset Levels, with primrose-covered banks and chestnut woods full of violets and hellebores.

The monastery of Visoki Dečani (to give it is full name) is set at the foot of a mountain range. When those intrepid Victorian ladies, the Misses Muir Mackenzie and Irby, came here in the 1860s 'At the great gate of the monastery courtyard stood Hadgi Seraphine, the portly abbot, and with him three priests carrying banners and clad in scarlet, crimson and white. As we alighted these priests turned about and marched before us to the church, the abbot beckoning us to follow in procession'. But the ladies came on horseback with a glittering escort of dragomen and cavalry while we arrived in our little car wearing jeans. In any case we had come too early in the morning and forgotten that it was Sunday. Not realizing that Mass had just finished and that because this was Lent it was the hour of the day's first meal, we blundered into a tiny kitchen where two stovepipe-hatted monks and three farm-workers were sitting at table. The Igumen Justin, a tall and dignified figure, rose and assured us in German that he had just finished and would be delighted to show us the church.

We could not help noting how delicious the Lenten meal smelt. This surprised us since during the fast the Orthodox abstain from all meat, eggs and dairy produce and confine themselves to a diet of beans, greenery, potato soup, sauerkraut and nuts; olive or corn oil is used only on Sundays, even if a little wine is permitted, and coffee and šlivovica. It is said that six-and-a-half weeks of such abstinence each year is a wonderful cure for a surplus of cholesterol, and that in consequence heart attacks are rare among devout Orthodox.

At first sight the church at Dečani seems astonishingly Western, with its Romanesque façade, doors and windows, and carved animals which include lions, rams and a cockatrice. One would expect to find it in Apulia rather than in Serbia. The exterior's white marble walls gleam, as does the pink and white stone of the floor inside, which must have come from the bed of the torrent in the Rugovo Gorge.

It was founded by two formidable men, King Stephen Uroš III Dečanski – who took his name from the monastery of which he was so proud – and his son and murderer the Emperor Dušan. In 1214 Stephen was goaded into revolt against his own overbearing father, the redoubtable King Milutin, by his young stepmother Simonida (at twenty, nine years his junior) whom he afterwards blamed openly. Milutin crushed his rebellion with ease, banished him to Constantinople, and before he left, had him blinded. There were six methods of blinding in Byzantium, all intended to avoid killing, the most usual being with special tools like pricket candlesticks which were heated red hot. On this occasion the operation was bungled; but Stephen pretended that he had lost his sight during six years of exile at the

Pantocrator monastery and for another year after his return to Serbia, when he was reconciled with his father. As soon as Milutin died in 1321 he recovered the use of his eyes publicly and ascended the throne. Once there he proved himself just as bloodthirsty as any other Nemanja, crucifying and sawing in half his half-brother Constantine for rebelling against him. Yet if no less ferocious than his father he was far less able. He fell under the spell of a new wife, the Byzantine Princess Maria Palaeologina, great-niece of the Emperor Androni-cus II, and became so excessively Greek that he alienated both his nobility and his son, who dethroned him. Ironically, before he married Maria Palaeologina Stephen Dečanski had seriously con-templated marrying a Neopolitan princess and had received a Papal Legate to discuss the possibility of the Serbian Church's submission to Rome.

King Stephen's architect was a Franciscan friar from Kotor called Fra Vid, who is plainly responsible for the church's Italianate exterior and for the marble lions within, a man who knew something of Western styles, Gothic as well as Romanesque. Yet despite Fra Vid and King Stephen's flirtation with Popery the interior of Dečani is profoundly Orthodox. The marvellous royal throne of white marble from Stephen's reign is a Byzantine throne on which, as stipulated in the monastery's foundation charter, the reigning monarch alone may sit. Some very fine icons from Dušan's reign (1331–55), from the original marble iconostasis, are on the present sixteenth-century carved wooden iconostasis which hides the former.

The principal impact made by the church is the sheer number of frescoes, all painted during the reign of Dušan, which cover it from the roof down to the marbled dado. Perhaps Dušan felt that by enriching his father's church he could expiate his murder. It is the largest collection of wall paintings in Serbia, nearly all of them from between 1335 to 1350; there are 46 scenes from the Book of Genesis, 43 from the Passion, 26 from the Last Judgment, 32 from the Miracles and Parables and 15 from the life of the Virgin. More unusual are the 21 scenes from the Acts of the Apostles and a composition entitled 'The Immoral Life of Cain's Descendants' with musicians and dancers. In all there are over 1,000 paintings.

As at Manasija not only the walls but the piers are covered with frescoes, many of warrior saints but also the Virgin, and there is even one of Christ with a sword in his hand. One saint whom we were to see again and again was a wild old man, naked save for a white beard and hair reaching down to his feet. This was Onuphrius (known in the West as Onfroi or Humphrey), a fourth-century hermit who spent 70 years in the Egyptian desert feeding on palm leaves and roots, clad – apart from hair and beard – only in a palm leaf loin-cloth, until he grew fur. An Orthodox acquaintance tells us that up to 30 years ago Onuphrius's way of life was emulated by a handful of hermits on Mount Athos, the 'Naked Grazing Monks'.

Stephen Uroš built Dečani as a mausoleum for himself, and his body lies in the church, brought there by his son and successor Dušan. On the southern wall father and son hold a model of the church between them while Stephen appears again on the pier above the sarcophagus with his relics. One is very conscious that this is a Nemanja church. In procession with the founders are Stephen Nemanja, St Sava and King Milutin. On the West wall Dušan is accompanied by his wife Helena, sister of the Bulgarian Tsar Ivan Alexander, and their two children. The body of Stephen Uroš's sister Anna, the first wife of Ivan Alexander's uncle Tzar Michael Šišman, lies in a sarcophagus covered with red velvet. The unfortunate Tsarina was divorced by Michael (who subsequently married the Byzantine Princess Theodora, sister of the Emperor Andronicus III); then on the death of her former husband at the battle of Velbuzd in 1330 her victorious brother Stephen Uroš restored her and her son Ivan Stephen to the Bulgarian throne, where they remained for less than a year. After their expulsion by the Bulgarian boyars and replacement by Ivan Alexander they returned to Serbia where the unhappy empress ended her days. Her nephew Dušan promptly married the sister of the usurper.

The frescoes in the narthex were commissioned by George Pecpal, a member of Dušan's court – who is shown being presented to Christ by St George. The founders of the church stare down from above the Royal door (the entrance to the nave), and there is another portrait of Dušan, this time with his wife and son, on the north wall. On the east wall twenty two members of the Nemanja dynasty from Stephen Nemanja to Uroš V appear in a family tree identical to the Tree of Jesse in the nave. The martyrdoms in the Calendar for the entire Liturgical Year are not for the squeamish: two saints tied to the tails of runaway horses, one being shod with iron, others being decapitated with their haloed heads rolling in the grass like gold plates.

The artists, whose work is of very uneven quality, seem to have given full reign to their imaginations. In consequence Dečani is a true 'Bible for the Illiterate'. We spent an entire morning in the church and left it with the greatest reluctance.

The Turks sacked Dečani after Kosovo, whereupon Lazar's widow Milica re-endowed it, renovating the vast chandelier (choros) given by Dušan which still hangs from the cupola. If gutted by fire more than once, the monastery otherwise escaped Turkish attentions. There are tales of a stone dropping from the coping onto a sacrilegious Imam's head, of the founder St. Stephen Uroš Dečanski (canonized locally on account of many healing miracles) setting fire to an evil Pasha with fatal results; but the real reason for such immunity was probably that the neighbourhood round about bred and trained falcons for the Sultan.

Both Dečani and Peć tell us a good deal about Byzantine arms and armour, which must have differed little from those of Serbia. At Dečani the archangels and warrior saints wear gilded jupons (leather tunics) over short mail shirts, gilt plate knee-pieces and leg armour, and carry long Western swords like those used at Crécy or Poitiers; one even has a visor, while St Nikita carries a small flat-iron shaped shield of a sort then going out of fashion in the West. On the other hand many are equipped with long Turkish lances and short curved Turkish bows for shooting from the saddle. One saint has an open Turkish helmet with a tall gilded crest, and some of his comrades wear short corselets of gilded metal scales over their jupons. Much of the equipment is neither Frankish nor Turkish, such as great round shields slung on the back. At Peć, although the artists generally prefer 'Grecian' armour, many of the Heavenly Host carry Turkish bows, while one saintly warrior holds a mace with a long wooden handle and a head like a multi-bladed axe – the mace is pure Byzantine, as is a helmet with ear-flaps.

So enthralled were we by the frescoes that we did not allow ourselves enough time to look for the hermits' cells which are dotted about the slopes of the River Bistrica. The Misses Muir Mackenzie and Irby were offered fragment of frescoes from the walls of the cells but some may still remain.

Our visit to Gračanica, a few miles south of Priština (capital of the Kosmet) where we had lunched on the ubiquitous čepavčići sausages – loosing their charm by now – was not one of unalloyed pleasure.

The flat and dreary landscape of maize fields is depressing in the extreme. It was a Monday, when many museums and historic buildings are closed, so that we had to use considerable powers of persuasion to get into the church. Then, when it had been re-locked after our visit, we discovered that we had left a notebook in it. Pleas to be let in again to retrieve it were met with shouting and a torrent of abuse, presumably pious, from a Sister Euphrosyne, who failed (not altogether surprisingly) to understand our German. When the proprietor of the café over the road was at last able to translate, everything ended in reconciliation and fond farewells. Later we heard that not only was Sister Euphrosyne seriously ill but that she was having to work a sixteen-hour day as well.

The nuns of Gračanica are plainly a great improvement on the monks whom Miss Muir Mackenzie and Miss Irby met there in the 1860s. 'To ignorance they added stupidity, dirt and disorderly conduct; they were also cowards with that furtive expression one sees in the hunted animal or in a dog that knows he has done wrong.'

Built between 1313 and 1321 by King Milutin, Gračanica is the last and finest of the forty churches which he is known to have founded. Badly damaged by the Turks after Kosovo and during the two World Wars, apart from sixteenth-century alterations to the exo-narthex (when the arcades were walled up to provide a surface for more frescoes) it has retained its original form. Of the cross-in-square type, with a central cupola and four lesser domes, it is taller than any previous church in Serbia and subtly composed of grey and ochre stone, very pink bricks and white mortar.

Sir Steven Runciman considers the frescoes at Gračanica the finest examples of the Serbo-Byzantine school to survive from the four-teenth century. John the Baptist, in the northern aisle, and the Raising of Lazarus are both unforgettable. There are 365 'Medita-tions', one for every day of the year, together with yet another Nemanja family tree – like most of the dynasty Milutin seems to have been obsessed with his pedigree – which constitutes an entire portrait gallery. The narthex is almost filled by a Last Judgment, which covers its west wall, parts of the north and south walls and the vault of the central bay. If not of the same quality as those in the church's main body it has its charms; in one scene children are queueing up to enter Abraham's bosom.

Certainly the oddest thing in the church is the portrait of St

Mercurius the Holy Warrior. One legend tells us how St Basil dreamt that this Scythian-born Roman legionary had been sent by God to kill the pagan Emperor Julian the Apostate; another how despite winning the Emperor Decius's favour through his prowess in battle he was tortured and executed for refusing to sacrifice to Diana. His fanciful 'Grecian' helmet with its weird crest looks so ridiculous on top of a face which is both weak and comic that one wonders if the painter has deliberately introduced an element of caricature.

The founder King Milutin is depicted with a long and forked white beard; in Imperial robes and crown, he holds up a model of his church. There is also an enchanting portrait of his fourth wife Simonida in robes which are encrusted with pearls, emeralds and rubies, with an enormous top-heavy crown similarly adorned and a great gold halo behind her head; but the eyes are missing. The paint may have been scraped off and swallowed by peasants – a well-known local cure for diseases of the eye.

Rebecca West was fascinated by Milutin, whom she compared to a Tudor – 'a murderer and a lecher, as red-fanged a husband and father as our own Henry VIII'. Elsewhere in *Black Lamb and Grey Falcon* she writes 'There is a robustness in him that charms from the yonder side of the grave, but without doubt his vitals were eaten by the worm of melancholy'. Beyond question he was a great monarch. He came to the throne in 1282 after his brother King Dragutin – a pious prince who habitually slept in a grave lined with thorns and sharp stones – abdicated. He had no scruples about keeping in prison their father, the former King Uroš, who died the following year. Although Orthodox in faith and culture he was a nephew of Philip of Courtenay, titular Latin Emperor of Constantinople and he had no hesitation in attacking the Eastern Empire. He began his reign by capturing Skopje and later overran all Macedonia. Eventually he transferred his capital from Ras to Skopje, styling himself 'King of Serbia, the Land of Hum (Herzegovina), Dioclea (Upper Albania) Albania and the Sea Coast'. At the same time he Byzantinized the Serbs still further, giving his officials Byzantine titles, introducing Byzantine etiquette at his court and phrasing his decrees like Imperial chrysobulls.

As Dame Rebecca puts it, Milutin 'hungered hotly for women, but was as cold as ice when he discarded them or used them as political instruments'. Orthodoxy allows only three marriages, so when he wished to marry for a fourth time he claimed that his first divorce had been invalid, thereby invalidating his subsequent marriages and his children by them. He married Simonida when she was only five and he himself was nearly fifty, rendering her barren by insisting on consummating the marriage too soon. He was so jealous of her that he is said to have had a secret staircase hidden in one of the columns, so that she could hear the Liturgy without being ogled by young courtiers. (Since he died in the year of the church's completion she is unlikely to have used it.) When her mother died in Serbia Simonida accompanied the body to Constantinople in order to escape and tried to enter a nunnery, but Milutin bullied her father into returning her and she was dragged back to the court at Skopje.

Simonida has, for some unknown reason, bequeathed a sinister reputation in popular legend. She was undoubtedly on bad terms with her stepson Stephen Dečanski, as has been seen. Despite his technical bastardy Milutin recognized him as the heir to the throne, calling into question the validity of the Queen's marriage, which may well have been the origin of her hostility. He afterwards accused her of bearing false witness against him to his father. Certainly it was Milutin who, by invading his lands, provoked Stephen into the rebellion which ended in his blinding and exile.

Just before we reached Prizren, after a long, wet drive from Gračanica, we passed what we later learnt was a Vlach shepherd. He wore a high cap of red felt, a short brown homespun cape, black-braided brown breeches and black leggings. Only afterwards did we realize how lucky we had been to see him.

The *kaljaja* or citadel towers over Prizren, first garrisoned by Byzantine troops, later by Serbs and then Turks. For a time Prizren was a dependency of the little maritime republic of Ragusa. From an old map we could see we were now on the frontiers of Illyria and Illyria Deserta.

Once the town possessed 360 monasteries and churches, but even today mosques are much more in evidence; a century ago it contained very few Christians and had an almost entirely Turkish population. Its greatest splendours were in the reign of the mighty Emperor Dušan (1331–55), who often kept his court at 'goodly Prizren'. It has been suggested that when he was here he lived in a wooden palace or even a pavilion, though it seems more likely that his residence was another *kaljaja*, the Byzantine castle in a valley not far away which guarded the road to his capital of Skopje. Next to his castle he built a vast monastic complex, which he intended as his resting place and which he fortified. Its church was covered in porphry and gold, and the outline may still be traced; it was very large, consisting of three apses, a nave and a narthex. Unfortunately there is little to see as the Turks removed the stones to build their mosques in Prizren.

Stephen Uroš IV Dušan, to give him his full name, was the mightiest of all the not insignificant Nemanja. He too fascinated Dame Rebecca West. She writes of his accession to the throne of Serbia 'Thus dreadfully was it announced that this family of amazing genius, which had now been reinforced with Byzantine and French and Bulgarian and Asiatic blood of proven worth, had reached its moment of divine positiveness.' (Later she compares him rather oddly to Queen Elizabeth I.) Like nearly all his dynasty's males he was given the Greek name of *Stefanos*, signifying 'crown'; but he wanted a crown greater than that of a mere king – he dreamt of that at Constantinople, where he had spent much of his boyhood. In 1331, when he was twenty-two, Dušan seized the throne from his father Stephen Dečanski, whom he imprisoned at the castle of Zvečan. Here Stephen met a violent death, supposedly strangled by his son – whose name Dušan means 'the strangler'. At his crowning he asked his nobles which he should attack first – 'Hungary or Constantinople?' During the Byzantine civil war of the 1340s he conquered Epirus and Thessaly, hiring Catalan, Turkish, Greek and German mercenaries to supplement his troops. In 1346 the Archbishop at Peć was promoted to Patriarch of Serbia, and on Easter Day that year at Skopje he crowned Dušan 'Emperor of the Serbs and Romans'. Three years later he promulgated the Zakonik, a new legal code which was a mixture of Serbian common law and the Roman law of Byzantium. Eminently sensible among these new laws was one designed to protect women; in a case of rape the rapist had his nose amputated, and a third of his property was given to his victim.

The language of Dušan's court was Greek, while his lieutenants were styled Despot or Caesar in the Byzantine fashion. In 1355, while he was preparing to seize Constantinople, he was suddenly struck down by a fever and died at the age of forty-six. In person he was a huge man, taller than any of his contemporaries with a handsome head and the burning black eyes of St Sava, prone to terrifying fits of rage and also to roars of laughter which convulsed his entire body.

If Dušan were the greatest of all medieval Serbs, he was nonetheless entirely Byzantine in outlook. The monk Ioasaph of Mount Athos wrote a history of his own life in which he recalls a visit to Dušan's court in the 1340s, in the days when he himself had been the Emperor John VI Cantacuzenus. Nobody could have been more Constantinopolitan than this great and cultivated Byzantine noble, a former Grand Domestic. He records the splendour and luxury which he saw, the rich robes and gems of the courtiers, and the perfection of the food which was served. Above all, he remembers the exquisite courtesy with which he was received. In the light of the mandarin etiquette and punctilio which was observed at the court of the Golden Horn there could be no greater testimony to the Serbs' membership of the Byzantine world.

Dušan is said to have built more than 30 churches to atone for the murder of his father. He did not, however, replace the imposing church built in Prizren on the site of an earlier church by his grandfather Milutin in 1307, the Bogorodica Ljeviška (Virgin Falling Asleep). Clearly it reflects the contemporary Serbian view of ecclesiastical splendour; it has five aisles and an open narthex as well as five cupolas and a bell tower. The Turks have done their worst to the interior; when converting the building into a mosque they hacked even more holes in the frescoes to hold the plaster than at Studenica, and a most painstaking restoration has been unable to obliterate them. It is a tragedy since some of the painting here is of the very finest, especially those executed in the narthex between 1307 and 1309, notably a Crucifixion and a Last Judgment which has such fascinating details as souls being strung up on ropes to be weighed in the angels' scales. In the main body of the church there are no fewer than nine frescoes of the Virgin, one – a Virgin Orans – very good; in the cupola a superb Christos Pantocrator and on a pillar a noble green-clad Christ known as 'The Guardian of Prizren'. There are some charming angels swinging censers and the familiar Nemanja portraits – Stephen Nemanja, Stephen the First Crowned and Milutin, and many saints, some dressed in the style of great noblemen of the Imperial court (though it is a little surprising to find Plato and Plutarch among them). A fresco of the Virgin and Child, surviving from an earlier church, has a wicker basket of a type still seen in the streets of Prizren. An inscription records that during the building of Milutin's new church Astrapas was the painter and

Nicholas the architect, and that they were paid four buckets of flour with salt and a pail of ale every month.

Drinking mastika (mastic flavoured raki) in a back street bar in Prizren, and watching a Tom and Jerry cartoon dubbed in Macedonian on the television, we met two Albanians. They bought us coffee and tried to make us drink some Albanian brandy called Skanderbeg which, so they said, has 'a nose like chocolate'. We declined, firmly. One, Redčep, told us he had Arab blood, while the other, Adni, said he was of Catholic Tosq descent. The former worked in a factory which made flowery scarves (of the sort we were to see worn by the women of Has); the latter owned his own baby clothes shop. They were proud of Yugoslavia and its high standard of living. 'When we go to their countries for a holiday,' they boasted, 'Poles, Czechs, East Germans, they all call us Americans because we seem so rich to them.' But they were deeply worried about Yugoslavia's inflation and the future. We were impressed by their knowledge of local history. They knew that the citadel above the town had once been a Byzantine fortress and that the Ragusans had been there long ago. Redčep told us where to find the ruins of Dušan's monastery.

We were glad to have met Albanians since they are so typical of this area. The Kosmet is a poor region, little visited by bureaucrats from Belgrade or by foreign tourists. The bureaucrats are reluctant to get involved in the Albanian problem, which is worsening daily, the Albanians being great believers in large families, eight children being considered a reasonable number. Tourists on the whole seem to prefer lakes or sea and the Kosmet has neither. What it does possess, apart from beautiful churches, is lovely scenery and colourful people.

In every village the women appear to have their own way of dressing, and although in Prizren we saw two or three shops selling fashionable Western clothes, for each one of these there were two shops next door crammed with long gold-embroidered velvet dresses and shiny satin gowns smothered in sequins. The most striking clothes we saw were worn by two Muslim Serb women in Prizren: black felt coats, calf length and tight waisted with beautiful, intricate red, gold and white embroidery down the front and round the hem, were worn with white veils and trousers. Less elegant but more cheerful were the extraordinary skirts of the women of Has, who originally carried wooden yokes at the waist for transporting buckets of water up from the mountain stream below the village. With the advent of pumps and piped water the yokes, no longer serving any useful purpose, have shrunk in size but keep their shape; under brightly coloured over-skirts they are worn with vivid shirts, flowered shawls and scarves and pill-box hats. Less picturesque, though in their day even more practical, are the long padded waistcoats still worn by some old women, designed to deflect kicks from the Turkish horsemen as they rode by. The materials for Turkish trousers vary from village to village; enormous checks near Debar, tartan in Peć and stripes in Prizren. Women from the mountains dress in snow leggings of dark brown or black wool.

We had been fortunate to see our Vlach shepherd outside Prizren, although they roam all over the Balkans. In Yugoslavia they are as common and as elusive as wolves. The only other one we saw was tending his sheep up by the source of the river Crni Drim – the 'Black Devil' – on the Albanian border, in the back of beyond. He wore a tall shapeless cap of black felt and a long brown homespun cloak. It is hard to imagine a more archaic figure, no doubt a sight well known to Byzantines.

We left Prizren with genuine regret. Its people have every right to call it beautiful and interesting. We followed the river Bistrica, preferring to use the Emperor Dušan's road to Skopje and passing the ruins of his monastery of the Holy Archangel. Then we went along the Lepenac valley through the Skopska Crna Gora, the Black Mountains of Skopje.

# Macedonia, the debatable land

'Whose goodly vineyards and gardens are these'?

John Bunyan, *The Pilgrim's Progress*

'On earth there is no difference in power between God and Emperor; kings are allowed to do everything, and they may use without any distinction that which belongs to God along with their own possessions because they have received the Imperial power from God, and between God and them is no difference'.

The Emperor Isaac II Angelus
quoted by Nicephorus Choniates.

AT SKOPJE we called on General Mihailo Apostolski, an octogenarian historian, at the impressive new Macedonian Academy of Arts and Sciences. We had brought a present of malt whisky, but he told us he did not touch alcohol. Nevertheless, although it was only 9 o'clock in the morning he was kind enough to offer us šlivovica, so gracefully that one felt bad mannered in declining. Still very much the professional soldier, once an officer in the old Royal Army, he was an immaculate figure. He was also very much a Macedonian patriot.

Macedonia, the southernmost of the Yugoslav republics, has had a blood-stained history, fought over by Bulgars, Serbs, Turks – and Byzantines. For a moment it had its own Emperor, Tsar Samuel, who was a Macedonian even if he called himself Emperor of the Bulgars. In 1014 his army was destroyed near Strumica by the Byzantine Emperor Basil the Bulgar Slayer, 14,000 prisoners being blinded and sent home to Prilep, one man in every hundred left with an eye to guide the rest. The spectacle of their return killed Samuel. Later the land was conquered by the Serbs, then the Turks. During the first half of the twentieth century its covetous neighbours the Bulgars, whose language is very similar to Macedonian, inflicted more devastation and committed more atrocities than had even the Turks. (Cutting off women's breasts was a Bulgarian speciality.) Bitter ethnic disputes persist, particularly over the Slav Macedonians in Greek Macedonia. On the whole, however, the years since 1945 as an autonomous republic have probably been the happiest in the country's entire history.

Skopje, the Macedonian capital, was a Byzantine city long before Tsar Samuel's brief occupation, and the birthplace of the Emperor Justinian. At the end of the thirteenth century Milutin joined the anti-Byzantine alliance of Charles of Anjou, John of Thessaly and the Bulgarian George I Terter. The Serbian king invaded Macedonia and captured Skopje. With this Byzantine defeat Charles of Anjou seemed certain to fulfil his ambition of obtaining the East Roman throne, but he had reckoned without the diplomatic genius of the Emperor Michael VIII.

In 1266 the Angevin king had snatched Sicily from King Manfred. Michael, foreseeing the danger of attack from the West, became a secret ally of Manfred's son-in-law Peter III of Aragon. Over the years he provided Peter with gold and a fleet as well as fomenting unrest in Sicily. On 31 March 1282 rebellion broke out in Palermo and Peter, as had been agreed, attacked Charles of Anjou in the rear; the rebellion was the Sicilian Vespers, which caused Charles the loss of Sicily and removed the threat to Constantinople.

Milutin continued to nibble away at Byzantine territory until his marriage with Simonida. As dowry he received all the lands he had conquered north of Ohrid and Prilep. Serbia now stretched from Belgrade to well south of Skopje and from Bulgaria to the Adriatic.

After Kosovo, Skopje passed to the Turks, who ruled 'Uskub', as they called it, not always with ease, until 1912. The terrible earthquake of 1963 killed a thousand people and left another 100,000 homeless. The world responded and in consequence Skopje is a gleaming metropolis which nonetheless retains a Turkish quarter. Its supermarkets are bursting, its citizens smartly dressed, while at the same time it still possesses considerable old world charm.

General Apostolski, who commanded the Macedonian partisans during the war, told us that history had prepared his fellow countrymen to face anything that the Nazis could throw at them. He told us of the *hajduks*, or outlaw mountain horsemen, who for hundreds of years raided the Turks from dizzy strongholds, and of a heroic seventeenth-century leader Karpos, who ended by being impaled by the Turks on the bridge at Skopje. He told us of the guerrilla warfare by the secret nationalist organization IMRO at the beginning of this century against the Turks and how, despite the expulsion of the Turks in 1912 after the First Balkan War, his country had suffered horribly during the 1914–18 war. He spoke of the Salonica Front (where so many Englishmen had died). In 1941 the Germans, Bulgarians and Italians – who were occupying Albania – invaded Macedonia, whose people rose against them the same year; by 1945, despite appalling casualties, the partisans had built up an army of seven divisions with 66,000 fighting troops including a cavalry brigade. He described the atrocities inflicted on peasants who fed the partisans – hangings, shootings, massacres and the burning of entire villages – of which the worst were committed by SS Skanderbeg Division (Albanian quislings). His most dangerous opponent had been the Royal Bulgarian Air Force. He had been very grateful to the British pilots who flew from Cairo to drop supplies to his men – always a tremendous boost to their morale even if the bulk of their weapons were those captured from the Germans. It had been a still greater boost when the first British Military Mission arrived in September 1943, in the person of Major George Quinney – 'a very brave man'.

The General passed us on to Dr Kosta Balabanov, the Director of the Museum of Macedonia. An archaeologist, a colourful and friendly figure who smoked a large Meerschaum pipe, he was surrounded by an enthusiastic team of young assistants. An extremely knowledgeable girl, very pretty and well dressed, showed us round his gleaming new museum. There was some rare Byzantine pottery from the fourteenth and fifteenth centuries, rough glazed, predominantly green, brown and cream although occasionally tomato, surprisingly inelegant if superior to anything produced by the contemporary West; it was faintly reminiscent of eighteenth-century English Whieldon. There was a wonderful silver drinking cup, a half oval in shape, made in Macedonia during the twelfth century, an exquisite enamel hanging-dove from the eleventh, also of local provenance, and a memorial tablet of 1355 to Princess Maria Palaeologina which had been found in Skopje. There were frescoes rescued from ruined Macedonian churches, together with many fine icons of the Macedonian school. Most exciting, however, were the clay 'icons' found by Kosta Balabanov himself when excavating a Roman *castrum* near Vinica in the summer of 1985, which we were the first foreigners to see. They were drying out in a locked basement with the word 'Treasure' painted over its door. There were 40 of them, depicting among other subjects the Archangel Michael, St George accompanied by St Christopher the Dog-Headed, St Theodore, Daniel between two fierce lions, deer drinking from the Water of Life, a bull (probably symbolizing Christ) and the Constantinian cross; they bear Latin inscriptions and were cast in wooden moulds. Fifth-century examples are already known from Tunisia, but these from Vinica have been dated to the late fourth and are the earliest known.

Kosta Balabanov then arranged for the principal restorer of frescoes in Macedonia, Dušan Miševski, to spend the day with us. He spoke hardly a word of any other language beside Macedonian or Serb, yet was so enthusiastic about his work that he somehow managed to communicate. He took us first to the monastery church of St Pantaleimon at Gorno Nerezi, high above Skopje though only a few miles from it. After so many churches showing traces of Western influence – albeit with Byzantine frescoes – it was a delightful surprise to be confronted by a purely Eastern building. Built of brick and stone, in design a cross in square and much smaller than anything we had seen since Kruševac, it is wholly Byzantine. It gave a great lift to our spirits. It was founded in 1164 by Prince Alexius Comnenus, a grandson of the Emperor Alexius I. The upper part was destroyed by an earthquake in 1555 and the frescoes in this and the conch are sixteenth-century restorations. Those in the remainder of the church are considered to be the most beautiful of all Byzantine wall paintings. Dušan is still restoring them, as they were badly damaged during a recent minor earthquake.

Nerezi was clearly decorated by the finest artists available at the court of Constantinople in the 1160s, perhaps as many as five. They seem to have had a leader who was allotted the church's most important and best lit areas, where he painted a superlative Pietà and Descent from the Cross. Their tenderness is deeply moving, with a poignant quality seldom seen before the Renaissance. His Raising of Lazarus is also most touching, with a genuine sense of wonder; we were fascinated to note that the tomb is almost identical with that of Archbishop Arsenius at Peć, and made of the same marble we had seen in the Rugovo Gorge.

Rebecca West visited Nerezi during its first modern restoration in 1937. The frescoes 'are being uncovered very slowly, to wean the peasants from the late eighteenth-century peasant frescoes which had been painted over them, for the peasants like these much better than the old ones, and indeed they are extremely attractive. They show tight, round, pink little people chubbily doing quite entertaining things, as you see them represented in the paintings on the merry-go-rounds and advertising boards of French fairs, and exploited in the pictures of Marc Chagall and his kind; and it would be a pity to destroy them if they were not covering fine medieval frescoes'. She was overwhelmed by what was revealed by the restorers.

Almost nothing remains of the monastery at Nerezi and, although impeccably maintained, the tiny church is now no more than a museum. One of the monastery buildings has been restored, however, and houses the restaurant next door. During a pleasant lunch, preceded by excellent šlivovica, we noticed a bearskin hanging on the wall. When we admired it the manager told us that it was not yet properly cured since it had only been shot the previous month. Apparently the mountains around Nerezi are well stocked with bears, as well as with our friends the wolves.

After lunch Dušan Miševski took us back to Skopje to a minute church, Sv. Svas, half hidden in a pretty garden. When St Saviour was built in the seventeenth century the Turks would allow no church to be higher than their own mosques. A strange, dark little building, it has an outstanding wooden iconostasis carved in the early nineteenth century by three brothers from Debar; in one scene they are shown working on their masterpiece, which took them ten years to complete. Animals, flowers, birds and little figures in Macedonian costume swarm all over the iconostasis in stories from the Bible. We could not help preferring the elegant marble simplicity of the twelfth-century iconostasis at Nerezi. We met the custodian, Zoran Nikolovski, an expert on wood carving. As so often in Yugoslavia we were struck by his enthusiasm and deep interest in the monuments in his charge.

Without Dušan we would never have found Sv. Nikita, near Gorgnane on the slopes of the Skopska Crna Gora, to the north of Skopje. Dušan had restored the frescoes so knew the church better than anyone. The village of Gorgnane, unmarked on most maps, lies in a fold of the hills a half-hour's drive from Skopje. The cross-in-square church, built entirely of greyish yellow stone, sits in a walled compound surrounded by poplar and apple trees, the monastic buildings now filled with farm implements instead of monks.

It was built in 1306 by Milutin and decorated by those prolific artists Eutychios and Michael – whose first recorded work is at Ohrid and whose last is at Gračanica. The frescoes at Sv. Nikita date from 1308. The Dormition is one of the finest (its colours more subtle than the palate used at Ohrid by the same artists) while the Pietà is unusual in that Christ is shrouded in grave bands and already prepared for the tomb – the Virgin clasps her son to her in a final farewell. The groom at Cana grasps a chicken in his left hand, carving it with his right; an old man next to him appears to be picking his teeth with a knife; children beg for food like dogs.

We sat at a long wooden table under an enormous walnut tree drinking tiny cups of coffee with Fr. Mome, the young priest who serves the church and lives with his wife and children in one of the old monastery buildings. With his olive face, burning eyes and slight black beard he looked remarkably like one of the warrior saints in his church. Chickens scratched around our feet, the evening sun slanting through the poplars shone on the whitewashed trunks of the apple trees, and we felt almost as though we had stepped into the pages of a Turgenev novel. Possibly our affection for Sv. Nikita was influenced by the idyllic circumstances of our visit, and perhaps we ought to return one day to see if its frescoes really are so good.

We came back to reality and April 1986 with a crash – literally. During dinner in the Turist Hotel's normally cheerful café-restaurant the television news reported the American bombardment of Tripoli. Since it was announced in Macedonian we could not make out what was happening, and wondered whether the Third World War had begun. The restaurant seemed profoundly uneasy, which was not reassuring; everyone stared at us. Then a Yugoslav at the next table explained coldly in halting French what had occurred, adding that he did not care for Reagan, Gorbachev or Thatcher. We realized all too well that we were in a 'non-aligned' country, theoretically in sympathy with the 'non-aligned' Colonel Gaddafi, and very nervous about its place in world politics. We also sensed that Yugoslavia is uneasy about domestic politics too. Although Tito died in 1980 his photograph hangs in a place of honour in every café, like that of Franz-Josef in Vienna – his name is picked out in lights on the *kaljaja* at Prizren. Sometimes one has the impression that Tito's memory is the only bond which still links the eight republics. It may or may not be justifiable to suggest that Yugoslavia has inherited something of Austria-Hungary's position in Mittel Europa; it is undeniable that Yugoslavia has inherited a sizeable number of the Empire's multi-national weaknesses. Much as we liked our hosts, we were anxious to escape as soon as possible back to our Byzantine day-dream.

We left Skopje early the following morning. Not far from the city, just off the road to Tetovo, is the village of Matka. A guidebook had assured us that there was a monastery at Matka with, a few kilometres away, the church of Sv. Andrija. We found the village without difficulty but after following several false trails failed to locate the monastery. We had to admit ourselves beaten and decided to look for Sv. Andrija instead. This was much easier. It stands on the shore of a long narrow reservoir, the river Treska having been dammed just below the church. It is only a short walk from where the public road ends, along a path cut in the side of the cliff. The valley was full of tiny forget-me-nots and matching blue butterflies, with wild lilac clinging precariously to the cliff opposite. Somewhat less romantically a young dam guard, in an ill-fitting khaki uniform and clutching an archaic carbine, hurried after us to demand if we were Czechs. (The only time in our lives that either of us had been asked this question.) He waved us on amiably when we assured him that we were not. For some reason Czechs are clearly unwelcome in the Treska valley.

The frescoes at Sv. Andrija date from the founding of the church in 1389. (The artist may have been the same Macarius who worked at Ljubostina.) The sleeping disciples on the Mount of Olives are painted in unusually natural poses, as they are in the Washing of the Feet. In the latter Christ wears an apron, though He is not portrayed in the act of washing; instead He raises a hand in blessing and with the other points to the water. In the sanctuary the infant Christ is shown on the altar in a basket, a chalice and a Gospel book beside Him – an elaborate symbol of the Eucharist. The little window above the real altar below has a central pillar on which is painted a dove with a halo and outstretched wings, a representation of the Holy Ghost.

The caretaker, who had been there for many years after doing the same job at Nerezi, was an ugly, melancholy man in his late fifties with large, dog-like eyes, wearing a cloth cap and gym-shoes. He was clearly fascinated by Sv. Andrija. He told us wistfully that at school in Skopje he had been taught some Byzantine history.

We had all day in which to drive to Ohrid, so for once we could afford to look at something non-Byzantine. We had not yet seen a market day. We stopped at Tetovo to find the streets packed with men in crocheted white cotton skull-caps.

Selling had almost finished, though a few men sat on the pavements with great sacks of dried peas and beans in front of them. The only women we saw were when a door into a courtyard opened to reveal four of them, in short white kilts, white stockings, elaborately embroidered flowery aprons and white veils. Beautifully decorated harness was for sale in one or two shops and even the painted wooden saddles contrived to look elegant. We passed many brightly coloured carts. A cow with her calf tied to her tail was in turn tied to one of these – they reminded us of ivory elephants holding each other's tails.

The mosque of the dervishes here is the only one of its kind left in Yugoslavia. The Tetovo dervishes were of the whirling as opposed to the howling variety. According to the Rev. George Fyler Townsend, who saw them at Constantinople in the 1870s, they whirled in white flannel vests and drawers and long flannel petticoats. 'The rotary motion was intended to express their acknowledgement of the ubiquity and to seek the presence of the Divinity on all occasions whilst the forward movement was designed to indicate the progress of human life, which commences feebly and slowly, and then hurries onward with irrepressible speed, until it is suddenly arrested by the hand of death.' The whirling chamber at Tetovo is a graceful building, well worth a visit. The adjoining monastery and quarters for the monks' concubines have been converted into an hotel with a large restaurant. The wooden mosque stands in a pretty garden. It has open sides and there is a cooling fountain in the centre of the whirling chamber – essential in summer if one is wearing flannel vest, drawers and petticoat.

The beauty of Yugoslavia never ceased to amaze us. It seemed impossible to find an ugly stretch of country, and the drive from Tetovo to Ohrid was no exception. We had climbed the northern slopes of the Sar Planina on our way from Prizren, and now we followed the eastern foothills through the forests up the valley of the Vardar. On our right Mount Titov soared up to 9,000 feet; ahead of us, to the left, was the 6,700 feet pinnacle of Dobra Voda ('Good Water') near whose summit the river Crni Drim ('Black Devil') rises. The range passes between Ohrid and Bitola, eventually petering out in northern Greece. We turned southward to reach Debar, the centre of the wood-carving industry and only a stone's throw from Albania. The Crni Drim has been dammed here, forming a long and rather beautiful lake, an intense aquamarine in colour, full of snow water. At that time of year there are countless lakes of such water all the way up to the river's outflow in Lake Ohrid, 2,250 feet above the Adriatic which is the Crni Drim's destination. Snow lay on the mountain tops but the sun shone and we realized that we had had no rain since our arrival in Prizren. Going south we were meeting the spring.

Ohrid, on a lake which is the deepest in Europe, has a fair claim to be considered the most attractive town in the entire Balkans. Both of us sensed a nostalgic pre-1914 air, something of Chekhov's Yalta. Admittedly there are some ugly modern buildings in the new part – it is a popular holiday resort – but on the whole these are tucked away behind the hill, out of sight of the old town which remains delightfully unspoilt. Yugoslavia seems to appreciate her artistic heritage more than most Balkan countries and Ohrid is a conservation area. The countryside around the twenty-mile long lake also possesses great beauty. The Galičica National Park, to the east, goes up to nearly 5,000 feet above the lake. It has flora found nowhere else in Europe and contains wolves, bears, lynxes and wild boar, though sadly we met none of these during our brief visit. On the far side the mountains of Albania – the border runs through the lake – look deceptively friendly.

The city lies on the old Via Egnatia, the great Roman road which was once the vital communications link between the Eastern and the Western Empire, along which legionaries marched to and fro for centuries during epic struggles for the throne of the Caesars. Long after the West had been lost the Via Egnatia enabled the Emperors at Byzantium to rush troops up into northern Macedonia or Serbia at very short notice.

All too many have found Ohrid attractive throughout its history. The Bulgar horsemen from the Volga, speaking a non-Indo-European language, were absorbed by the Slavs, whom they conquered in the late eighth century, but became their aristocracy and led them against the Byzantine Empire. In 864 the Emperor Michael

III abandoned Ohrid to them. Recaptured by the Emperor John Tzimisces in 971, it was quickly lost for a second time to the Macedonian Samuel who proclaimed himself Tsar of Bulgaria, carving out an empire which eventually included most of the Balkans, and setting up his capital of Veliki Grad ('Great Town') at Prespa. Understandably, he chose Ohrid for his personal residence, building a mighty fortress-palace, parts of which still stand on the hill above the town.

Unfortunately for Tsar Samuel, his reign coincided with that of the ferocious Emperor Basil II Bulgaroctonus – the 'Bulgar Slayer'. The Emperor first destroyed the Bulgarians and Macedonians militarily and then, when Samuel's nephew and successor died in 1118, marched into Ohrid. The city stayed Byzantine until occupied by King Dušan and his Serbs in the second quarter of the fourteenth century.

Basil (976–1025) was not admired by Edward Gibbon, who wrote of him: 'after the first licence of his youth, Basil the Second devoted his life, in the palace and the camp, to the penance of a hermit, wore the monastic habit under his robes and armour, observed a vow of continence, and imposed on his appetites a perpetual abstinence from wine and flesh. In the sixty-eighth year of his age his martial spirit urged him to embark in person for a holy war against the Saracens of Sicily; he was prevented by death, and Basil, surnamed the Slayer of the Bulgarians, was dismissed from this world with the blessings of the clergy and the curses of the people'. Yet the contemporary historian-bureaucrat Michael Psellus, while admitting that he 'was somewhat indiscriminate in the infliction of blinding as a punishment', speaks of him as 'that famous Basil, that treasure and glory of the Roman Empire who outshone all other sovereigns who ruled over it'.

Under Turkish rule very few foreigners visited Ohrid, an exception being the artist and nonsensical versifier Edward Lear. In his *Journal of a Landscape Painter in Albania* published in 1851, he recounts how he was stoned at Ohrid for wearing a white hat instead of a fez.

Unlike Lear, we spent two very agreeable days at Ohrid. On the whole we had not eaten badly in Yugoslavia, and would undoubtedly have fared better if we had been able to speak Serb. Fortunately for us, there is a genuinely good restaurant in the main square of Ohrid, *The Ohrid Trout*, where communication is no problem. On the first night we naturally ordered the local speciality, *pastrmka*, a 'pre-historic trout' which is found only in the lake here, in Lake Prespa and in Lake Baikal in Siberia; they are caught from special flat-bottomed boats with raised prows and used to be sent not only to the Serbian Kings at Kruševac but also to the Sultans at Constantinople – it is more than likely that they were served at the Byzantine Emperors' tables. Lear says 'The trout of the Lake of Akhrida are surpassingly fine'. It proved as good as we had been led to believe. Marinated in white wine and herbs, it is then stuffed with lightly sautéed vegetables and grilled over charcoal. With firmer flesh than a brown trout or a rainbow, it is quite delicious. We felt sure we had tasted authentic Byzantine cuisine.

On its rocky promontory overlooking the lake Sv. Jovan Kaneo has one of the most beautiful positions of any church in the world. Thirty years ago it was little more than a heap of rubble, but it has since been sensitively restored. Virtually nothing is left of the frescoes but it is a good example of a cross-in-square church of the Emperor Dušan's reign. Above is the public park containing the remains of a fifth-century basilica, still to be seen though the walls stand only a foot high. Unfortunately the mosaic pavement is covered with sand in order to preserve it. We were able to scrape some of the sand aside and found white, mauve and dark blue tesserae with a shelduck, two other birds and a doe – and felt all the excitement of archaeologists. The park runs up the hillside, whose slopes were then covered with the yellow candles of asphodeline, to Samuel's castle. There are also foundations of a tenth-century church in the park with fragments of frescoes. The Turks destroyed this church, dedicated to St Clement, and built a mosque on the site. The crypt, where the bones of the saint have been discovered, is open to the public.

Once Ohrid possessed 300 religious foundations, of which a fair number remain. On our first evening, just after we had driven in from Skopje, quite by chance we stumbled across the tiny church of Sv. Nikola Bolnicki, built by the Byzantines in about 1313 but decorated by the Serbs between 1335 and 1345 and again in 1375. There are portraits of Dušan and his Empress, Helena of Bulgaria. The Marriage Feast at Cana includes a guest with a forked beard, a fashion then much in vogue in the West, while the Miraculous Draught of Fishes has a net of the type still used to catch pastrmka in Lake Ohrid.

The two outstanding churches are are those of Sv. Kliment, on a hill next to that of Tsar Samuel's castle, and Sv. Sofije, the cathedral. The former is a cheerful building erected by the Grand Heteriarch Pragon Sgouros, a son-in-law of the Emperor Andronicus II Palaeologus in 1295, which has nicely patterned brickwork, slightly marred by a nineteenth-century porch. Until the 1950s the frescoes were hidden by centuries of candle smoke (Sv. Kliment became the cathedral when Sv. Sofije was turned into a mosque and remained in use all through the centuries of Turkish oppression). They were then cleaned, to reveal work comparable with that of Constantinople or Thessalonica. John Beckwith thinks the artists were almost certainly Greeks from one of these centres. The scene of the Betrayal is intensely dramatic, with Judas leaping forward to embrace Christ, and there is a most unusual Annunciation; the Virgin, almost fainting at the news of her role as the Mother of God, is supported by two companions. The warrior saints are especially effective with their gold-plated cuirasses and flat-iron shaped shields. The signature of the painter Eutychios is on St Procopius's belt, and that of his partner Michael on St Demetrius's sword – the first known instance of fresco painters signing their work. We had seen their last church at Gračanica and here we were seeing the earliest examples of their frescoes.

Next to Sv. Kliment is a modern icon gallery which, among others, contains icons formerly in the church. There are a St Clement and the Evangelist Matthew, which have both been attributed to Eutychios and Michael, and an outstanding Annunciation of the same date which is almost certainly by a leading painter from Constantinople. We did not see them, however. Ironically, as we drove from Skopje they were on their way there, preparatory to be shipped to Rome for an exhibition of Macedonian art.

'The beauty of an icon is the beauty of the acquired likeness to God and so its value lies not in its being beautiful in itself, in its appearance as a beautiful object, but in the fact that it depicts beauty'. To the Byzantines of the post-Iconclast period the holy icons were the focal point of worship. Unchanging in essentials until the fall of the Empire, they represented a tradition handed down by sketch books and written descriptions from the earliest period of Byzantium. St. Luke, they believed, had painted a portrait of the Virgin and Child and a number of Apostles had been painted in their lifetime –

unfortunately there is no archaeological evidence for portraits done before the reign of Constantine. Be that as it may, it is now possible to enter a church and, without reading the names, know exactly which saint is depicted – St Basil with his long, pointed black beard, the grey haired balding St Nicholas, or the warrior St George, clean shaven with curly locks reminiscent of a tea-cosy. The Church Fathers, SS. John Chrysostom, Basil and Gregory, are always shown with unusually large eyes, long thin noses and small mouths to indicate the highest spirituality, yet the Apostles Peter and Paul are tough peasants with strong broad features. Portraits of Christ were based on the miraculous veil, the Mandylion, with an imprint of the features of Christ, which He is believed to have sent to King Abgar at Edessa. The Mandylion was transferred to Constantinople in 944. At the monastery of St Catherine on Mount Sinai there is an icon of about this date showing King Abgar holding the Mandylion, on which one can clearly see Christ's head.

Theodosius the Hermit says 'The Divine Service of icon representation draws its origin from the Holy Apostles. The priest and the iconographer should be either chaste, or married and living in accordance with the law; for the priest, officiating with divine words, prepares the body of which we participate for the remission of sins; while the artist, instead of using words, draws and images a body and gives it life, and we venerate icons for the sake of their prototypes'.

Icons were so greatly venerated that most have suffered considerable damage over the centuries. Flakes of paint worked miraculous cures for various diseases, while the endless kisses of the faithful wore away the pigments. Consequently they have often been repainted or restored, the original artist's work considered of less importance than the subject. There must still be many early icons hiding under much later over-painting. Also waiting to be discovered are the portraits of prostitutes and actresses which according to written sources were used as advertisements in the capital to attract customers. It has been suggested that these panels may have been re-employed as a base for icons – so far none have been brought to light.

The most popular subjects seem to have been, apart from Christ and the Virgin, John the Baptist (whom from the fourteenth century frequently sprouted wings); St George on his white horse, often accompanied by the small figure of a slave boy rescued by the saint from the heathen; St Demetrius either on a strawberry pink horse or on foot; and St Nicholas. The Bishop of Myra, who was present at the First Ecumenical Council of Nicaea in 325, is not only the most revered and loved saint in the Orthodox hierarchy but sometimes venerated by Muslims as well.

Sv. Sofije is one of the most interesting and attractive churches in Yugoslavia. Built on the site of a pagan temple, this basilica dates from the eleventh century. What are so intriguing are the narthex and exo-narthex, added in 1314 by Archbishop Gregory, a friend of the Emperor Andronicus II and a man who knew Constantinople and Byzantine high society. The galleries over them were designed as apartments in which the Archbishop could entertain King Milutin, and may well be modelled on rooms in a Byzantine palace – the arcades of both the exo-narthex and the gallery above it bear a striking resemblance to those of early Venetian palazzi, themselves supposedly inspired by the palaces of Constantinople. The arcades were bricked up during the 500 years that the church spent as a Turkish mosque, and the entire building is now a triumph of sensitive restoration, inside and out. The frescoes were very badly damaged, though some have survived, among them a lovely Dormition with an awe-inspiring head of Christ dating from the 1050s. From the same period are various Old Testament scenes which include Jacob dreaming of his ladder. The colours are muted and subtle, reminiscent of those at Sopoćani. We met – on scaffolding – Djordje Krsteski, one of Kosta Balabanov's team, who was making tracings of the frescoes' outlines in order to obtain an exact record.

One should remember that 30 years ago the Ohrid churches were in a parlous condition, most of them more or less semi-ruinous. The frescoes at Sv. Kliment had disappeared beneath layers of candle smoke, varnish and repainting. A special detergent had to be developed – it took two years to do so – after which no less than 2,000 square feet of the original paint was revealed in only four months. Sv. Sofije's walls were on the verge of collapse, its arcades largely bricked up, the reconversion from a mosque in 1913 having done as much harm as good. Before its frescoes could be restored, they had to be transferred to canvas screens while the structure of the church underwent drastic repair. Sv. Jovan Kaneo was in an equally neglected state, its lines obscured by crumbling outbuildings. The rescue of these churches and their paintings seem little short of a miracle.

We returned to *The Ohrid Trout* on the second night to eat the other local speciality, eels. Due to the building of the Crni Dam these are unable to return from the Sargasso Sea to Lake Ohrid as formerly, so nowadays the elvers are brought by lorry from below the dam and released in the lake. Baked in the oven with vegetables, the eels were as good as the trout. However the best restaurant on the lake is said to be at Sv. Naum at the far end. An expedition can be made to it by boat, and we were tempted to make it. St Naum, with St Clement, was a disciple of Cyril and Methodius, the men who brought the Christian faith to the Slavs and who invented the Cryrillic script in order to translate the Bible into Slavonic. The church of Sv. Naum was founded in the tenth century and the saint's body is buried there. The building one now sees dates from the sixteenth century with later additions, while the frescoes are nineteenth century.

On the morning we left Ohrid the waves were crashing over the jetty, whipped up by a gale from Albania. We drove down the lake, over the Galičica Pass to Lake Prespa. Every time we came to a hairpin bend on the ascent the gale threatened to snatch up the car and hurl it over the edge of the unprotected road. At one stage, as we picked our way between the rock falls, we were blinded by dead beech leaves blown ceaselessly against the windscreen. Once over the pass, however, we were in shelter and it was a lovely drive down to the lake. Even higher than Ohrïd, Prespa is shared by Greece and Albania as well as Yugoslavia.

At the time we were puzzled to find no sign of the town of Prespa but later, on studying a map of the area in Leake's *Travels in Northern Greece*, we discovered that until at least the beginning of the last century Lake Prespa consisted of three small lakes some distance apart. The Via Egnatia followed the route down Lake Ohrid and over the Galičica Pass we ourselves had taken and then continued through the middle of what is now Lake Prespa. Tsar Samuel's capital must lie beneath the water. The islands covered with Byzantine ruins would have been surrounded by dry land.

The church of Sv. Djordje at Kurbinovo, near the Greek frontier, is on the slopes of Mount Pelister overlooking Lake Prespa. It is not easy to find, up a very rough un-metalled lane, through the untidy hamlet of Asmati, and in a remote, grassy valley full of rock thrushes. The tiny, unimpressive building, which from the outside could be mistaken for a cowshed, contains remarkable frescoes dating from when the church was founded in 1191. Although not of the same quality, they reminded us of those at Nerezi, painted some thirty years earlier. The faces, particularly those of the women, are almost caricatures of those at Nerezi, and the patterns formed by the folds in the clothes have been exaggerated to such a degree that they appear to dance. There is flowing movement everywhere: in the curls of Christ's beard, in the furrows of the Apostles's brows, in the angels' draperies, let alone in Christ leaping forward to drag Adam from the jaws of Hell. Yet although there is exaggeration there are also nice human details. The shepherds, who keep their flock of sheep and goats in a round wattled pen, have brought their four-tiered lunch tins with them – one has a comb for carding wool and a pair of hobbles slung at his waist. The colours are no less striking, strange brown ochres, grey greens and slate. The names of the three artists are unknown but two of them worked at Kastoria as well, in the church of the Anargyroi. They were undoubtedly Byzantines.

The craggy-faced custodian, a man of extreme amiability, asked us back to his house for a drink. It was some highly potent šlivovica, which we suspected came from an illicit still hidden in the mountains. He had fought with the partisans for a year during the War and remembered General Apostolski.

Our next destination was Prilep, where Tsar Samuel met his blinded army, which is approached through flooded fields with storks and water buffalo. It once had 77 churches and chapels, some of which remain. We were lucky enough to fall in with Goce Cakoski, who was guilding a party round the monastery church of Sv. Archangel. He turned out to be a former pupil of Kosta Balabanov. He first showed us the church, half way up a hill on which stand the ruins of the vast and still menacing castle of Marko Kraljevic, son of the self-styled 'King' Vukašin. He is a legendary figure, said to have carried invariably a mace weighing 200 lbs and a huge wineskin, who is supposed to have been killed fighting the Turks at the age of 300. There are many ballads about him. (In reality he died on 17 May 1395 at the battle of Rovine fighting, as a vassal, on the Turkish side. With him died Constantine Dragaš, the father-in-law of the Emperor Manuel II and governor of eastern Macedonia.) There are portraits of Marko and his father outside the church, which is currently being restored. Goce took us down a ladder beneath it and by the light of a candle showed us an earlier church, discovered only in 1985; it has fragments of frescoes which have been identified as being by the same Byzantine painters who worked at Kurbinovo.

Goce then showed us the pretty church of Sv. Nikola nearby, built in 1286 and partly rebuilt in 1975. The frescoes in the apse here are puzzling. The contorted draperies could almost have been painted by the artists of Kurbinovo, but the building is a century later than Sv. Djordje; the explanation may be that they were copied from those by the same painters in the original Sv. Archangel, fragments of which we had just seen. The Virgin Orans above two angels is particularly graceful. The frescoes in the nave are clearly by a different hand, the scenes from the Passion being slightly old fashioned though the colours are warm and glowing, while we are firmly in Byzantium with an Emperor and Empress begging for entrance into Eternal Life. One has the impression that all the figures are wearing contemporary clothes and armour. The Jews have head-dresses which look very like that worn by Yasser Arafat.

There seems to have been a spate of hotel building in Yugoslavia during the sixties. Our pleasant if shabby Ohrid hotel, the Palace, had started life in the 'A' category but – with the lack of maintenance which we noticed all too often – had been downgraded to 'B'; we had enormous, light rooms with comfortable beds and large balconies overlooking the lake, but tiles were falling off in the bathrooms, and chairs missed the odd leg. The receptionist had booked us into the hotel at Bitola with some reluctance. ' 'Orrible 'hotel', he warned us. Unfortunately he was right. The bedroom walls, no thicker than the dirty porridge-coloured paper peeling off them, were unable to hide the fact that the rooms next door were being occupied by those concerned with the pleasures of the flesh rather than the mind. The curtains flapped like washing on a line although the windows were shut and we were thankful we had to spend only one night there. At least our experience in Bitola was less painful that that of Edward Lear who, whenever he tried to sketch, was harrassed by the mob who considered his efforts 'the work of the Devil'.

Bitola (formerly Monastir) is a nice, sleepy place with a few villas and one or two mosques remaining from the days of the Turks who departed in 1912. In those days there was a military academy here which Kemal Ataturk attended. On Sunday we went to Mass at the Orthodox cathedral of Sv. Demetrius, not a very interesting building.

The liturgy was in Macedonian, since the cathedral belongs to the new Patriarchate of Macedonia founded in 1959 and carved out of the Patriarchate of Serbia. (The present incumbent, Patriarch Ange-larije – a former partisan – is not recognized by the Serbian Patriarch.) The singing sounded very like the Russian Liturgy. While the deacon sang the Gospel half a dozen very old men and women knelt at his feet, an oddly touching sight.

Although basically similar, the Orthodox Liturgy differs from a Western Mass in its symbolism, besides reflecting the disagreements which led to the schism between East and West – such as the use of leavened bread and omitting '*filioque*' ('and the son') from the Creed. One obvious difference is the iconostasis or screen; behind it the church is divided into three, each part being reached by a door in the screen. On the left is the prothesis, where the priest prepares the elements of bread and wine; in the centre the altar or sanctuary where the host is consecrated; and on the right the diaconicon which serves as a vestry.

The first part of the Liturgy, the preparation of the elements, is called the prothesis after the chapel where it takes place. It is far more elaborate than in the West. The bread – always leavened, the leaven symbolizing the Holy Ghost – has the monogram[IC XP/NI KA] signifying 'Christ the Victor' stamped in the middle, and it is this part alone which is consecrated. The priest cuts this away with a knife shaped like a lance, and also pierces the side of the loaf. Other pieces are cut, one for the Virgin Mary, nine for the Apostles, saints and martyrs, and some to commemorate the dead. The remainder of the loaf becomes the antedoron for distribution at the end of the Liturgy. The wine is then mixed with cold water to represent the water which flowed out with the blood when the lance pierced Christ's side. Finally the elements are covered with a veil supported by a metal asterisk – 'And lo, the star stood over where the child was'.

The congregation arrive toward the end of the prothesis, light their candles before a chosen icon, and taken their places. In larger churches the sexes are still segregated – either standing in the middle of the church or, if infirm, sitting round the walls. (During the later centuries of the Byzantine Empire services became longer and longer, sometimes lasting for eight hours, at which even small children were expected to remain on their feet; but the modern Liturgy – for the congregation at least – takes only about an hour.)

The Liturgy of the Catachumens is now celebrated, followed by the Liturgy of the Faithful Original. There used to be an interval between the two while the unbaptised left the church and the doors were locked against them, but nowadays, since members of the Orthodox Church are usually baptized at eight days, the second liturgy follows immediately.

The Royal (or Holy) doors in the iconostasis are used first for a procession from the prothesis carrying the Bible to the altar where the Epistle is read. This is the Little Entrance. The Liturgy of the Faithful begins after the deacon has sung the Gospel. The bread and wine are now brought in procession – the Grand Entrance – and placed on the altar. After the Lord's Prayer the curtains above the Royal doors are closed and the doors shut to show that Christ is in the tomb and the seal has been put upon it. The stamped bread is now cut into four and placed on the paten, and a little warm water is added to the wine in the chalice. After the clergy have taken the sacrament in both kinds, the remainder of the consecrated bread – the Lamb – is cut up and mixed with the wine and the water in the chalice. The people are now invited to come forward, each in turn giving his name to the deacon, who repeats it to the priest. Each communicant stands with his hands crossed on his breast while he receives the sacrament with a spoon. At the end of the service the congregation files up to receive the antidoron and kiss the priest's hand.

Some of the Liturgy is inaudible to the congregation (although Justinian specified that all of it should be read in a loud voice) but one prayer which we liked especially was the request for a Guardian Angel. 'For an Angel of Peace, a faithful guide, a guardian of our souls and bodies, let us entreat the Lord.' Devout Orthodox pray daily to the 'Guardian Angel who alone knows my despondent soul and passionate life'.

As a Papist one of us felt a little disloyal in not attending Sunday Mass in the local Catholic church – we looked in as we passed and the entire congregation consisted of a handful of nuns. Yet Mass in Albanian seems outlandish to someone who remembers the days of Latin, when Catholic services were the same the world over. The other, an Anglican, felt no such scruples. Curiously, during our frequent wrangles over religion we always found common ground on which we could agree in Orthodoxy.

On coming out of the church we saw a bread queue. There is a 35 per cent unemployment rate in Macedonia, as in the Kosmet. A long line of shabby men and women were waiting patiently in front of an office window from which huge round loaves were being handed to them.

If anything, we liked the Macedonians even more than the Serbs. While just as tough they are not so dour and have that light-heartedness, desire to please and volubility which so often goes with a southern temperament. Nor were there any offhand hotel reception-ists. They are certainly one of the reasons why one would like to go back to their lovely country.

We spent our last morning in Macedonia exploring all that is left of Heraclea Lyncestis, which is just outside Bitola. On our arrival a dear old custodian hastily donned his uniform, consisting of a grey military tunic, a grey cap with a red partisan star and pin-stripe blue trousers. Founded by Philip of Macedon, and in classical times one of Macedonia's most important cities, it was destroyed by an earthquake in AD 580 and never rebuilt because of the Slav invasions. Its glory is the mosaic floor in the foundations of the narthex of the larger of the two basilicas, which dates from the end of the fifth century. There is a moufflon beneath a cherry-tree watching a bull (Christ) fight a lion (the Devil) under an apple-tree (the Tree of Knowledge). There are two deer drinking from the Fountain of Life with peacocks above them, a red hound (Cerebus) tied to a fig-tree, and a leopard killing a doe beneath a pomegranate-tree. In the borders are ducks, pelicans, barbel, trout (*pastrmka?*), lamphreys and squid. Everything is in pale green, ochre, blue grey and terracotta against off-white. We thought it the most attractive pavement we had seen in all our travels.

By now we had grown convinced that medieval Serbia and Macedonia had been quite as close to the Byzantine world as Venice. Perhaps closer, since the Southern Slavs depended entirely on Byzantium for their civilization, and since they shared the Orthodox faith. But we had not yet seen Byzantium.

# Kastoria and Thessalonica

'The position of Kastoria is as follows: there is a lake named after the
place, and a promontory broadening at the tip and ending in rocky
cliffs juts out into it; on the promontory towers and battlements have
been built by way of fortifications'.

Anna Comnena, *The Alexiad* Book VI

'From Thessalonica to the river Danube where stands the city called
Belgrade, is a journey of eight days, if one is not travelling in haste
but by easy stages'.

Constantine VII Porphyrogenitus, *De Administrando Imperio*

NORTHERN Greece, or Greek
Macedonia, has been fought
over no less than Yugoslav Macedonia. During the Middle Ages it
was constantly changing hands between Byzantines, Serbs and
Bulgars. Its capital of Thessalonica stayed firmly Byzantine until
1423, however, save for a few years at the beginning of the thirteenth
century when it was a so-called 'Crusader' kingdom. As one would
expect, its frescoes have much in common with those north of the
border.

Crossing the border into Greece we saw a little owl, exactly like
those on ancient Athenian coins, perched on a telephone wire, and
we hoped it was a good omen. In any case we were taking a break
from fresco hunting and looking for birds. Our destination was Little
Lake Prespa, a bird sanctuary whose shores are bounded by Greece
and Albania. We were lucky to meet a professional ornithologist at
once, the warden. To our joy we saw both species of European
pelican, the white and the Dalmatian. According to the warden, apart
from the Danube Delta, Prespa is their only breeding site in Europe –
it seems they feed on the innumerable frogs here, whose croaking is
almost deafening. We also saw a brace of marsh harriers, pigmy
cormorants and a great white heron.

On a little island near the shore there is the church of St Achilles,
dedicated not to Homer's hero but to yet another warrior saint – a

Roman legionary of the first century who after his conversion to Christianity refused to fight and shed blood, and was martyred in consequence. Dušan Miševski had suggested that we try to see it, as there are traces of frescoes, but that morning the only boat on the lake was monopolized by a government minister who had come to inspect the bird sanctuary. We wondered if it had always been on an island or whether this had in Leake's day been merely a small hill on a plain.

A narrow isthmus divides Little Lake Prespa from Lake Prespa. Here, on a beach covered with wild, short-stemmed yellow chrysanthemums, we found a restaurant where we ate fish and chips. We drank retsina with them, our first experience of the resinated wine which is the everyday drink of the country. It came in metal-capped half-litre bottles, an ideal size for lunch for two when preceded by what became our customary glass of ouzo. Much nonsense has been written about 'mouth-puckering' retsina, which is wine – usually white – flavoured with pine-tree resin as a preservative. Mildly acidic, it is not unpleasant and can make even the greasiest Greek food almost bearable. (Hugh Johnson believes retsina's 'ordained role' is to take away the taste of musty oil and soggy hopelessness which characterizes Greek cooking.) This is the same wine which in the eighth century BC the poet Hesiod called 'glad Dionysus's gift' and is undoubtedly what most Byzantines knew as wine. It is best from the barrel.

The weather was rain, snow and sunshine, changing from one moment to the next. Although still mountainous, the landscape began to seem subtly gentler – it is sometimes described by English writers as 'Greece's Lake District'. Yet it put us more in mind of Scotland after the Clearances. It must have been fairly well inhabited in the not too distant past, but now great tracts are empty of any vestige of human life; we noticed the scant remains of crofts, most of them no more than small piles of rubble. Suddenly, below us, we saw a beautiful sheet of water, Lake Kastoria.

There can be no more agreeable approach to Kastoria than from the north-west. Not only does it enable one to make the short detour to Little Lake Prespa, which quite apart from pelicans, is most attractive, but the view from the mountains above Lake Kastoria is very lovely. After the horrors of Bitola we chose a slightly classier establishment, booking rooms in the pleasant Hotel Tsamis on the lakeside at Dispilio about two miles outside the town, where night-ingales sang in the garden.

Tamara Talbot-Rice had told us not to miss Kastoria on any account as an unusually good example of a Byzantine town, still possessing 32 churches and chapels from the medieval period out of the original 72. It is built on a peninsula which reaches out into the lake, surrounded by mountains on every side save the south-east; once the peninsula was defended by a strong Byzantine wall running right across it, reinforced by towers and bastions. Ruled like most of this region by Byzantines, Bulgars and Serbs, then Turks until 1912, for a short period during the late eleventh century it was garrisoned for the Emperor by Varangian Guards, who lost it to Norman invaders; these guardsmen, who fought on foot with long two-handed axes, were mainly Anglo-Saxons, and such a defeat must have been all the more bitter for men who had lost their own country to the Normans at Hastings only a few years before.

The Normans under Robert Guiscard sailed from Bari to Dyr-rachium (now Durrës in Albania) and put to flight the Imperial army led by the Emperor Alexius I Comnenus. Alexius escaped to Ohrid where his general, the eunuch Taticius, held the citadel with Turkish mercenaries. From thence he returned to Constantinople to raise money for a larger army. Alexius had inherited an empty treasury and an empire surrounded by enemies, but through his genius as a diplomat he succeeded in acquiring gold through the sale of super-fluous church plate and from the rich, and in gaining the friendship of Venice, who supplied him with a navy. His greatest success was with Germany; the Emperor Henry IV attacked the Normans in Lombardy, causing Robert to return to Italy. Robert's eldest son Bohemond, left in charge of the newly conquered territory, estab-lished himself at Ioannina with many deserters from the Byzantine army. Alexius, on returning to the attack, was once more forced to flee to Ohrid. Not only was the Byzantine army hopelessly outnum-bered but it was no match for the Norman cavalry.

A third defeat for Byzantium came at the river Vardar followed by the seizure of Skopje, Kastoria and Trikkala. From Kastoria Bohe-mond moved to Larissa, arriving there on St George's Day 1083. A six-month seige ensued during which the inhabitants had to eat human flesh. The governor wrote: 'We are deprived of victuals which Christian men may eat; we have even touched what is not lawful'.

The battle to relieve Larissa became the first success for Alexius. Bohemond retreated to Kastoria while the Emperor sowed dissension among his followers. The Norman troops had not been paid for a considerable time (Anna Comnena says four years) and the wily Alexius bribed them to demand immediate payment. Bohemond was forced to depart for Italy, leaving Raoul of Brienne, Constable of Apulia, in charge of Kastoria. By October 1083 Alexius had equipped himself with siege engines and men. He appeared at Kastoria and, dividing his army into two groups, one to attack from the land and the other in small boats from the lake, took the town.

Robert Guiscard, on learning of this loss, sailed for Illyricum, attacking Corfu on the way where his fleet was routed by the Venetians. The Doge of Venice, Domenico Selvo, was rewarded with the title of Protosebastos and a pension, and all the churches of Venice received an annual payment in gold. Venetians were given workshops in Constantinople and exemption from customs dues in any part of Byzantium. Alexius had saved the Empire from attack from the West for over a century, but in doing so made Venice the power which overthrew Constantinople in 1204.

Bohemond returned to Kastoria where he spent the winter of 1096, requisitioning animals for his baggage train. On this occasion he was no longer the enemy of Byzantium but a leader of the First Crusade to the Holy Land. On their journey through Asia Minor the Crusaders were accompanied by Taticius, the eunuch from Ohrid.

Under Byzantine rule Kastoria often served as a place of exile for courtiers who had fallen foul of the regime by the Golden Horn. It was, after Constantinople and Thessalonica, the most civilised city in Greece, with one of the most important icon workshops in the Empire, producing icons of the highest quality during the twelfth and fourteenth centuries.

During the fifteenth century Sephardic Jews, banished from Granada in 1492 by Ferdinand and Isabella, established the fur trade which has flourished here for nearly five hundred years. Most of its products are made up from scraps of rejected fur imported from all over the world. Yet we passed many shops whose windows were full of clumsily stuffed bears, wolves, beavers, badgers, wild cats, beech martens, pine martens, squirrels and otters.

Naturally we did not have the time, let alone the stamina, to see 32 churches. However the Tourist Police put us in touch with a gruff –

extremely gruff – old café proprietor who acts as custodian for six of the most important. In fact it was unclear whether there are other Byzantine churches in the town or only those dating from the Turkish occupation.

We were fortunate in coming to the tiny twelfth-century basilica of Hagios Nikolaos tou Kasnitzi with the frescoes of Kurbinovo and Prizren fresh in our minds. While lacking the turbulence of the draperies in Macedonia, the angels in the frescoes here bear a great resemblance to them. Particularly beautiful is the angel of the Annunciation to the left of the apse. An inscription tells us the church's founder was Nicephorus Kasnitzes, a courtier from Constantinople who had been banished to Kastoria. There is a portrait of him in the narthex – tall, slender, dark-bearded, in blue robes, holding a model of his church, his wife Anna standing next to him. The frescoes are among the best of the Macedonian school. The Virgin in the Dormition is unusual in that she is facing to the left, whereas the opposite is the norm. She has an unmistakably Greek face, as does each one of the very fine warrior saints on the south wall, the latter in scale armour and carrying kite-shaped shields. Outside, the ornamentation on the brickwork includes a series of large 'N's, either the donor's initial or that of the saint to whom the church is dedicated.

The church of Hagios Athanasios is as small, though much later. It was built by command of two Albanian brothers, Stoias and Theodore Mousakes, in 1384 during the decade between Serbian and Turkish rule when these two held Kastoria as an independent lordship. Its frescoes belong to the Thessalonica school and are good examples. Christ is portrayed in an Imperial crown and stole. Many of the saints wear court-dress, with costly robes and strange, high plumed head-dresses, while the Two Theodores are armed very much like contemporary Western knights apart from holding kite-shaped shields. St Barbara is in a close-fitting coif like a 1920s wedding veil, banded round with three rows of pearls. A Roman virgin, she was imprisoned in a tower for being a Christian by her pagan father, who starved and beat her before finally killing her; he was then consumed by fire from Heaven – in consequence Barbara is invoked against lightning. She is also the patron saint of gunners.

The three-aisled church of the Taxiarches of the Metropolis is much older, dating from 860. Many of its frescoes were repainted about 1359 under Serbian rule and are very like those in Serbia. There is an extremely lifelike portrait of Princess Irene Palaeologina, mother of John Asen, who commissioned the redecoration. Irene, daughter of the Byzantine Emperor Michael VIII, married a Bulgarian who as Ivan Asen III became tsar for less than a year in 1279 – a not uncommon occurrence during the Second Bulgarian Empire. Another of their sons, on the death of John Cantacuzenus, became governor of the Peloponnese.

The founder and his mother appear with the Archangel Michael on the exterior of the church, which is covered with portraits from various dates giving a fascinating glimpse of different styles of fashionable dress. It is thought that the Taxiarches was a cemetery church and that Irene Palaeologina was buried there. The frescoes in the narthex and the side aisles – all in very bad condition – date from the tenth century while the redecoration of 1359 is confined to the central aisle and the sanctuary. As one might expect in a frontier town, they include some splendid warrior saints. The scenes of the Passion are particularly intense and dramatic, the tortured faces bewailing the death of Christ portray the very deepest grief. Even the Virgin Orans in the conch of the apse has enormous power – a far cry from the sentimental Virgins of the Roman Church.

The little church of the Panagia Koubelidiki is another mid-ninth century building. It has three projecting semi-circular apses on the east, north and south, forming a design termed a 'tri-conch' by architects, to which a narthex was added, lengthened in the fifteenth century by a much larger exo-narthex. There is a most unusual Trinity from the thirteenth century which depicts a bearded God the Father holding on his knee the Son who supports a disc on which is painted a dove (the Holy Ghost). Equally unusual is the Dormition: instead of standing behind the bier of the Virgin, Christ is shown ascending into Heaven with the baby which represents her soul. Many of the frescoes, including the Annunciation, all those in the sanctuary, and most in the narthex, date from the Turkish occupation. The church was bombed by the Italians during the War and the unusually tall dome had to be rebuilt. It is currently being restored.

The seat of a bishop, the church of Hagios Stephanos is one of the largest in Kastoria. It is unique in possessing a gallery for the women and is the only church in the town with frescoes dating from its foundation in the ninth century. Sadly they are in appalling condition. It is thought that while the outlines were painted when the plaster was wet, the details were worked on a dry ground, and have subsequently flaked off. In the narthex it is still possible to make out one of the earliest scenes of the Last Judgment, with souls being weighed in the scales and rows of Apostles lined up with Christ. A second layer of frescoes was added in some places in the thirteenth century, and these are in better condition. The latest work dates from the fourteenth century and consists of two dedicatory portraits, one of which is of the priest Theodore Lemniotes, who may have re-endowed the church. A bald, bearded man in late middle age, his eyes have a profoundly spiritual expression.

The most impressive church we saw at Kastoria, both in terms of architecture and painting, was that of the Anargyroi – who in the West are better known as SS. Cosmas and Damian. They were two Syrian physicians, early martyrs who in the Middle Ages had a considerable reputation as wonder-workers; according to the Golden Legend one of the miracles wrought by their relics was to replace the cancerous leg of a Christian as he slept with the sound leg of a dead Moslem. Sometimes the sick would spend a night in a church dedicated to them, hoping for therapeutic dreams. A three-aisled basilica, the only church in the town decorated with marble, Hagioi Anargyroi was built at some time between 950 and 1050; the Bulgarian Tsar Samuel is sometimes credited with being the founder. Among the few frescoes which it keeps from its early period are those in the narthex of 'St Constantine' the Great and his mother the Empress Helena. The church was repainted in about 1180 by an earlier Theodore Lemniotes and his wife Anna Radene, who dedicated it to the Anargyroi in order to be deemed worthy of 'the healing of the flesh and the gift of physical well-being'. Lemniotes also dedicated the new paintings in the north aisle to St George – there is a very fine portrayal of the saint on his white horse as well as scenes from his miracles and martyrdom. An inscription in verse reads

> You were already painted in my heart,
> Cruelly-tried martyr, with secret hues of longing
> And now, with more material colours,
> I paint the pictures of your miracles
>
> Asking your help in the judgment to come
> Your suppliant Theodoros Lemniotes'.

The frescoes of the second phase include some which are outstanding not only at Kastoria but among Byzantine art as a whole, in particular the Entombment. Some of these are by one of the artists who worked at Kurbinovo. By another hand there are portraits of the opulent donor, of his wife and of their son John; Anna Lemniotes is sumptuously dressed, with a gold turban and rings on each finger and thumb. There is also a portrait of the monk Theophilos Lemniotes – presumably a cousin – shown holding a model of the church; he was the donor of the frescoes in the south aisle. It is thought that the family were not exiles but belonged to the local nobility. An unusual (possibly unique) feature of the decorations is that each artist painted his own version of the Annunciation. One shows the Virgin standing with the Angel approaching from the right, the other a scene from the Apocrypha where the Virgin is drawing water from a well.

We recovered from our six churches with a pre-lunch glass of ouzo – which had already become established as the ritual of the 'morning ouzo'. It is a much better drink for a hot spring day than šlivovica. After a truly awful lunch of greasy meat balls and disintegrating vine leaves, swallowed only with the aid of retsina, we cheered ourselves up by walking beside the lake to the monastery of the Panagia Mavriotissa. We saw distinctive local fishing boats, flat-bottomed with high, square prows and sterns, spotted an elegant black-necked grebe amid the feathery rushes, and heard a nightingale sing in broad daylight. After half an hour we suddenly met a stork, unusually tame even by the standards of those friendly birds. It turned out to be the pet of a Fr. Gabriel, priest-in-charge of the monastery. We asked them to pose for a photograph, but the stork fled as soon as its pastor donned his stovepipe hat.

The monastery by the lake, surrounded by gigantic plane trees, has not retained any conventual buildings, but its two churches remain. They are the church of the Panagia dating from the eleventh century, and the adjoining chapel of St John the Theologian from the sixteenth. The well preserved frescoes on the first of these are from the early thirteenth century – it is thought the upper part of the church collapsed and these frescoes copied the earlier ones – and, while some are impressive, they are on the whole rather crude. The frescoes on the exterior of the narthex include two figures tentatively identified as the Emperor Michael VIII Palaeologus and his brother the Grand Domestic John – unfortunately they have both lost their heads. The paintings in the chapel of St John are interesting in that the boats in one scene are identical with those we had noticed on Lake Kastoria.

We had to return our car to Yugoslavia, having hired it there. Bitola seemed the obvious place to do so, since it was possible to cross the border by train to Florina and then continue the following day to Thessalonica, the next Byzantine centre on our list. We left our luggage at the King Alexander hotel outside Florina and drove over the border to Bitola, rather pleased to be back among the Southern Slavs. With its mosques and shady parks, Bitola is pleasant enough for idling away half a day. There were gypsies everywhere, not the tinkers and vagrants of Western Europe but zingari straight out of Ruritania. Children with wreaths of flowers round the headscarves covering their curly black hair brought their tambourines with them into the public gardens to beg. There was a large band of them at the station, shouting at each other, their gold ear-rings and the gold coins sewn on their embroidered waistcoats and brightly coloured Turkish trousers gleaming in the sun.

As we left Bitola, from our train window we could see still more gypsies. They were in the field sitting in two circles, men in one, women in the other. They had tents and one or two goats but, unlike English 'travellers', no horses, no lurchers and no caravans. We were to meet many more in Greece. Their numbers have in fact declined in the last half century. Proportionally they suffered far more than the Jews from the Nazis, 400,000 out of a mere two million being herded into the gas chambers. They still speak the Romany language and are much swarthier than gypsies in England, more Indian in appearance. The younger women are very striking indeed, with raven black hair and glittering eyes, especially on great holidays when they wear ropes of gold coins. The Byzantines knew the gypsies as the Zatts. After being settled in Syria and Cilicia by the Abbasid Caliphs, they first entered Imperial territory in 855. Peace-lovers and fortune-tellers then as now, they were confused with a demon-worshipping sect of Gnostics who practised magic, the *Athingani* – from whom they derive the name 'Tsiganes'.

The train took two-and-a-quarter hours to cover the twenty-five miles to Florina. It travelled so slowly that one could see the fledgelings in their nests in the bushes beside the line. Hens wandered over the tracks, water buffalo grazed next to them. It was not just one train but three, since we had to change at the frontier and again at the branch line, yet the pace throughout was the same, lurching along in spurts or else drowsing at halts.

Florina, in the mountains, has been totally rebuilt, having been completely destroyed during the civil war of 1945–47. The sole item of interest was a stuffed honey buzzard in a chemist's shop. We stayed at a splendid but moderately priced new hotel run by some cheerful Melbourne Greeks who spoke classic 'Strine'. (Melbourne has the largest concentration of Greeks in the world next to Athens and Thessalonica.) The family pet was an elderly, reserved and dignified Alsatian called Bobby. They told us how one night during the previous March, when there was a deep fall of snow, they had heard Bobby growling and saw him glare at the car park. Then they saw five pairs of eyes glaring back – wolves. But no-one in his right mind could be deterred from staying in so excellent an hotel by a small hazard like wolves in the car park. There are no recent incidents of people being eaten, even if the occasional sheep is taken. We heard too that there are bears in the locality, though these at least have never been seen near the hotel. They served here a drinkable unresinated white wine made by monks on Mount Athos – one would like to think this was something which has been produced since Byzantine times.

The train from Florina to Thessalonica had rexine-covered seats which were uncomfortably hot. A woman got in after us, dressed in black wool from head to toe, and sat opposite. Before she sat down she crossed herself, dusted the whole seat carefully with a tissue, crossing herself again when the train began to move. Fortunately she had left the train before it hit a car on a level crossing. No-one was hurt, but we sat in the sweltering heat for an hour while the police were called to sort everything out. The country seen from the windows was dull and rather flat. We had never met such a profusion of Judas trees anywhere, however. Their dark pink blossom was set off by acres and acres of white asphodel – no doubt very pretty, but a sign that the soil had been over-grazed for centuries.

Though it is Greece's second largest city and a busy modern seaport, Thessalonica is elegant and cheerful, with the best food in the country, though no-one can claim that Greek cuisine is competitive. (Jan Morris lists it among the world's great disappointments.) The Romans made Thessalonica the capital of Illyricum and, after

Rome, the most important city in the Empire – a role it was to retain under the New Rome, Constantinople. Sacked by the Arabs in 904 and again by the Normans in 1185, on both occasions with appalling carnage, the city became the capital of the Latin kingdom of 'Salonique' under Boniface of Montferrat in 1204. Most of the Western knights returned home with their spoils, leaving 'Salonique' easy prey for Theodore I Angelus, Despot of Epirus, who freed the kingdom in 1224, admittedly after a lengthy seige. Another long seige, lasting three years, resulted in Ottoman rule for a short time from 1387, but it returned to Byzantium in 1402 with the Turkish defeat at Ankara. Given to Venice in 1423, Thessalonica was finally conquered by the Turks in 1430. It remained a bastion of Ottoman rule for nearly five centuries (Kemal Ataturk was born here) before being at last retaken by the Greeks in 1912, when the churches which had been converted into mosques were reclaimed for Christianity. In August 1917, the old quarter was largely destroyed by a terrible fire, accidentally started by a French soldier, which swept through the entire city. In 1917, after the evacuation of Gallipoli, the Allies – English, French, Russians, Italians and Serbs – had landed at Thessalonica. By 1918 they had assembled 600,000 troops there but because of sickness only 100,000 of these were on their feet; with some justice the Germans described the 'Salonika Front' as the 'greatest Allied concentration camp of the War'. At last General Franchet d'Esperey (known by British Tommies as 'Desperate Frankie') broke out in September and annihilated his Bulgarian opponents.

The city's Turkish population was expelled in 1923, to be replaced by a far more numerous population of Greeks driven out of Asia Minor. These brought with them their 'Bouzouki' music which, contrary to popular opinion, is not a product of the Greek mainland. There was another change in the ethnic mix of the population – or rather loss – during the Second World War. After their expulsion from Granada in 1492 a large colony of Sephardic Jews had settled here, continuing to speak their archaic Spanish. Misses Muir Mackenzie and Irby reported in the 1860s that 'All the richest people are Jews'. They comment: 'The Hebrews settled in Salonika are handsome, many of them auburn-haired, and their women often delicate and even fair. In beauty the latter exceed the Helene.' These Jewesses dressed in 'curious cut-down pelisses . . . of scarlet cloth lined with fur and bordered with gold'. A rabbi told the admiring ladies: 'We came here from Spain, and at first all wore black like Spaniards. What we wear now is Turkish and some of us are beginning to imitate the Franks.' The community continued to flourish after the departure of the Turks, still speaking their curious Spanish, but in 1943–4 the Nazis dragged most of them off to Germany and the gas-chambers. A few were saved by the Spanish consul, who demanded their repatriation to Spain as Spaniards, apparently on the instructions of General Franco who was himself a quarter Jewish.

Despite many disasters and drastic rebuilding, for those who have determined imaginations it is still possible to visualize Thessalonica as a Byzantine city. The heart is an area running up from the sea to the acropolis around which the fourteenth-century walls stand, linking sturdy towers; the gate of Anna Palaeologina, Empress of Andronicus III (1328–41) is more or less intact though most of the Heptagyrion, or 'Seven Towers', are in ruins. It was here that in 1430 the Turks stormed in, to massacre the inhabitants. The former Turkish quarter, on the site of what was once a Byzantine quarter, lies beneath these ramparts, with steep un-numbered streets full of wooden houses and gardens. And, if not perhaps quite so exciting as some writers claim, there are many interesting churches.

The first we visited was the eighth-century Hagia Sophia. Half way between an aisled basilica and a cross-in-square with a dome, it has columns whose magnificent acanthus leaf capitals may have come from a pagan temple. A mosaic of the Virgin in the apse is impressive, even if her head is much too big; behind her may dimly be seen the outline of a great cross which she has replaced, the cross being the sole form of ecclesiastical decoration permitted by the Iconoclasts (the 'image breakers' of the eighth and ninth centuries). The Christ of the Transfiguration in the dome is also impressive though undeniably crude, while the Twelve Apostles below have their admirers despite a curious awkwardness – they seem to be performing a clumsy dance. Beneath them are inscribed the words 'Ye men of Galilee, why stand ye gazing up into Heaven?' They were made in either the ninth or the tenth century.

Before the Turkish occupation the Paraskevi was known as the Acheiropoeitos – 'Not made by human hands' – on account of an icon of the Mother of God which wrought so many wonders that people considered it could only have been painted by miraculous means. It is a fifth-century basilica reminiscent of St Apollinare in Classe and its two rows of huge marble columns have superb Ionic capitals which bear the chi-rho emblem. On the soffits (the surfaces underneath the arches joining the columns) there are vividly coloured contemporary mosaics of flowers, birds (notably pheasants) and baskets of fruit, while there are more of these in the narthex where there is also a fine plain cross of blue and gold. The Paraskevi is a noble building, still in process of a meticulous restoration which has revealed two early floor mosaics, but marred by a deplorable nineteenth-century iconostasis.

The Panagia Chalkeon ('Our Lady of the Coppersmiths') is in a corner of the Roman forum, the square named Plateia Dikastirion. Built in 1028 by Christopher the Lombard, this is the only surviving example of a Byzantine guild church (though not the guild of coppersmiths since the name commemorates the days when it was the mosque used by the Turkish coppersmiths of Thessalonica). Small and very holy, when we visited it Vespers was being sung with great dignity by the priest and a single member of the congregation. The marble slabs of the iconostasis have two strange birds rather like kiwis, but the eleventh-century fresco of the Last Judgment is too damaged to be of real interest, despite attempts at restoration.

Hagios Demetrios, the largest basilica in Greece, may be described without exaggeration as a replica of the building which once stood here. It was founded in the fifth century, rebuilt in the seventh and restored after the fire in 1917. It is essentially a reliquary church, designed to house the relics of Demetrios, Thessalonica's patron saint. Demetrios is above all a warrior saint. He was a Roman nobleman whose military abilities earned him the patronage of the Emperor Galerius (305–11). This was no mean achievement since Galerius was a brilliant commander who had risen from the ranks to the throne as a result solely of his own military genius. Demetrios forfeited the Imperial favour by becoming a Christian, however, though at first he was only imprisoned. Unfortunately his bosom friend St Nestor (they are frequently depicted side by side) killed Thessalonica's leading gladiator, who was the apple of the Emperor's eye. Nestor was summarily beheaded by the angry Galerius, who thought he had acted on his friend's instructions; Demetrios is said to have been despatched at the Emperor's command by his fellow-soldiers' spears. The place of execution was the public baths where he had been imprisoned and on whose site the church now stands. A phial of blood-stained earth was found when the original crypt was discovered earlier this century, after the fire. Demetrios, who is sometimes painted being speared to death, sometimes riding a red horse and carrying a lance, was regarded as one of the most efficacious of all heavenly protectors and was credited with securing victories over Arabs, Franks and Slavs. The latter also adopted him, but he remains essentially Greek, perhaps the most popular of all saints among the Greeks.

The first church here was built by Leontius, Prefect of Illyricum, after his prayers to Demetrios cured a palsy, which doctors had told him was incurable. The mosaics which are Thessalonica's greatest treasure date from the rebuilding some three hundred years later, in the seventh century. They are those of St Demetrios with the donor's two small sons (every visitor's favourite); St Demetrios between the city's bishop and its treasurer; St Demetrios with a deacon to whom he had appeared in a dream with a reassuring message that the church was soon to be rebuilt; the Virgin with St Theodore, who is portrayed in the robes of the Captain of the Imperial Guard; and St Sergius. André Grabar finds their colours 'sober almost to the point of meagreness, with cool tones predominating: whites and greys, greens mingled with a little gold'. Yet the effect is magnificent and one of the utmost richness. Moreover the figures are wonderfully alive, the faces those of real people.

St Theodore and St Sergius were two more popular Byzantine warrior saints whom one meets again and again. 'Theodore the General' is surrounded by stories of incredible wonder-working. The least unlikely account of him is that he was a Christian Roman legionary who tried to burn down a temple of Cybele at Amasea and who, having first endured revolting tortures, was martyred by being thrown into a furnace. Sergius, who is frequently depicted with his brother officer and fellow-martyr St Bacchus, was executed with Bacchus in the year 303 at Resapha in Syria; their crime being to have absented themselves from a parade at which the Emperor Maximian was sacrificing to Jupiter, the special protector of Rome.

The side chapel of St Euthymios, built in 1303 by Andronicus II's Master of the Horse, contains wretched fragments of once splendid frescoes of which – so far as one can judge – the best was the Communion of the Twelve Apostles. There are a few frescoes in the main body of the church, of which the most interesting depicts the hesychast St Gregory Palamas and the monk Iosaph (formerly the Emperor John VI Cantacuzenus), contemporaries who knew each other.

Profitas Elias has likewise suffered from unavoidable restoration. It is on a hill, since churches dedicated to the Prophet Elijah were always built on high ground, often on the sites of former temples to Apollo – both rode through the heavens in fiery chariots. This however is supposed to be on the site of a former Byzantine palace. Originally a monastery church, it dates from 1340–60, was converted into a mosque by the Turks in 1430 and given back to Christian worship in 1912. Few fragments of frescoes remain, but the brick-work ornamentation of the exterior is very good indeed. Learning that we were not Germans, its friendly old custodian insisted on shaking hands.

We had dinner at what in our opinion was one of the best restaurants in Greece; Stratis, on the sea-front. We had very good fried mussels and a strange but excellent mixture of green vegetables, which seemed to include nettles. There is every reason to suppose the Byzantines ate similar food. When Constantine moved his capital to the Golden Horn Byzantine cuisine was Roman, and remained so for many years, but gradually the influence of the East made itself felt. By the reign of Justinian the Imperial court was importing chefs from Syria, Persia and even India. Fish played a large part in their diet – especially outside the capital. They ate three times a day. A meal consisted of hors d'oeuvres – cheese from the Vlach shepherds, olives, cold ham and pork and vegetables stewed in olive oil. This was followed by various soups – tripe such as we had sampled in Venice, meatballs in a lemon sauce like the avgolemono soup of modern Greece, or fish soup flavoured with saffron. Next came grilled fish and pig's trotters, veal, game, duck, and lamb stuffed with raisins and pistachios or pine kernels. Fruit included pomegranates, grapes and oranges (introduced from China) and apples from Persia. Cucumbers were grown extensively but tomatoes and peppers – now so popular in Greece, Turkey and Southern Italy – were, of course, unknown. The New World had yet to be discovered.

The Rotunda, later the church of St George, was erected by the Emperor Galerius at the beginning of the fourth century as a mausoleum or as a temple to his patron Jupiter. It is a vast, domed, circular building, whose huge size is disguised by perfect proportions.

Once a colonnaded triumphal way led to the mighty Arch of Galerius nearby, commemorating a crushing defeat which he had inflicted on the Persians. (A companion arch has long since disappeared.) The Emperor built on this grandiose scale because he intended to move the Empire's capital from Rome to Thessalonica.

Gaius Galerius Valerius Maximianus was born near Sofia and started life as a shepherd. Entering the Roman army, he rose from the ranks to become one of its most formidable generals – intrepid, bloodthirsty and an inspired strategist. In 293 the Emperor Diocletian appointed him Caesar (Is he one of the four red porphyry tetrarchs outside St Marks?) while in 305 he became Emperor of the East, ruling what are now the Balkans and Turkey; for a moment it seemed he might become Emperor of the West as well. A firm pagan, it was he who persuaded Diocletian to unleash the last full-scale persecution of the Christians by the Roman Empire. His characteristic suggestion that anyone refusing to sacrifice to the old gods should be burnt alive immediately was not, however, adopted. He died in 311 after a lingering illness during which his body, hideously swollen, was covered with ulcers and devoured by worms. Suspecting this horrible disease to be the vengeance of the Christian God, just before he died he issued an Imperial edict in which he begged his Christian subjects to pray for him. To judge from statues Galerius appears to have been a tiny little man with strangely small, almost Puckish features.

The Rotunda was converted into a Christian church dedicated to St George about 400, when an apse was formed out of a recess opposite the entrance. Later a narthex was added and also an ambulatory around, though this disappeared long ago. It was lavishly decorated with mosaics at the time of its conversion, those in the dome alone comprising not fewer than 36 million tesserae. Many of the surviving mosaics fell down during the earthquake of 1979, since when the building has been closed for restoration, which is expected to take another ten years; the interior is covered by scaffolding. Most of the mosaics are being reconstructed. We were especially sad not to be able to see the famous panels of saints against backgrounds of fantastic architectural perspectives which are in the dome. We did see a magnificent Iconoclast's cross in blue and gold, however, together with some motifs of birds, palmettes and fringes (which in André Grabar's opinion are in imitation of Persian silks and carpets).

Fortunately we had an introduction to the director of the restoration, a learned, friendly, heavily moustached young archaeologist called Sotirios Kissas (a name which, correctly pronounced, sounds a little odd to English ears). He told us that what was being done at the Rotunda was only part of a gigantic programme of restoration currently being undertaken in Thessalonica by the Greek government, involving ten monuments. As someone who spent five years at the University of Belgrade he was particularly interested in the relationship between Byzantium and the Southern Slavs. In his view the latter's culture during the Middle Ages had owed everything to the Eastern Empire. He placed great importance on the contribution of Ohrid, which he believed to have been a centre from which Byzantine ideas spread to the Slavs. He emphasized the significance of Archbishop Gregory (who built Sv. Clement's there in 1314) having been the personal friend of both the Emperor Andronicus II and King Milutin of the Serbs. It was he who explained to us that the frescoes at Mileševa are almost certainly by artists from Thessalonica.

On climbing the hill towards the Turkish quarter we came upon Hagios Nikolaos Orfanos. The latest of Thessalonica's Byzantine churches, it was built between 1314 and 1317 by an exiled Serbian prince. It is small in size, and both the building and its frescoes are charming. There is a Crucifixion which is typically Byzantine and yet reminiscent of many Italian Primitives; an Ascent of the Cross in which a movingly dignified Christ goes up a gallows ladder; and a delightful saint removing a thorn from a lion's paw.

Much further up the hill, nearly at the top and just below the (uninteresting) monastery of Vlatodon, after some searching we eventually found what we thought the most memorable of all Thessalonica's churches. This was Hosios David, in the depths of the Turkish quarter and not easy to locate. Little more than a chapel, it is sometimes called the Oratory of Christ Latomos, since it is all that remains of a church which once served the vanished monastery of the Latamou. It probably dates from the late fifth century, although according to tradition it was founded by the daughter of that scourge of fourth-century Christians, Galerius. Its cross-shaped plan was ruined when it was turned into a mosque by the Turks, who also applied their customary plaster to its walls. In 1921, however, a wonderful fifth-century mosaic was uncovered in the apse. It is of a beardless, youthful Christ of great majesty, from whom emanate rays of light. He is seated on a rainbow, the Prophet Ezekiel on one side and the Prophet Habakkuk on the other. There are also the beasts who represent the Evangelists (in the *Apocalypse*), together with birds who symbolize the Apostles. But it is the face of Christ which is so haunting; as Grabar puts it: 'His face conveys not so much the imperiousness of Godhead as the eternal youth of Emmanuel the promised Son.'

The custodians of Thessalonica's churches are unusually pleasant people. That of Hosios David was no exception. Perhaps it was not just the beauty of what he had to guard, but the cheerful little garden in which it stands, and his canary who lives in a cage just outside, that made him so friendly. He told us, in a species of German, how when the Turks burst into the church in 1430 with murder in their minds the priest in charge had welcomed them, plied them with communion wine till they were dead drunk, and then made his escape through a trapdoor into the catacombs below which communicate with every other church in the city. We were very disappointed when Sotirios Kissas told us that the tale was a complete myth.

The White Tower on the front was built by the Turks soon after their capture of the city. It is now an exhibition centre. When we visited it a collection of Early Christian and Byzantine art was on display. There were some good pieces of pottery – not that Byzantine ware was ever of the same high standard as Persian, silver and ivory being considered more suitable for elegant dishes. Perhaps the most striking exhibits were a fourth-century tomb painting of Susannah and the Elders, a forerunner of the Byzantine fresco, and two wonderful gold and cloisonné enamel armlets decorated with birds, leaves and rosettes. The latter date from the ninth or tenth centuries and were found during excavations in the city in 1956.

Very few Byzantine enamels have survived, having been melted down for their gold by the Turks, by the 'Crusaders' of 1204 or even by their owners themselves, desperate for money during the last days of the failing Empire. Very few of those which remain are in Balkan museums; these armlets are the supreme examples. The best collections are in the Treasury at Venice and at Dumbarton Oaks in Washington DC. After the Fourth Crusade many found their way to France, nearly all of them reliquaries, and were destroyed as relics of superstition – and also for their gold content – during the Terror. Fortunately they are still being discovered from time to time. That from the hoard in the Piazza della Consolazione at Rome is at Dumbarton Oaks, part of one found in Cyprus being at the British Museum while the rest is at the Metropolitan Museum in New York. Perhaps the most interesting is the crown formed of seven enamel plaques, which was found in a field in Slovakia. It was the gift of the Emperor Constantine IX Monomachus (1042–55) to either King Andrew of Hungary or his consort, a daughter of the Grand Duke of Kiev. It may have been buried when the King was fleeing from Bela I in 1061, or alternatively when King Solomon was besieging Neutra in 1074. It is now in the National Musuem at Budapest.

The Rotunda, Hagios Nikolaos Orfanos, Hosios David and the White Tower were enough for one morning. We lunched at the reassuringly named Tottis Tea Rooms in Plateia Aristotelou. Full of red plush, it seems to be where well-heeled Thessalonicans go but is reasonably priced. We found the food excellent value if scarcely remarkable – only later did we realize how good it was for Greece.

The churches we saw in the afternoon were not of the same quality as those of the morning, yet were nonetheless worth visiting. Hagia Ekaterina, an early fourteenth-century edifice built on the ruins of a monastery and dedicated to 'the Great Martyr and all-wise Saint Catherine', contains miserably damaged frescoes dating from the Palaeologan revival. At Hagioi Apostoloi, from the same revival, there are frescoes which are not in quite so bad a state, together with several mosaics of this period, including a fine Nativity and an even better Transfiguration. The brickwork outside is much admired, with elaborate patterns. The church derives part of its charm from having escaped excessive restoration. We were there during Vespers on a sunny spring evening, and the singing, taken up by many enthusiastic young people among the congregation, lifted our spirits.

The train, second class only with no restaurant car, sleepers or couchettes, left Thessalonica at 9.30 a.m. for its twenty-one-hour journey to Constantinople. Making stop after stop it crawled slowly along a circuitous route toward the Turkish frontier, at first through flat, dull country enlivened by the blossom of countless orchards, then through miniature canyons and the magnificent rocky gorge of the river Nestos. We saw a flock of storks, a marsh harrier, a beautiful blue-chested roller. We had brought bread, meat, cheese and olives, ouzo and red Nemean wine, and were prepared to enjoy our journey. But the ticket clerk at Thessalonica had booked us non-existent places and at about 5.30 p.m. we were ejected from our reasonably comfortable seats. For a moment we wished that the Ottomans still ruled Thessalonica so that the clerk could be bastinadoed. After a wrangle in his – and our – amazing German the amiable Greek guard found us new places. An hour later our new compartment was invaded by wild women in black robes, white veils and slippers who, with much shouting and screaming, installed their luggage of huge black plastic bags over our feet, after which they squatted in the corridor brewing coffee in scarlet enamelled coffee pots – offering cups to male passengers, though not to female. They appeared to be a mother, and three daughters who were in their twenties, all looking so outlandish that someone asked if they were Bedouin.

At dusk the Bosnian sitting opposite us took his shoes off, then knelt on the seat to say his prayers. Before night came finally we trundled through mountains, marshes and dense woods – once past a Frankish hilltop castle. The wild women's leader, a tiny old crone of forty with a delightful grin who flirted with every man on the train and who asked us to fill her coffee cup half full of wine – probably to shock her daughters – grew noticeably uneasy as we approached the frontier. At Pithion we were lined up below the customs house under floodlights so that a Greek customs officer could throw the passports down into the crowd – bellowing out the names as he did so, Turkish names being shouted with marked contempt. We felt like refugees. The wild women were allowed through; but at Uzun Kupri the Turkish customs men opened the black bags to reveal hundreds of scarlet enamelled coffee pots, no doubt destined to be sold at some remote village in the back of beyond. The wild women, very subdued save for their mother and leader, who winked non-stop at male passengers, were herded off the train by customs men plainly trying hard not to laugh. The last we saw of any of them was at midnight through the window of the customs house at Uzun Kupri as the train drew out. The little crone was at bay, seated in front of a table under a strong light and facing two fierce uniformed officers, a sight which reduced the entire compartment to fits of laughter. We were all of us quite sure that she would emerge triumphant.

The night grew very cold, the rexine-covered benches very hard. We ached all over as a grey, foggy morning came very slowly. Then, at the side of the track, we saw ruined ramparts. We had reached the city of the world's desire.

# Constantinople, city of the world's desire

'They never thought there could be in all the world so rich a city,
when they saw the high walls and magnificent towers that enclosed it
round about, the rich palaces and mighty churches, of which there
were so many that no one would have believed it who had not seen it
with their own eyes.'

Geoffroy de Villehardouin, *La Conquête de Constantinople*

The spider weaves the curtains in the palace of the Caesars; The owl
calls the watches in Afrasiab's towers.'

Sultan Mehmet II – 'The Conqueror' – (quoting Saadi) as he walked through the
ruins of the Imperial palace in 1453.

T HE EASTERN Empire's former capital has an incompara-
ble setting and a vile climate. On its north-eastern side is the superb
harbour called, from its shape, the Golden Horn; on its southern is
the Sea of Marmora. The Bosporus, which separates it from Asia,
links the Mediterranean with the Black Sea. During its Imperial days
no city in the world was better sited commercially, commanding
trade routes which reached north and south, east and west. Such
advantages more than compensated for bitter winters and sultry
summers.

Constantine may have decided to build his New Rome at Byzantium not only because of its perfect strategic position but also
because, like his former capital, it was build on seven hills. As far as
possible his new city was copied from the old (churches replacing the
temples), with thousands of statues removed from Rome to Constantinople to adorn the palaces, gardens and the Hippodrome. Within a
hundred years the population was greater than that of Rome and the
walls had been rebuilt in their present position. By the sixth century
500,000 people lived in the capital. There were strict regulations to
preserve the rights of householders. Every private owner had a right

to an uninterrupted view of the sea, gardens or public monuments, but those claiming a right to a view of a particular antique statue must prove they had the education to appreciate it. There were no rich or poor quarters, palaces being beside hovels and nine-stored tenement blocks. The houses of the rich, usually two or three stories high and built of brick, had glazed windows overlooking a large courtyard at the back surrounded by stables, hen houses and cattle sheds. Also in the courtyard would be the bath house and a lavatory. There were also public bath houses in the city, rather like clubs, where men could spend the day with their friends.

The Eparch was the governor of Constantinople, responsible for maintaining law and order, for providing the city with food from the provinces, and for controlling trade and industry. The trades were divided up into many guilds — five for different branches of the silk industry alone — and there were heavy penalties for those who tried to engage in two businesses, however similar (for instance, dealers in raw silk could not make or sell silk dresses). Idlers of all classes were discouraged, jobs being found for them weeding the public gardens, cleaning the streets or working in the bakeries. The infirm were looked after in state hospitals which by the eleventh century employed female as well as male doctors.

Even ladies of the Imperial court were encouraged to lead a useful life. The daughters of Constantine VII Porphyrogenitus did secretarial work for their father. In the gynaikeion (or women's quarters) trade was permitted. The Empress Zoë made scent for the guild of perfume, wax and soap sellers and for many centuries silk was manufactured for the retail trade. In the thirteenth century the Emperor John III Vatatzes bought his wife a crown called 'Eggy' with the proceeds of her poultry farming.

Women of the upper and middle classes were better-off in Byzantium than anywhere else in the medieval world. Unlike their Western counterparts they were not treated as chattels and, even in cases of divorce, were practically on an equal footing with men in respect of property and guardianship of children. Girls had the same basic schooling as boys but were not allowed to attend university, relying on tutors for further education. The Byzantines were intellectual rather than social snobs. Until the eleventh century there was no real aristocracy in the Empire, and lowly birth was no barrier to the Imperial throne. Justinian was the son of a peasant, Basil I a groom at the stables of the Great Palace. Equally the daughter of a publican could become Empress. Often brides were chosen for Emperors or their sons at Brideshows. Agents scoured the Empire for beautiful girls of respectable family who were then lined up for inspection in Constantinople. The bridegroom handed a golden apple to the winner – Leo VI found one of his four wives in this way. But although the Byzantines valued education in women, this must not be taken to extremes. Kasia, the only really gifted poetess in Byzantium and a great beauty, was turned down by Theophilus just as he was about to give her the golden apple because she was too intelligent. Picking a bride in this fashion may seem odd, but until the twelfth century (with the exception of the Khazar wives of Justinian II and Constantine V) no foreigner had been considered worthy of marrying an Emperor.

Thanks to their education, women could be very powerful. Theophano, sister of Basil II, ruled Germany at the end of the tenth century, while a hundred years later Anna Dalassena, mother of Alexius I, governed the Empire in her son's absences on campaign. Women could never wield quite as much influence at court as the eunuchs, however. These were not servants as in other countries but usually high officials or generals. Parents who had ambitions for their sons often had one or two of the younger ones castrated in youth. The only positions a eunuch could not fill were Eparch of Constantinople, Domestic of the four Imperial regiments and the throne itself. Otherwise they took precedence over non-eunuchs. Many worked in the Great Palace as advisers to both the Emperor and the Empress.

The Great or Sacred Palace occupied a site stretching from the sea to the Hippodrome and including the present Topkapi Saray. In its extensive grounds were many churches, chapels and six other palaces, among them the Magnaura Palace used for the Imperial honeymoon, the Purple Palace where the Empress gave birth in the Purple Chamber – hence Porphyrogenitus, Born in the Purple – and the Daphne Palace, the gynaikeion or private quarters of the Empress and her women.

The gynaikeion could be entered only with permission. Sir Steven Runciman compares it with a Victorian lady's boudoir where close male friends and relatives could be entertained. In that respect it was less exclusive than some modern gentlemen's clubs where no women are ever allowed to darken their doors. Ladies of the court rarely left the Palace grounds, and when they took the air they were usually veiled – this was more for the sake of their complexions than modesty. Maria of Trebizond, wife of John VIII, certainly appeared without a veil, a contemporary noting her great beauty as she rode to Hagia Sophia but regretting her excessive use of cosmetics. The Empress had her own officials, many of whom were eunuchs, and her own treasury. If her husband should be deposed she could either marry his successor or retire to a convent where she was not forced to take her final vows. Unlike her deposed spouse she would not be mutilated by the amputation of hands or feet, the slitting of the nose or, most common of all, blinding. Very few women in Byzantine history lost their lives by political murder, an exception being Maria of Antioch, whose unfortunate young son was forced to sign her death warrant.

The Byzantines could be accused of almost oriental cruelty both to man and beast. In the Alexiad, Anna Comnena, the blue-stocking daughter of Alexius I, recounts how her father and uncle fled from Constantinople with horses taken from the Imperial stables. 'Some of the horses they left there, after first cutting off their hind-feet with their swords.' For political opponents and felons, mutilation was preferred to the death penalty to allow the victim time in which to repent of his sins and as a warning to others. Perhaps this should be considered an enlightened approach to punishment.

They were equally enlightened in their attitude to the Saracens and the Persians, holding both races in great respect and borrowing many of their ideas in art and medicine. Although they were intensely religious and well read in theology they were tolerant of other religions, allowing freedom of worship for Muslims and Jews. The first mosque in Constantinople was completed in 717, the second built by Constantine IX Monomachus, and a third (at Saladin's request) by Isaac II Angelus in 1189. The Jews had their synagogues in the Blachernae quarter and were responsible for all transit trade. At the end of the eleventh century a church was built for the English (presumably for the Anglo-Saxon members of the Varangian Guard) where lamps burnt before an icon of St Augustine of Canterbury.

We arrived at the New Rome on a Saturday without money, or at least without Turkish currency. There had been a bank strike on our last day in Thessalonica which had prevented us from buying Turkish lira. However the taxi driver who took us to our hotel had no objection to our paying him in drachma. Then the hotel refused to change travellers' cheques. Being in the old centre of Constantinople, after a quick bath we made our way to the Covered Bazaar and – beating off countless touts circling round us like bluebottles – found a kindly carpet merchant who was only too pleased to change some British banknotes. Much to our surprise, he asked if we were Hungarians. (On our return to our very cheap hotel we found it crowded with Magyar tourists; plainly the pre-war sense of 'Turanian' kinship survives despite the Iron Curtain.)

We would have liked to spend longer in the Covered Bazaar, which is on the site of the Byzantine bazaar. It was partially destroyed by fire in 1954 and again, though to a lesser extent, in 1975, but has been rebuilt and covers an enormous area. According to one well known (if admittedly often misinformed) guide book to Constantinople, there are 4,000 little shops and 90 streets totalling 40 miles in length. It is certainly very easy to get lost in, as we discovered when, weak with hunger after our train journey, we tried to find somewhere for breakfast. An endless succession of shops filled with carpets, leather goods, antiques, jewels or junk could not tempt us when all we wanted was food, any kind of food. Eventually, on the edge of the bazaar we found a snack-bar selling kofte and aryan which we fell upon. Back in England we had never dreamt that one day we might actually enjoy grilled meatballs and watered down yoghurt first thing in the morning.

In the street outside boys were selling peeled cucumbers and simit (rings of hard bread sprinkled with sesame seeds) threaded onto long sticks. Across the road the merchandise was cheap watches and shirts which, on our way back to our hotel later in the day, were almost forced on us. In the streets near the centre we had a running battle with the salesmen. We discovered that a polite 'No thank you'! was more effective than shouting or assumed deafness, the Turks being a courteous race.

Still on foot, we made our way to Hagia Sophia. Constantinople is hilly and its pavements are not designed to let two people walk abreast. Passing Topkapi Park we saw two men with dancing bears – sad moth-eaten creatures, their teeth torn out and ropes thrust through their nostrils, shambling in a pathetic night-club shuffle at a word of command. We were depressed that human beings could pay to watch such a spectacle, even if we had to admit to ourselves that it must have been a familiar enough sight in Byzantine times.

Part of the Forum of Augustus near Hagia Sophia has been turned into a garden filled with viburnum, cherry and judas trees, all in full bloom at the end of April. There are many such green and leafy oases, as there were in Imperial days, even in the twelfth century when the population was a million. Now only 19,000 are resident in the old city while two and a half million live in shanty towns outside the walls. Slums have been cleared to be replaced by numerous parks, and the Golden Horn is being transformed into beaches and marinas. During the clearances many churches and mosques disappeared.

The church of Hagia Sophia – 'Holy Wisdom' – staggered us by its vast, overwhelming, annihilating size. Almost incredibly, it took less than six years to build; 10,000 workmen, some say 100,000, were employed in its construction 'whose payment in pieces of fine silver was never delayed beyond the evening'. One can understand why on the day of its consecration, 25 December 537, the Emperor Justinian exclaimed 'Glory to God who hath deemed me worthy to complete so mighty a work. Solomon, I have outdone thee!'

Justinian was the last Eastern Emperor to speak Latin as his first language. (Henceforth the Imperial tongue was Greek.) His reign was one of the most successful in Byzantine history. As well as Italy his armies reconquered North Africa and southern Spain, while he promulgated a corpus of law which has shaped most of the world's legal codes. In David Talbot-Rice's view 'no greater or more enlightened patron of the arts than Justinian has ever lived'. Yet personally Flavius Anicius Justinianus was in many ways contemptible. Born in 483 in Skopje, a peasant of Gothic stock, he reached the throne solely through being adopted by his uncle the Emperor Justin, a rough old professional soldier. As a ruler Justinian proved unstable – prone to panic, haughty, ungrateful, suspicious and cruel. He overtaxed his subjects mercilessly while he employed a host of informers and torturers. He owed his success to those who served him and to his wife.

In 532 the so-called 'Nika riots' between the two circus factions of the Blues and the Greens devastated Constantinople, Constantine's church of Hagia Sophia being destroyed by fire. After seven days of rioting, when a nephew of a former Emperor was proclaimed

Emperor in the Hippodrome, Justinian prepared to flee. It was his low-born consort Theodora (whose portrait we had seen at Ravenna) who stopped him. 'If flight were the only means of safety, yet I should disdain to fly' said she proudly. 'Death is the condition of our birth, but they who have reigned should never survive the loss of dignity and dominion. I implore Heaven that I may never be seen, not a day, without my diadem and purple; that I may no longer behold the light when I cease to be saluted with the name of queen. If you resolve, O Caesar! to fly, you have treasures; behold the sea, you have ships; but tremble lest the desire of life should expose you to wretched exile and ignominious death. For my own part, I adhere to the maxim of antiquity, that the throne is a glorious sepulchre.' The revolt was put down, 30,000 rioters being slaughtered in the Hippodrome by Belisarius's loyal troops.

Hagia Sophia began to rise from its ashes in the very same year. The architects were an engineer, Anthemius of Tralles, a Greek from Asia Minor, and Isidore of Miletus. The church's most impressive feature is its great dome 107 feet wide; a contemporary wrote that it seemed as if hanging from Heaven by a golden chain rather than supported by solid masonry. The curve of the original dome was too shallow and it collapsed within twenty years following an earthquake, to be replaced by the more rounded dome we now see, constructed by Isidore's nephew, another Isidore. In 1682 Sir George Wheler, in the course of an unusually elaborate Grand Tour, visited the church. He commented: 'St Peter's at Rome may excel this Cupalo in height, but not in Breadth nor Beauty.' The ceilings were decorated with gold mosaic edged with fruit, flowers or geometric patterns; the re-built dome had an enormous cross against a golden background. The walls were covered with countless rare and many coloured marbles (famous for a mirror-like sheen) from all over the Empire while the pillars supporting the galleries came from ancient temples – six of green jasper from the Temple of Diana at Ephesus and eight of porphyry from the Temple of the Sun at Rome. The altar was of gold studded with jewels – and later with enamels – while the canopy over the altar, the iconostasis and the ivory pulpit were plated or inlaid with silver. Costly hangings of silk woven with holy images adorned the walls. Throughout the twenty-four hours of the day the church was brilliantly lit, serving by night as a welcome beacon to ships sailing toward the Golden Horn. It had a clerical staff of 600. (Today the only priest resident in Constantinople whom the Turks allow to dress as one is the Orthodox Patriarch.) It was the supreme expression of Byzantium – no civilization, not even that of ancient Egypt, has taken religion more seriously.

During the ninth century the cross in the dome was replaced by Christos Pantocrator, while in the apse the enthroned Virgin with the Child on her knee demonstrated to the Faithful that she was the guardian of the city as well as the Mother of God. This placing of the Christos Pantocrator in the dome and the Virgin in the apse set the pattern for all subsequent Orthodox churches. Underneath Christ were prophets, saints and bishops in rows while on either side of the Virgin were the Archangel Gabriel and the Archangel Michael. Those which remain are dwarfed by the building's size, and although beautiful enough in illustrations look distant and insignificant in reality. The Christos Pantocrator in the dome is hidden by layers of yellowing whitewash and by a great green disc with inscriptions from the Koran. In the past travellers were offered handfuls of tesserae by the guides whom they had bribed to let them enter. (This could be dangerous; the Sieur du Mont writing in 1690 says that 'if a Greek or Jew were found in the Mosque, he wou'd either be immediately put to Death or constrain'd to save his Life by renouncing his Religion'.) The most beautiful things in the church today are the marbles; Procopius, who saw the church in the year of its completion, tells us 'One can only marvel at the purple of some, at the green of others and at the gleaming white of yet others . . . one might think that one had come across a meadow filled with flowers in full bloom.' Equally outstanding are the exquisitely carved capitals of the pillars, though not everyone has praised them. Writing of Hagia Sophia in 1789, Captain Sutherland comments: 'The dome only is tolerable . . . The capitals are by no means chaste, and the architecture throughout is very indifferently executed.'

In the narthex, over the royal entrance, is the mosaic of the Emperor Leo VI crouching at the feet of Christ, from whom he is receiving the gift of Holy Wisdom. Leo 'the Wise' supported the prohibition of third marriages yet married for a third time when his second wife died. Then, three days after the death of his third wife, he married his mistress. On Christmas Day 906 he was met at the royal entrance by the Patriarch and refused entry; he tried again at Epiphany and was again refused. The Emperor finally obtained a dispensation from the Pope. He made the Patriarch resign, replacing him with a more pliable cleric.

Over the door of the south vestibule there is another ex-voto mosaic. It is a late tenth or early eleventh century double portrait of Constantine the Great and Justinian; one Emperor presents his city to the Virgin and Child, the other his church. We had not so far seen a city depicted like this and wondered if it could have been presented by an Eparch (Prefect) of Constantinople. John Beckwith suggests Basil the Bulgar Slayer as the most likely donor, after his defeat of Tsar Samuel in 1017.

Hagia Sophia's galleries are enormous open spaces compared with the narrow marble maze which is the gallery of St Mark's at Venice. From here the women for whom it was reserved – and no doubt some men as well – watched in horror as sacriligious enemy troops burst in to kill, loot and desecrate in 1204 and again in 1453.

On the first occasion they were Christians, Catholic 'Crusaders': a drunken horde who rode their horses up to the altars, seizing the chalices and tearing the vestments off the priests, then breaking up the altars and iconastases for the sake of the jewels and precious metals, and wrenching the gold covers set with jewels and enamels off the Gospels. More discriminating, the Venetians under the blind Doge looted systematically in organized bands. (With unbridled arrogance Dandolo had himself buried in Hagia Sophia when he died in 1205. His tomb is still there. On recapturing the city the Byzantines threw his bones to the dogs, but those patriotic animals refused to eat them.) Finally they seated a tipsy whore on the Patriarch's throne where she sang filthy songs. The Pope excommunicated the 'Crusaders', calling them 'worse than dogs', then gave a tacit blessing to the sack by recognizing a Latin Emperor and installing a Latin Patriarch. As recently as this century the Holy See insisted that, should Constantinople be re-conquered from the Turks and Hagia Sophia restored to Christian worship, the cathedral must go to the Catholics. It is scarcely surprising that Orthodoxy has little love for Catholicism – had Orthodox 'Crusaders' sacked St Peter's and installed an Orthodox Patriarch at Rome, expelling the Pope, Catholics would no doubt feel the same about Orthodoxy.

In 1261 the Byzantines recaptured Constantinople and Hagia Sophia was restored to Orthodox worship. Both the church and the palace of the Blachernae had been left in a deplorable state by the

Latins, the palace being so filthy that the Emperor Michael VIII Palaeologus moved his court back to the Great Palace which, since the days of Alexius I, had been used only for guests. Ninety years later the Grand Duke of Moscow sent money for the restoration of Hagia Sophia, but the Emperor of the day spent the money on hiring Turkish mercenaries for his struggles in the civil war. The apse had been badly damaged by a serious earthquake in 1346 and was in fact restored; the Virgin and Child are thought to date from this period. So poor was the Imperial House that when John VI Cantacuzenus gave his daughter in marriage to John Palaeologus the bride and groom were crowned with lead, and at the wedding feast the guests were served on pewter and earthenware.

In 1453 the spectators in the galleries witnessed – no doubt all too briefly – the second and final desecration. On Tuesday 29 May the Emperor Constantine XI fell at the Romanus Gate, his mutilated body only recognizable by the red buskins on his feet. The bronze doors of Hagia Sophia came crashing down and the Turks poured in. The Liturgy had been celebrated but Matins was still being sung. This time not only was the church looted but, apart from a few whom they cut down, the conquerors roped the worshippers together and dragged them off to the slave markets. The priests continued chanting until they were seized. (It is said that one who was celebrating the Liturgy at a side-altar picked up the holy vessels and vanished into the sanctuary wall, and that he will return to finish the Liturgy when the cathedral is restored to Christian worship; during the seventeenth century a secret passage was discovered in the sanctuary wall.) The great church was converted into a mosque forthwith by command of the Sultan.

In Constantinople's antique shops one occasionally comes across a fifteenth-century Byzantine coin, a battered silver hyperperion or copper follis, bearing the head of Christ and with a hole punched through its rim. Such coins were worn round their necks by the defenders of 1453, who wished to die beneath an icon of Our Lord.

No-one could have withstood the fury of these 'infernall Impes', as the seventeenth-century Scots traveller William Lithgow calls the Turks. His late nineteenth-century fellow-countryman Sir Charles Eliot, who knew and understood the last Ottomans, sums up the dynamism of the early Sultans as 'that wild brilliancy and vigour in which no ordinary ideas of humanity, morality, or economy find a place'.

As was their usual custom the Turks obliterated all mosaics with whitewash. During the secularization of Turkey under Kemal Ataturk in the 1920s the building ceased to be a mosque and became a museum instead. A colourful American, Professor Thomas Whittemore – who had acquired an interest in Orthodox art from helping White Russian refugees – persuaded Ataturk to let him uncover the mosaics, and rich compatriots to finance the operation. He secured the services of a Clerk of Works to the House of Lords, Mr Hawkins, who had a genius for restoration; his methods involved the use of cobwebs in large quantities. In consequence one may now see sufficient masterpieces to gain some idea of what was destroyed by infidel invaders.

All the mosaics in the galleries and narthex are ex-voto offerings (although unfortunately there are no inscriptions to tell us what events they commemorate) and, apart from the lovely Deesis in the south gallery, form a portrait gallery of Emperors and Empresses. In the north gallery stands Alexander I, Leo VI's dissolute brother, who ruled for only thirteen months before dying in 913. He is shown here in Imperial full dress, clad as he would have been for the procession to Hagia Sophia on Easter Sunday – rather as a life peer in England might have himself painted in his parliamentary robes. It is strange that someone who ruled so briefly, and so badly, should be thus immortalized.

The best portraits are in the south gallery, which was reserved for members of the Imperial family. The earliest, from the first half of the eleventh century, is of the Emperor Constantine IX Monomachus and the Empress Zoë with Christ. Zoë and her sister Theodora being heirs to the throne, it was essential that one of them should marry a man capable of ruling the Empire. Theodora took the veil and Zoë, at the age of fifty, chose as her first husband the Eparch of the City, Romanus Argyrus. He soon neglected her and kept her short of money. After six years of ill treatment she fell passionately in love with Michael, the young brother of the eunuch John the Orphanatrophus, who had slyly contrived for them to meet. Romanus was found dying in his bath, and Zoë and Michael were married the same evening. Zoë did not profit from this black deed since, having donned the purple, her new husband spent as much time away from her as possible. When he died from an illness contracted while campaigning in the Balkans the eunuch John, determined to retain power, persuaded Zoë to adopt his nephew – another Michael – as her heir and co-Emperor. Michael V promptly rewarded his uncle by exiling him. Encouraged by his success at removing the most hated man in Constantinople he then banished Zoë to a nunnery. This was too much for the people, who took Zoë and Theodora out of their respective convents and acclaimed them as their rightful rulers. Michael, who had taken refuge in the church of St John in Studion, was lured into the street and blinded. The two sisters, who in any case loathed each other, proved incompetent rulers and Zoë was persuaded to marry yet again at the age of sixty-four. Her third husband was Constantine IX Monomachus, with whom she does not seem to have been greatly in love; she did not object to his mistress, the niece of one of his former wives, being given a title and attending all the court ceremonies with the two Empresses. In consequence of this complex marital saga the heads in the mosaic had to be remade again and again. Constantine was previously Romanus III, and may have been Zoë's second husband. Michael IV, as well. Zoë herself had her head removed from the mosaic at the time of her banishment, while that of Christ must have been renewed several times to match the style of the new Imperial heads – probably at least once by a different mosaicist. Zoë looks remarkably pious for a murderess.

In complete contrast to this mosaic is a family group with the Virgin and Child portraying John II Comnenus and his wife Irene and, on the wall next to them, their son Manuel I. John, according to Ostrogorsky the greatest and most pious of the Comnene, was the brother of Anna Comnena, the authoress of *The Alexiad*, who hated him; she and her mother made their father's death even more painful by trying to induce him to disinherit John. This able and honest Emperor was fatally wounded by an arrow while out hunting – probably not by accident. His very attractive wife Irene, shown here with red gold hair, grey eyes and lightly rouged cheeks, became a saint, as did her father King Ladislas of Hungary.

The most beautiful mosaic in the cathedral is unquestionably the Deesis in the south gallery, depicting Christ with the Virgin and John the Baptist. Probably it was done as a thank-offering for the church's restoration to Orthodoxy in 1261. Gentle and restrained, it is a prelude to the Palaeologan renaissance.

All these treasures were so absorbing that for a moment we forgot the squalor of our surroundings. We had only to look over the gallery

*Top:* The lion of St Mark. From a sixth-century mosaic at San Vitale at Ravenna. *Bottom:* The Sacrifice of Abel, Melchizedek and Abraham. From a sixth-century mosaic in Sant' Apollinare in Classe at Ravenna.

*Top:* The fifteenth-century ramparts of the fortress monastery at Manasija. *Bottom:* The Patriarchate of Peć, looking towards the Rugovo Gorge and the Čakor Pass.

*Top left:* A handmaid at the Birth of the Virgin. From a fresco in the church of St Demetrius at Peć. *Top right:* St Simeon at the Presentation of the Infant Jesus. From a fresco of 1164 at Nerezi. *Centre:* Spectators at the Ascension. From a fresco of 1194 at Kurbinovo. *Bottom:* Christ raises the widow's son. From a fresco of 1348–50 at Dečani.

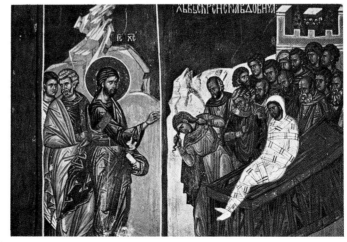

*Top:* The Virgin of Mileševa. From a fresco of c.1230. *Bottom:* The Angel of Mileševa. From a fresco of c.1230.

*Top:* The thirteenth-century castle of Maglić near Studenica. *Bottom:* The Deposition. From fourteenth-century frescoes at Prilep.

*Top:* An angel, from
fourteenth-century frescoes
at Prilep. *Bottom:* The mid-
ninth-century church of the
Panagia Koubelidiki at Kastoria.

Top: The city of Monemvasia. From a drawing of 1686 by Frà Marco Coronelli, Geographer to the Venetian Republic. *Centre:* A church at Geraki. *Bottom:* Two Empresses of Byzantium. From a twelfth-century fresco in the church of St John Chrysostom at Geraki.

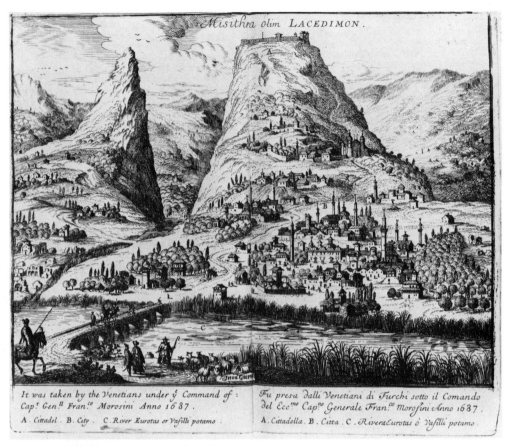

*Misithra olim* LACEDIMON.

It was taken by the Venetians under ỷ Command of : Cap.ᵗ Gen.ˡˡ Fran.ᶜᵒ *Morosini Anno* 1687.

A . *Cittadel* . B . *City* . C . *River Eurotas or Vasilli potamo* .

Fu presa dalli Venetiani di Turchi sotto il Comando del Ecc.ᵐᵒ Cap.ⁿᵒ *Generale Fran.ᶜᵒ Morosini Anno* 1687 .

A . *Cittadella* . B . *Citta* . C . *River Eurotas o' Vasilli potamo* .

*Top:* Mistra in 1687. From *The Present State of the Morea, Called Anciently Peleponnesus*, by the Smyrna merchant John Randolph. *Bottom:* Mistra as it is today.

parapet to be brought back to earth. However inspiring the church of Holy Wisdom may be, it filled us with sadness, a sense of emptiness. Here is truly the Abomination of Desolation. The Muslim adornments from the days when it was a mosque – the mihrab, the Koranic texts, the box for the Sultan, can be tolerated. What revolted us was that such a wonderful monument should be so badly treated, with almost deliberate insensitivity. The air of neglect, of sheer lack of appreciation, is horrific. The whitewash covering the dome, yellow with age, and the whole building are desperately in need of soap and water on a vast scale. We had only to go into the beautifully kept Blue Mosque nearby to see what a holy place should be like. Having always thought of Hagia Sophia as the epitome of not just Constantinople but of all Byzantium, we had to admit to ourselves that this is no longer true, and cannot have been for hundreds of years, so thoroughly have the Turks exorcized the Byzantine ghosts.

Mehmet II the Conqueror, an enlightened patron of the arts who spoke six languages fluently, permitted the churches in the areas which had surrendered first to remain in Christian hands. Others, in areas which had resisted, were turned into mosques immediately. The church of the Holy Apostles became the Patriarchal church for a few months, but since it was already falling into disrepair the Patriarch Gennadius moved to the church of the Pammakaristos the following year. He became a valued friend of the Sultan, who would visit him at the Pammakaristos; to stop the Turks using Mehmet's presence in the church as a pretext for taking it over they always met in the side chapel. The ruinous Holy Apostles was eventually razed to the ground and a mosque built on the site.

Sometimes a Sultan's benevolence caused trouble with his co-religionists. 'Foreign News' in *The Lady's Magazine* of January 1775 tells us that on the occasion of his favourite 'sultanessa' becoming pregnant the Grand Signior gave permission for Christians in his dominions to repair churches that, with the passage of time, had become ruinous. The gesture aroused furious Muslim resentment:

> One of their emirs, however, viewing this privilege with a jealous eye, employed every artifice to instigate the people to revolt; insomuch that the Sultan found himself at length constrained by policy to revoke the permission he had given to the Christians, and to issue an order that such of their religious edifices as had been repaired, should be instantly demolished.

On the whole, as much damage has been done in this century as during all the preceding centuries. In 1954 rioters burnt so many churches in Constantinople in a single night that the cost of the damage was put at £60 million. Since then other churches have disappeared beneath the tarmac of new roads, the Turks turning a deaf ear to protests by the Greek Government.

We had been led to believe that there was a restaurant in the Topkapi Park but, after a lengthy search which seemed to cover the entire park, we gave up and went to the Archaeological Museum. In any case it was a bit early for lunch. To keep us going we drank a glass of Turkish tea at the kiosk, amid the antique and Byzantine statues of the museum garden. In the courtyard were some colossal porphyry sarcophagi from the church of the Holy Apostles, until the eleventh century the final resting-place for the Emperors, as equals of the Apostles. The museum itself was a disappointment. The ivories we had hoped to see were upstairs, which was closed for restoration. The only outstanding exhibits we could see were a magnificent carved marble sarcophagus from Lycia, and the so-called Tomb of Alexander (probably that of a King of Sidon), which was quite staggeringly beautiful.

By now it was definitely lunch-time, and we were lucky enough to find a restaurant near Hagia Sophia whose proprietress spoke excellent French. She was small, plump and fair haired, in her early forties with curiously light brown eyes. The restaurant had been her family's 'kiosk' or house for 150 years and was built on the site of a lunatic asylum. She told us that her great-grandmother had come from the Caucasus and had been in the Seraglio, but the Sultan had allowed her to leave and marry. She also said that her grandfather had been one of the tutors of Mehmet VI Vahdettin, the last Ottoman to reign over the Golden Horn, who abdicated in 1922. She had an impressive knowledge of the Sultans, her favourites being Murad Celebi ('Murad the Gentleman'), Mehmet II (the Conqueror of Constantinople, whose portrait hangs in every other shop in the city), Selim the Sot, who composed a thousand songs (many are lost but 300 are still sung today), and Selim the Grim (apparently much cosier than is generally appreciated).

Vahdettin's sons had bought houses in London, though they had been allowed to return to Constantinople since 1963. She asked us if we knew the Viennese operetta *Die Rose auf Stambul* of 1916 – a year when Austria-Hungary and Ottoman Turkey were allies – and gave us roses. She explained that Turks believe there is a special affinity between the rose and the nightingale or *bul-bul*, but added that the true flower of Turks was the tulip, even if it had been appropriated by the Dutch. Her food was excellent and she bought us enormous glasses of her own raki, much less fiery than the normal product, more like ouzo.

After lunch we walked through the small square which is almost all that is left of the enormous enclosure that was once the Hippodrome. William Lithgow wrote (in his *Rare Adventures and Painefull Peregrinations*) that during his visit to Constantinople in 1609 'I saw also the famous Hyppodrome and the Theater whereupon the people stood, when the Emperours used to runne their Horses, and make their Princely shewes on solemn dayes, which is now altogether decayed'. It had been decaying for a long time; even before the fall of Constantinople young men had been playing polo in its ruins. It is worth remembering that by then the city's population had sunk to fewer than 100,000, of whom a mere 7,000, including monks and foreigners, were capable of bearing arms. It must have been a city of women, children and old men. Indeed it was no longer a city as such; within its walls were huddled thirteen large villages, some with their own walls, separated by fields and orchards. Seven thousand men were expected to defend fourteen miles of wall against the Sultan's army of 80,000 (many of them Christian mercenaries), and 20,000 Bashi Bazouks.

The horses of St Mark once graced the Hippodrome's gates, and its walls were adorned with statues brought from Rome and the isles of Greece. All that remains in situ on the Spina – the central dias around which the horses raced – are an obelisk from the Temple of Tuthmosis at Karnak brought from Rome and set up on a plinth carved with scenes from the victories of Theodosius; the Pillar of Constantine (a battered column restored by Constantine Porphyrogenitus and stripped of its bronze casing by the Crusaders); and the remains of the Serpent Column. Sir George Wheler illustrates this in 1682 when the serpents had their heads, but by 1700 they had disappeared. They formed a bronze tripod, made to celebrate the Greek victory over the Persians at Plataea in 479 BC, which stood outside the temple of Apollo at Delphi; originally the snakes were surmounted by a golden dish found in the baggage train of the

Persian King Xerxes after being abandoned in the battle. The snakes' heads formed a fountain from which flowed milk, wine and water on festive occasions. The Hippodrome was the great centre of Byzantine entertainment. On one occasion the Emperor Manuel I had it flooded and a naval tournament was staged in honour of the Seljuk leader Kilij Arslan. A less successful entertainment consisted of a man in an enormous garment inflated with air who claimed to be able to fly. He jumped from a high platform and crashed to the ground before the assembled thousands.

The last time races were held in the Hippodrome was in 1204. Its final destruction came when the Turks removed the stones in order to use them in the building of the Blue Mosque.

We were very keen to visit one of the enormous subterranean cisterns which held the water brought by the aqueduct of Valens from the hills of Thrace to the City. The largest of these is near the restaurant where we had had lunch. It was closed for restoration and the workmen were going home at the end of the day's work. We were determined to see it, however, and with the restaurant proprietress's help arranged to return in the morning. The other great cistern, that of One Thousand and One Columns (in reality 224) lies further west and according to contemporary travellers was used as a silk factory, having been empty of water for many years.

By now fairly exhausted, we set off back to the hotel. En route we passed another pillar of Constantine, this time of the founder of the City. Scorched and cracked, held together by iron bands, it is in the Old Forum. Once a gilt bronze figure of Apollo cast by Phidias surmounted it, converted into Constantine's likeness. This endured until the twelfth century, when it was replaced by a gold cross – to be torn down soon after by the Crusaders. There is what appears to be a reference to this statue in that best seller of the 1360s, *The Travels of Sir John Mandeville*:

> And there [at Constantinople] dwelleth commonly the Emperor of Greece. And there is the most fair church and the most noble of all the world; and it is of Saint Sophia. And before that church is the image of Justinian the emperor, covered with gold, and he sitteth upon an horse y-crowned. And he was wont to hold a round apple of gold in his hand: but it is fallen out thereof. And men say there, that it is a token that the emperor hath lost a great part of his lands and of his lordships; for he was wont to be Emperor of Roumania

and of Greece, of all Asia the Less, and of the land of Syria, of the land of Judea in the which is Jerusalem, and of the land of Egypt, of Persia, and of Arabia. But he hath lost all but Greece; and that land he holds only. And men would many times put the apple into the image's hand again, but it will not hold it. This apple betokeneth the lordship that he had over all the world, that is round. And the tother hand he lifteth up against the East, in token to menace the misdoers. This image stands upon a pillar of marble at Constantinople.

However confused, the tale probably gives a true enough glimpse of how fourteenth-century Englishmen thought of Byzantium.

We also passed a sign reading 'To Europe'. This seemed especially ironic in view of reports in the newspapers that Turkey was hoping to join the European Community.

At dinner in a cheap restaurant near the hotel we sat next to a Tunisian school mistress who was by herself. She told us that her speciality was teaching French. She never took her holidays in Paris, however, as she felt so much safer in Istanbul or Cairo. Two days later Sue had reason to find her confidence reassuring.

On Sunday morning we were woken hideously early by the call to prayer – taped – from the many muezzin in the neighbourhood. Nothing could have reinforced more strongly our feeling of being Christians in an infidel country. We began to realize something of the miseries of Orthodox Byzantines under the Turkish occupation.

After breakfasting on the ubiquitous hard-boiled egg and tea-bag tea, we set off for the Yerebatan Serai cistern. The foreman had forgotten having promised to let us in, but after nearly a quarter of an hour's arguing and wheedling, despaired. 'One minute only,' he said. It was enough. From the top of the thirty-nine steps leading down we could see a forest of columns, each one topped with a beautifully carved Byzantine capital, stretching away into the floodlit gloom. There were 150 workmen, toiling waist deep in parts, clearing out the mud and restoring the stonework. It is unlikely that any of them had ever heard the name 'Justinian'.

We paused in the gardens in the Forum of Augustus, where we had to decline the services of countless shoe blacks. Eventually we succumbed to the eloquent gestures of a boy of about eight. He could manage the small blue shoes of one of us but was too little for his brushes to go easily round the gigantic black feet of the other.

Banging a brush on the foot rest when he wanted us to change over shoes, he did a wonderful job. He took tremendous professional pride in shouting at his competitors that he had obtained our custom because of his sheer skill, not on account of his small size. He beamed most unprofessionally when at the end of the operation we over-tipped him and shook hands.

Then we went to Küçük Ayasofya Camii, the former church of SS. Sergius and Bacchus (the Roman officers martyred by the Emperor Maximian) which is now a mosque. After decorously removing our shoes, somewhat incongruously we said our Sunday prayers here, having failed to find an Orthodox Liturgy. Reluctantly we had to admit that the church, unlike Hagia Sophia, lends itself very sympathetically to Muslim usage; the whitewash and blue Islamic decoration are neither unsightly nor incompatible. In plan it resembles San Vitale at Ravenna, a great central dome and an extended apse, two circular rows of marble columns one above the other with very fine capitals, and a gallery for women. The sole reminder that it was once Christian is an ornate cornice around the bottom of the dome with an inscription praising Justinian and Theodora, yet it retains a profoundly Christian air – unlike Hagia Sophia and despite generations of Imams. In a corner there is a comically antiquated fire-fighting machine of Keystone Cops vintage, painted an Islamic green, no doubt very unfunny and a matter of life or death in its day. At the side of the mosque there is a small burial ground for Imams, which is unusual since most Turks prefer to be buried in Asia Minor. The Rev. George Fyler Townsend, in his *A Cruise on the Bosporus* tells us: 'The Turks, it is well known, entertain great dislike to be buried in Europe, under the prevalent impression that they will some day be obliged to resign possession of Constantinople and return into Asia.' More than a century later they are still there.

Nearby is the Mosaic Museum on the site of the Great Palace of the Emperors. The museum was closed for restoration but we had already seen some of the mosaics it normally contains, striking evidence that secular as well as religious art flourished in Byzantium. All are before the end of the sixth century and are very similar to ancient Roman mosaics – pastoral scenes predominate. During the restoration they have been heaped in the passages of Hagia Sophia.

According to the *Secret History of Procopius*, the Empress Theodora kept her enemies in dungeons deep beneath the Great Palace, torturing them and disposing of them without trace. We owe to Liudprand of Cremona, a tenth-century Italian prelate-diplomat, an eye-witness account of the impression made upon the sophisticated visitor by an audience with the Basileus at the Great Palace – the Emperor in this instance being the pedantic Constantine VII Porphyrogenitus, an expert on court etiquette. 'Before the Emperor's throne stood a tree made of gilded bronze, its branches filled with birds likewise made of gilded bronze who sang, each one according to its kind. So marvellously fashioned was this throne that at one moment it was on the ground and at another had risen high into the air. It was huge, guarded by lions of gold-plated bronze or wood, who beat the ground with their tails and roared horribly with quivering tongues. I was led into the Emperor's presence by two eunuchs. As I approached the lions began to roar and the birds sing according to species. I was neither frightened nor taken aback since I had made enquiries about this performance among people who knew all about it. I prostrated myself in front of the Emperor, my face touching the ground. When I raised my head it was to find that the man whom a moment before I had seen sitting on a moderately elevated throne had changed his robes and was somewhere up near the ceiling. How this was done I cannot imagine, unless he had been lifted by machinery of the sort we use for raising a wine-press. On this occasion he did not address me directly – the distance between us would have made direct conversation undignified – but through an interpreter.'

As a distinguished diplomat Liudprand was invited to dinner by Constantine. The party was at a small palace near the Hippodrome. There were places for only nineteen diners, who reclined on couches in the ancient Roman fashion (as opposed to the Byzantine fashion of sitting down to a meal). Liudprand was deeply impressed by the gold plate on which the food was served and by gold dishes 'too heavy for men to carry' filled with fruit which were lowered from the ceiling on purple and gold cords after dinner. On another occasion he was enchanted by the Byzantine cuisine, notably a dish sent from the Emperor's table consisting of 'a fat goat, of which he had already taken a generous helping, richly stuffed with garlic, onions and leeks, in a lavish fish sauce'. Liudprand and Constantine's enthusiasm may have been because the 'fish sauce' was caviare, for which the Byzantines had a passion.

Bishop Liudprand's experiences at Constantinople have dazzled

Westerners down the centuries, if not necessarily at first hand. Indirectly they must have inspired the final lines of Yeats's *Sailing to Byzantium*:

> But such a form as Grecian goldsmiths make
> Of hammered gold and gold enamelling
> To keep a drowsy Emperor awake;
> Or set upon a golden bough to sing
> To lords and ladies of Byzantium
> Of what is past, or passing, or to come.

Ironically both the roaring lions and the singing birds were copied from those made at Baghdad for the Caliph Haroun al-Rashid.

The Great Palace was a rambling collection of buildings and courtyards (like the old Palace of Westminster though on an infinitely larger scale) which stretched from the present Blue Mosque to the Sea of Marmora. Alexius I moved his court to the Blachernae Palace near the Land walls (of which the so-called Palace of Constantine Porphyrogenitus is a twelfth- or thirteenth-century annex), the Great Palace becoming a royal guest house until the reign of Michael VIII Palaeologus. By 1453 it had been abandoned by the Emperors and was falling into ruin. Today nothing is left apart from the mosaics in the museum and a few fragments of wall. Much of it lies beneath the seventeenth-century Blue Mosque of Sultan Ahmet with its six minarets. About 1170 Benjamin of Tudela visited the Blachernae and was deeply impressed by the pictures of the exploits of Manuel I and his ancestors with which Manuel had recently redecorated its walls. There must have been many mosaics and frescoes of this sort in the Great Palace.

Unluckily St Irene, not far from Hagia Sophia, which in its present form dates from 740, was shut for restoration. In an evil hour we returned to the restaurant of the friendly lady with Ottoman sympathies. Her food, especially a curiously flavoured species of meatball, *tasted* as good as ever, and so did her raki. She introduced us to her nephew, who took us off to his carpet shop next door; his prices were so tempting that we arranged to go back the following day, by which time he would have 'some really old pieces' to show us. (Any carpet made more than thirty years ago is considered 'old'.) He also recommended an 'old fashioned' Turkish restaurant where a blind singer sang traditional Turkish songs. 'He sings with his heart,' the nephew told us. 'He always cries.'

We had been warned before leaving England that when we took a taxi to look at a church it was advisable to give the name of the mosque it had later become. Our taxi took us to the Fethiye Camii, passing on the way the extensive remains of the aqueduct of Valens which was enlarged by Justinian.

The early twelfth-century church of the Theotokos Pammakaristos (or All-Blessed Mother of God) was the cathedral of the Patriarchs of Constantinople after they lost Hagia Sophia until 1586. In that year half of it was confiscated and turned into the mosque of Fethiye Camii. The turbaned mullah who took us into the Muslim half showed us how its apse had been rebuilt so as to point towards Mecca. The Christian half was a *parecclesion* (side chapel) added in the fourteenth century as a funerary chapel for her late husband by Maria Ducaena Comnena Palaeologina, as a touching inscription informs the learned. The main church had from its foundation been a royal burial place, both Alexius I and his daughter Anna Comnena lying there. Outside, its three small domes and elaborate decoration of blind arcades, niches and striped brickwork combine to give the church's exterior considerable charm. Inside it is even more pleasing, with some fine mosaics which include a Christos Pantocrator in the main dome and in the apse a Christos Hyperagathos – the Christ of Extreme Kindness. Some of the mosaics on the soffits of the arches are joined to the marble columns by encaustic capitals picked out in blue, while a frescoed frieze of very western-looking lions seems all but heraldic: we wondered if the latter were due to Frankish influence. The custodians are a kindly, very simple Turkish family. The father, pointing at the buttons on the boating jacket Desmond was wearing, asked if he were a sailor – 'You Captain?' Apparently this is the ultimate compliment.

The final church we visited was the Kahriye Camii (the church of Christ in Chora). There had been a monastery on the site from the sixth century. Then in the eleventh century Maria Ducaena, eldest daughter of the Bulgarian Tsar Samuel and mother-in-law of the Emperor Alexius I Comnenus, founded a new church. A second was built in the following century. It was extended and redecorated during the Palaeologan renaissance of the fourteenth century by the Grand Logothete Theodore Metochites, who is portrayed here on a lunette wearing the huge turban of his office (a Byzantine fashion long before the Turks adopted it). In plan the building is a Greek cross, to which a *parecclesion* and two narthices were added by Theodore. Apart from the Dormition over the west door the former has lost its mosaics, but it keeps its many-coloured marbles.

The Kahriye's real glories, however, are the mosaics and frescoes in the *parecclesion* and the narthices. Most are of great originality as well as being superbly executed, such as the First Seven Steps of the Virgin from the cycle of her life, and the Enrolment of the Virgin and Joseph for Taxation in the outer narthex. (The governor Cyrenius wears one of those strange, high feathered hats of office we had seen at Kastoria.) There are two fascinating mosaic portraits in the inner narthex, of the Sebastocrator Prince Isaac Comnenus – brother of the Emperor John II – and of Princess Maria Palaeologina, who married Hulagu's son and became a Mongol *Khanum*, coming home after his death to enter a convent under the name of Melane. Yet everything paled into insignificance before the fresco of the Anastasis in the apse of the side chapel, in which the risen Christ tramples down the Gates of Hell and releases the righteous dead. The triumphant vigour of the dazzling white Saviour who pulls Adam and Eve out of their graves is overwhelming. The fresco is one of the world's great paintings and alone makes the Kahriye worth a visit. But there was so much else that we left only with great reluctance when the church had to be closed. The mosaics and frescoes, especially the latter, are the supreme examples of the new Palaeologan style, partly inspired by the drawings in Classical manuscripts, with an extraordinary feeling of movement.

During the Ottoman seige the icon of the Virgin Hodegetria was brought to the Chora to be near the fiercest of the fighting. The Turks sacked the church and hacked the icon into four pieces; but they cannot have destroyed as many holy relics as is perhaps imagined. On their return to the City in 1261 the Emperors had been so poor they had been forced to sell the relics they had managed to save to Louis IX of France, a saintly king who would have paid a good price. Unusually, the Turks did not cover the mosaics in the Chora with whitewash. Although it was turned into a mosque the decorations were preserved under boards mentioned by various travellers in the last century.

As we walked away in the late afternoon sun we noticed, not for the first time, exquisite little pigeons even smaller than turtle doves. They had bodies of burnished copper, with spots of pale blue on the chest, and steel blue wings. According to our bird-book these were palm doves, which in recent years have colonized Constantinople just as collared doves have settled in England.

We had been looking forward eagerly to our dinner at the 'old fashioned' restaurant recommended by the young carpet dealer. It sounded untouristy, and we promised ourselves an authentic Turkish meal by the Sea of Marmora. When we arrived in the dark it looked so dauntingly glossy and expensive that we would have eaten somewhere else if the exchange had not been so much in our favour. The blind singer was there, but our friend had omitted to tell us that he always used a microphone. We couldn't hear ourselves think, let alone speak, while he howled and wailed interminably, like a wolf in agony. The clientele – exclusively Turkish apart from ourselves – enjoyed his 'music' thoroughly, clapping wildly; there were no apparent intervals since the man never seemed to end. At least the food looked delicious, especially the fish. No sooner had we ordered our meal than we were hit by what were in fact the first stabs of food-poisoning. (Those meatballs at lunch!) Attempts amid the singer's deafening howls to order glasses of water only resulted in the waiters trying frenziedly to tempt us with countless exotic dishes. At last, against all hope, the singing ended, though only for a moment, and we stumbled out into the night. Soon we were to regret having eaten anything at all.

We each spent the day after in bed, thankful that our cheap rooms ran to bathrooms. Our appointment with the carpet dealer had to go by the board. We could only lie there and pray that the pills prescribed at home by the family doctor were as infallible as he promised. We were determined to be in Greece for Orthodox Easter the following Sunday and, if we were going to catch the ferry to Chios, dared not leave later than the next day; we believed there was a weekly service on a Wednesday but even the main ferry office was not sure. In consequence we had to miss seeing the remains of Constantine's Palace near the Theodosian walls, and did not visit the church of St John in Studion, the Golden Gate and several lesser churches. We would also have liked to make the short trip by boat to the Princes' Islands where the Empress Zoë was banished; off whose shores Sultan Mamoud II had his brother's 300 concubines drowned (instead of following the normal practice of sending them off to the Eskai Serai); and where the Empress Irene – deposed before she could accept Charlemagne's offer of marriage – was imprisoned prior to ending her days on Lesbos.

Having taken the decision to go to Çeşme by bus the following morning Sue, never one to miss a meal, tottered out to a nearby grocer's to buy provisions for the journey. Unable to speak a single word of Turkish she rubbed her stomach in an attempt to indicate that she needed food for a delicate constitution. The shopkeeper thought that she was penniless and starving. He made her sit down on a box at the back of the shop, brought a glass of tea he had been about to drink himself, and prepared a huge sandwich filled with goats' cheese and black cherry jam which she was expected to eat on the spot. Each time she tried to escape he, together with two other men who had come into the shop, forced her to stay sitting on the box. Our hotel was uncomfortably near the red light district, and she grew frightened at finding herself trapped in a tiny shop by three men. Remembering the Tunisian teacher's sense of security she tried to persuade herself her own fears were groundless, but was very relieved indeed when she reached the street outside. She was allowed to leave only after opening her wallet and showing the men that she had plenty of money. However the shopkeeper refused to let her pay for the sandwich or for a bottle of mineral water. The Turks are a strange mixture of cruelty and kindness. Fortunately we never saw first-hand the other side.

The bus station is by the Theodosian walls. These walls take their name from the Emperor Theodosius II (408–50), in whose reign they were completed. Four-and-a-half miles in length at this western end, they stretch from the Golden Horn in the north down to the walls along the Sea of Marmora. Despite the ravages of time – and gaps for the railway and main roads – they are still imposing because of their height and multitude of towers and bastions; once there were 96 towers, each 60 feet high. These walls daunted Arabs and Avars, Crusaders and Turks. As late as 1422 they enabled a tiny garrison to beat off an attack by Murad II, and it was only because a postern gate was left open that Mehmet II's Janissaries were able to storm them in 1453. They have now been cleared of the slum dwellings which until recently obscured them from view.

Turkish buses are to be recommended unreservedly. They are very modern, very comfortable, manned by excellent drivers and very cheap; we travelled nearly 300 miles for the equivalent of £7 each. At intervals a boy came round with rose water to bathe our hands and faces. To begin with we went through an unexpected amount of hideous ribbon development, but then the country opened up into valleys and rocky gorges covered in rock-roses, alternating with lush plains. We caught glimpses of storks, egrets, blue-chested rollers and a single bee-eater. We noticed that many mosques were being built and saw women washing clothes in wayside streams. We passed through Bursa, from where the Ottomans imposed their rule over the other Turkish emirates and *ghazi* warlords, and through the country of Ataturk's 1922 campaign where he routed the Greeks and ended their dream of restoring the Byzantine Empire. The bus stopped for lunch, though we could scarcely keep down a mouthful of aryan. We reached Smyrna during the evening rush-hour and after some fraught moments of enquiry found the right bus, to arrive at Çeşme in the dark after a journey of thirteen hours.

Çeşme is a pretty little seaport with a resort a few miles outside the town. We booked in at a clean modern hotel on the quay with rooms overlooking the castle. The Ertan Hotel cost us £6 a night, and we were not too disappointed to learn that the ferry sailed only on Thursdays and that in consequence we would have to spend two nights there.

A Turkish tourist brochure informed us that the Aydinogullari Turks had 'liberated Çeşme from the Byzantines' in the fourteenth century (just as the Normans liberated England from the Anglo-Saxons). There are no obvious Byzantine remains, although the citadel built by the Genoese and restored by Selim the Grim is on the site of an earlier Byzantine castle.

Our stomachs began to recover. We had excellent meals by the sea and at a restaurant in the main street. On one occasion we were served by an old waiter who looked very like the unfortunate dancing bears we had seen in Constantinople; most of his life had plainly been spent on a fishing boat or behind a plough, and there could have been no more vivid symbol of the revolution brought by tourism. We had to stand siege by cats, as many as a dozen sitting round our table. It seems as if the Islamic revival extends to felines – after all, Muhammad once cut off a corner of his prayer mat rather than disturb a sleeping cat.

Nevertheless, we were not altogether sorry to leave Turkey. Constantinople had been a disaster, and not just because of our outraged stomachs. For Islam has been all too successful in banishing the shade of Byzantium from 'The City'. Nothing could bear more eloquent testimony than the pathetic shell of what was once the cathedral of the Holy Wisdom, with its dirt and stifling air of neglect amid the Muslim *bondieuserie*. Far from being the climax of our journey, it had been a sickening disappointment. So we were far from unhappy to board the battered little ferry for our hour's voyage to Chios. Even if it was pouring with rain the sea was as flat as the proverbial millpond. We were now slightly more than halfway through our journey.

# Chios, the chewing-gum island

'But the Lenticke tree, which is wel-nigh proper to Sio, doth give it
the greatest renowne and endowment.'

George Sandys, *A relation of a journey begun in An. Dom 1610*

'Fill high the cup with Samian wine!
Leave battles to the Turkish hordes,
And shed the blood of Scio's vine!'

Lord Byron, *The Isles of Greece*

**A** PASSION for chewing-gum is
not what most people associate
with Byzantines. Yet a thousand years before chewing-gum became
widespread in the United States during the 1860s the Eastern
Romans had their own habit. For centuries the prosperity of Chios
depended on the scented resin 'tear drops' of the mastic tree. It may
have been mastic which motivated Arab conquest of the island in the
seventh century and re-conquest by Byzantines in 961. Gum was
certainly the basis of Chios's flourishing condition during the Imperial centuries which ensued, and the reason for take-over attempts by
Venetians and Genoese. The latter ruled it from 1346 to 1566, when
the Turks took it. They lost it only in 1912. For several hundred years
there was a patrician class, half Byzantine and half Genoese, which
was unique in Greece – even if its pretensions were sneered at by
Western visitors – and whose crumbling mansions may be seen in the
Kambos (or 'campus') district just outside the city amid huge overgrown gardens full of orange and olive trees. Most of these patrician
families were wiped out in the Turkish massacres of 1822, when over
25,000 Chiots perished – nearly a quarter of the island's population
at that date. There were only a very few survivors, such as the
distinguished Ralli clan. Chios suffered further devastation during a

terrible earthquake in 1880, and has never regained its former opulence.

The island of Chios – or Scio, as the Genoese called it – is big (842 square kilometres, with a population of over 50,000) and not to everyone's taste when compared with other Greek islands. Yet it has sandy beaches and beautiful country inland, with some interesting Byzantine churches. For over a quarter of a century it has been waiting for a tourist invasion which has never materialized; its airport is small and does not cater for package tours. In consequence it has something of a sleeping-beauty air. Even the city of Chios has a pleasantly dated 1950s atmosphere, of a sort which has long departed from resorts such as Rhodes.

Our hotel had been built in the early 1960s in anticipation of a great tourist boom. Although comfortable enough it already showed considerable signs of neglect. The plumbing was unreliable and the iron railings of the balconies were almost rusted through. Every morning a large, obviously elderly and really rather respectable-looking rat was to be seen washing its face within a yard of the main entrance. 'When the package tours come all will be different' was the manager's sad refrain. One had a sneaking suspicion that he had been saying it for the fifteen years he had been on the island. He was in despair that particular weekend since, although it was the Ortho-dox Easter, only one couple besides ourselves was staying in the hotel, compared with 'a full house' the previous year. This was clearly due to the accident at the Russian nuclear power plant at Chernobyl which had just occurred. The television news showed pictures of deserted main streets in Thessalonica and Athens – the inhabitants had fled to the country. We were reassured by the manager's thirteen-year-old son, a bespectacled fount of wisdom, who explained that everything would be all right so long as the rain held off, and that even if it didn't Greece would become dangerous only after we left. He also confided, in surprisingly good English learnt at the local school, that the Elgin marbles were much better off in the British Museum – 'You look after them proper'.

His father was the most helpful hotel manager either of us had ever met, a tall, bald and sad sceptic in his mid-fifties who painted in his spare time. Although not a religious man he seemed obsessed by the Crucifixion, several versions of which hung on the hotel walls. Full of stories, he told us about an American artist, a friend of Gertrude

Stein and Alice B. Toklas, who came to Chios 50 years ago and locked herself in a village church to copy its frescoes in a 'Cubist' idiom; when the doors were unlocked and the peasants saw her canvases she escaped lynching as a witch only by a miracle. He also referred us to a nobly named official, the 'Byzantine Officer', who was in charge of all Byzantine remains on the island; but since it was a public holiday he proved uncontactable. In addition the manager arranged for us to hire a car, though we refused when we learnt that local hire terms did not include insurance for accident. We had to rely on buses, the odd taxi and thumbing lifts.

We took a taxi some five miles from the city to what for us was Chios's greatest attraction, the monastery of Nea Moni. A visitor in 1700, the Sieur de Tournefort, recorded that it 'is on a little Hill . . . very lonely, amidst huge Mountains, very disagreeable to the View'. We by contrast found the setting delightful, the yellow flower spikes of tall mullein (used as fish poison in Greece) standing like a guard of honour as we drove past. The church here is generally regarded as one of the most important in the Byzantine world, not because of its architecture but on account of its mosaics, which put Nea Moni on a level with Daphni and Hosios Loukas. They have not always been admired; Tournefort reports that 'the Paintings are so horribly done, they'd frighten ye, in spite of the Gilding they are loaded with'. Tastes change, however, and 70 years later the Irish Earl of Charlemont admits that the church 'pretty enough for the age in which it was built . . . has some tolerable mosaics'. It is a miracle they have survived, since the building was nearly destroyed in the earthquake of 1880; we were shown two baskets of tesserae which had fallen from the dome.

The Nea Moni was built between 1042 and 1056 by architects and mosaicists from Constantinople sent by the Emperor Constantine IX Monomachus – the Empress Zoë's third husband. Some years earlier three hermits had found on the burnt out slopes of Mount Privation an icon of the Virgin hanging from an unharmed myrtle bush. They took it to Lesbos where Constantine was living in exile and obtained a promise that if he ever became Emperor he would build a church on Chios. These hermits are buried at the Nea Moni. In style the surviving mosaics are most unusual, with excessively pronounced outlines and very strong colours; David Talbot-Rice suspected they were made by provincial craftsmen, but this is unlikely. We were particularly struck by the three Maries under the Cross in the

Crucifixion, by the Harrowing of Hell where, as well as Adam and Eve, David and Solomon in Imperial robes stand beside Christ, and by a wonderful angel with a timeless face in the north apse. It is sickening to reflect on just how much was lost in the earthquake, such as the head from the Virgin in the apse and, above all, the entire Christos Pantocrator in the main dome, apparently an unusually benign and kindly interpretation.

Adjoining the church are the extensive ruins of what was once an enormous monastic establishment. Tournefort tells us that in his day it 'looks more like a Town than a Religious House; it is said to possess an eighth part of the Revenue of the whole Island'. There is an eleventh-century cistern, a minute version of the one we had seen at Constantinople, and a disused refectory with long polychrome marble-topped tables flanked by marble benches, plainly designed to discourage long sittings – we shivered at the thought of how monastic posteriors must have suffered in cold weather. There is also an ossuary with a large kitchen cupboard which contains a hundred or so skulls, the heads of monks massacred by the Turks in 1822.

The pavement outside the church is overgrown, with many wild flowers among the grass. An aged nun, bent double and with a single immensely long snaggle tooth remaining in her upper jaw, spoke to us in halting French. She told us that a small white flower growing outside the church was called 'Tears of the Virgin', and offered us sweet biscuits and Turkish delight. She and the two other sisters who together comprised the entire community appeared sublimely happy with their life. That day being Great (Good) Friday, they were busy preparing their ancient church for the Easter Vigil.

Nea Moni is surrounded by pines and must be in constant danger from woodland fires during the summer. Just beyond the east end of the church some very tall cypress trees shade a bench on which we sat looking down on a vista which dropped slowly to the sea seven or eight kilometres away. We shuddered at the prospect of what charter flights will one day do to this beautiful and lonely place.

That evening the invaluable hotel manager suggested we go to the mastic-growing villages in the south of the island. Pyrghi and Mesta both had very old churches, and it was an easy excursion by bus. At the same time he said that Chian wine, unobtainable at restaurants and shops in the capital, might possibly be found at Mesta. This tallied with the statement of the Sieur de Tournefort that 'The

Vineyards most in esteem are those of Mesta, from whence the Antients had their Nectar'. He thought the wine produced by them 'pleasant and stomachical'. Early next morning, long before the manager's appearance, we set off for the bus station. It was Easter Saturday so the bus was filled with people returning to their villages. Much to our disappointment there were no pigs or hens, not even a Paschal lamb, to share our journey.

The road climbed between patches of artichokes and beans up into hills yellow with the blossom of sage and broom, and russet with a euphorbia which appeared to be unique to the island. Occasionally we had glimpses of the sea far below. Beside the pump at Armolia a sign in English announced 'Water isn't proper'. There were few villages. It was an enchanting countryside, covered with flowers and wild fig, and if only the buses had run on Easter Monday we would have explored more of it.

We found Mesta to be a fascinating little medieval village in the depths of the country, a stone beehive of twisting, arched alleys, whose houses are built in blocks for protection from pirates. Some houses have been restored and are let as holiday cottages; a tempting idea until we went inside one. What banished all thoughts of renting it was not Spartan furnishings but the height of the doors, suitable only for the young and supple or for a race of dwarves – we had to bend double to pass from one room to the next.

The local bar did not sell Chian wine but referred us to the village shop next door. Here we succeeded in buying some, in a Johnny Walker whisky bottle still bearing the label. It was red and sweet, with a high alcohol content. Although neither of us normally care for sweet red wine (apart from vintage port, for which we share a cautious passion), we thought it excellent, very unlike the treacly Mavrodaphni which is what sweet wine usually means in Greece. As in Tournefort's day, the grapes are left to dry in the sun on straw mats for at least a week after picking.

During our search for Chian wine we met a very likeable couple from Athens with their two children. We sat with them in the tiny square drinking ouzo and eating mezze of cold calamari and olives. The wife, a native of Chios but obviously a shadow of her former self (see p.152), took us to the tiny church of Palaios Taxiarchis, a twelfth-century skete of Nea Moni, originally an aisleless basilica. It was partly destroyed by the Turks in the eighteenth century and when it was rebuilt in 1794 an aisle was added; there is an iconostasis completed in 1834 which took ten years for one man to carve. The caretaker was far more interested in the iconostasis than in frescoes, ignoring any queries about these as, with the aid of a taper on the end of a long pole, he pointed to one figure after another in the carvings. Yet it was still possible to make out fragments of what were once good, early frescoes. (There is a fine fourteenth-century icon in the nearby modern church of the Meghas Taxiarchis, which once belonged here.) The church, now being restored, is well worth a visit.

Our new friends gave us a lift to Pyrghi, some three miles away, stopping en route to show us clumps of lentisk or mastic trees growing by the side of the road. Both Mesta and Pyrghi stand among extensive groves of them. Only in southern Chios – although they grow elsewhere – does the bark of these curious little trees with dark-green bushy foliage, whose squat misshapen trunks, gnarled and contorted, are never more than six feet high, exude the resin or gum which is so prized. Cuts are made in the bark between June and September, from which the 'tears' are collected. Until recent times the resin constituted the principal wealth of Chios. Lord Charlemont tells us 'The Turks set a great value on this gum. They put it into their bread to give it a flavour, and burn it as a perfume. The women of the Seraglio are continually chewing it from a supposition that it is beneficial to the teeth and to the breath.' It was also credited with assisting in the conception of male children. So greatly did the Turks prize it that the peasants of the mastic villages were deliberately spared during the otherwise merciless massacres of 1822. The gum was chewed long before the Ottomans by the ladies of the Byzantine court, and it must have been they who bequeathed the habit to the Turks. It is known that the Catalan freebooter Roger de Lluria seized two cargoes of Chian mastic in 1292, while the Venetians' short-lived occupation of the island a century earlier was undoubtedly inspired by lust for the precious resin. Although the demand has greatly declined a Gum Mastic Growers' Association still exists on Chios. Nowadays it is mainly used to flavour the raki known as Mastika, and also made into a jam-like sweet which is eaten with a spoon.

At Pyrghi we lunched most suitably, since it was Lent, on fried calamari. According to Clark, writing in the early nineteenth century about the Peloponnese in Lent: 'Fish too is forbidden. Only one exception is made in favour of the cuttle-fish which has been pronounced to be, in an ecclesiastical point of view, a reptile, and lawful food accordingly.' He adds in a footnote: 'It is at all times a very abundant, cheap and disgusting article of food.' He probably means calamari as the word seems to have been applied to all members of the squid and cuttle-fish families. At Pyrghi one could almost agree with his assessment. But being Lent there was literally no other choice; no fish, certainly no meat. All that accompanied it was beans, so we drank rather a lot of retsina from the barrel and then, in a cheerful mood, went in search of the church. Pyrghi is an attractive village whose houses are painted with strange geometric patterns in shades of grey, pale blue or green; even modern houses are bound by law to conform with the custom.

The red-brick church of the Holy Apostles – which does not conform with the custom – is hidden from the main square, approached by a tunnel-like arcade, so that it comes as a delightful surprise when at last one succeeds in tracking it down. The external decoration is totally Byzantine, remarkably well preserved, with blind arcading, curved pediments and pilasters along the side of the walls, brick arches, saw-tooth bands and small marble double columns on the domes. The church dates from the twelfth century, but its frescoes were all painted in 1665 by the Cretan Antonios Domestichos Kynigos. They are a bit 'folksy' yet nonetheless effective, especially the Christos Pantocrator in the main body of the building, which has been over-restored. The Christ who presides over the Eucharist in the apse is unusual in wearing an Imperial crown. This church too has a link with Nea Moni, whose abbot Symeon – also Metropolitan of Chios – seems to have restored it in 1564.

On the way back to Chios we saw terebinth trees, which once produced another crop that was exported to Constantinople. 'The Turpentine Harvest is likewise made by cutting cross-ways with a Hatchet the Trunk of the biggest Turpentine Trees,' Tournefort (Botanist to King Louis XIV) informs us. Apparently the Chians, and presumably the Byzantines, took it as medicine. We learn from the same source that 'this Liquor is an excellent natural Balsam, a sovereign Stomachick, and good for provoking Urine'.

At eleven that night, having first eaten a forbidden snack since we were not used to dining at 1.30 a.m., we made our way through dark streets to a church on the hill above our hotel. If most un-Byzantine in either shape or decor it was nonetheless not unattractive, bright with lighted tapers held by an already large congregation. The gallery was filled with young women, the side aisle with their mothers and grandmothers. The Byzantine tradition of segregation has been preserved in many places. Clark describes a similar service at Nauplia over 150 years ago. 'The back seats on the ground floor were occupied by the married women; the unmarried sat in a gallery with lattice-work before it, as if their presence at church was like the presence of ladies in the House of Commons, not allowed but winked at.' Everyone lit a taper when they arrived, sticking it in a brass bowl filled with sand. Children sat on the stairs of the pulpit, as though watching their elders in the ballroom of some great house. At midnight the young women released a shower of rose petals over the congregation and all the candles were extinguished. The Easter service's great moment is when the priest emerges from the sanctuary carrying two long lighted candles from which everyone in the congregation lights the gaily beribboned ones they have brought with them. Then he cries joyfully *Christos anessi* and the fireworks begin. A child near us clutched two rockets in the same hand as her lighted candle, touch-papers level with the flame; but before we could all be blown to bits we had streamed out into the night. Rockets shot skyward, squibs jumped and spluttered among the crowd. The icon of Christ which since Good Friday had lain supine on a rose bedecked bier, covered with a richly embroidered epitaphios of purple velvet, was now raised to be shown to the people and carried through the streets. We joined the throng making its way to the best restaurant in town for a proper Easter dinner (traditional from Byzantine days); soup made from lamb's offal, beaten eggs, rice, bay leaves and bitter herbs, followed by roast lamb and red wine.

We decided to spend Easter Sunday visiting the thirteenth-century church of the Panagia Krina near Vavyloi, not far from Chios, which has important mosaics of whose existence we had been unaware. The taxi took us down a road of pink shale into a lonely but lush green valley, where we were confronted with an exterior which was a most beautiful example of Byzantine brickwork, pink and convoluted. We were miserable at finding it closed for restoration. We had brought a picnic so we went up into the hills below Nea Moni instead, finding a perfect spot on the terraced hillside outside the village of Karies. Irises and anchusas set off the blue of the distant sea, and the butterflies were magnificent. There were painted ladies, commas, red admirals and large skippers, so that one might have thought oneself at home. There were also southern white admirals and false commas. What we had never seen before was the exquisite kite swallowtail which, with its cream colouring, exaggerated 'tails' and curious gliding flight – dipping and swooping like a kite – can never be confused with the ordinary swallowtail, for all its zebra stripes.

We sat in the shade of a wild fig, our backs against the terrace wall, and ate our Easter eggs (their shells died red with cochineal), bread and cheese, salami and oranges, and drank our Chian wine which although good was not really suitable for a picnic in the heat of the day, making us sleepier and sleepier. After our siesta we walked back to the village square looking for coffee, which we drank under a most venerable walnut tree. At the next table, beneath the same huge tree, an old man who had lost most of both forearms (a common enough sight in this part of the Aegean where fishermen use dynamite) gesticulated wildly with his stumps as a story he was telling plainly became more and more improbable.

On Easter Monday we wandered round the city of Chios. There was much more to see than we had expected. Although rebuilt by the Genoese the Kastro (the fortified city centre as well as citadel) is basically Byzantine in origin. The Archaeological Museum was firmly shut; we were told it contains early Christian and Byzantine carvings. The Kastro was ample compensation, with a massive dungeon, the great Gothic Giustiniani Palace, Turkish houses and curious tombstones in the little Turkish cemetery. In the public gardens of Vounaki Square, the heart of the city, with its crowded coffee houses, disused mosque and plane trees, there are the mournful ruins of a basilica which for a time was the island's cathedral; it is dedicated to St Basil (330–79), one of the four great Greek doctors of the Church, on whose Rule all Orthodox monasticism is based – the altar is still there and in honour of Easter someone had stuck up a cheap card of the saint, placing some flowers and a wax lamp beneath it. What interested us most was watching the Chians themselves. In the majority of cafes men sat without women, as is normal all over Greece. On Chios, when the sexes sat together it seemed to be with the object of making women and girls consume as many cakes as possible. We could not help wondering if there was some special reason for this eagerness on the part of Chian men to nourish their womenfolk.

Time and again we saw husbands and boyfriends assiduously pressing cakes on nearest and dearest of already Rubens-like proportions. We were constantly staggered by the enormous size of Chian female bottoms, clearly a much admired asset. Later we discovered that the Chiots have always appreciated 'the fuller figure'. As long ago as the 1670s Bernard Randolph remarked of the island's girls 'their bodies [are] short and thick wasted' and that 'They esteem great Leggs'. Lord Charlemont makes the same observation – 'their petticoats are so short as to show a great part of the leg, a circumstance of which we certainly should not complain, if they did not render it disadvantageous by a prediliction for thick legs which they esteem a beauty'. What they omit to mention is that as well as hind quarters of noble proportions Chiot women on reaching puberty are prone to wear fierce moustaches – a fashion which is not shared by their menfolk.

Turks, and no doubt Byzantines before them, loved these ample curves, and during the seventeenth century Western observers were no less keen admirers of Chian womanhood – which was well aware of its allure. In his *Rare Adventures and Painefull Peregrinations* Walter Lithgow, a Scot from Lanark who visited the island in 1609, tells us: 'The Women of the Citty Scio are the most beautifull Dames (or rather Angelicall creatures) of all the Greekes upon the face of the Earth, and greatly given to Venery,' he writes. 'They are for the moste parte exceeding proude and sumptuous in apparell and commonly go (even Artificers wives) in gownes of Sattin and Taffety, yea in Cloth of Silver and Gold, and are adorned with precious Stones and Gems, and Jewels about their neckes and hands, with Rings, Chaines and Bracelets. Their Husbands are their Pandors, and when they see any Stranger arrive they will presently demand of him if he would have a Mistresse; and so they make Whoores of their owne Wives and are contented for a little gaine to weare hornes, such are the base minds of ignominious cuckolds. If a Stranger be desirous to stay all night with any of them, their price is a Chicken (sequin) of Gold, nine Shillings English, out of which this companion receiveth his supper, and for his paines a belly full of sinfull content.'

The city of Chios – or Chora as the inhabitants call it – is filled with patisseries, favourite cakes being chocolate sponge covered with melted chocolate and crammed with chocolate butter icing. Various confections based on filo pastry and the island's famous pastry abound, as do small tarts brimming with glacé cherries, though chocolate seems to be the runaway winner. In the interests of research we tried one or two, finding them unbearably sweet and sickly. What intrigued us most were chocolate rabbits and hens, often life-size, which presided over every shop window, and an Easter bread plaited to represent the Crown of Thorns with in the middle an egg dyed red symbolizing the Blood of Christ. These are seen all over Greece and were remarked on by Clark when in Sparta at Easter during the 1850s. He compared the coloured eggs to 'the "pace eggs" or otherwise by corruption "Paste eggs" of the north of England'.

Since it was Easter Monday there were no seats available on flights to Athens and no berths on the ferry, so we had to travel deck class to Piraeus on an eight-hour voyage through the night. Our sensitive hotel manager was genuinely shocked, muttering over and over again 'stinking' and 'very 'orrible', just like Mr Youkoumian in Evelyn Waugh's *Black Mischief*. He insisted on driving us to the dock himself to show sympathy. We were consoled by the cheerful discovery that there was an excellent restaurant on the dockside, where we ate a very agreeable dinner of roast kid with good clean retsina. Then we merged into the teeming multitude boarding the ferry, a vessel of several thousand tons, climbing awkwardly with our luggage up an unusually high and nerve-racking gang-plank like emigrants in an old film. Once on board even ouzo lost its power to solace. One of us slept on deck, the other draped over four stools in the bar. There was none of the jollity which so many travel writers claim to have seen on sea voyages between Greek islands and the mainland. Everybody on the ship seemed subdued, though this may have been the consequence of too many good parties in celebrating Easter – which means far more than Christmas in what is still an Orthodox country.

It is difficult to imagine a more ghastly prospect than the port of Piraeus on a grey drizzly morning with a chilly wind. Breakfastless, we groaned in spirit as we approached the gloomy modern buildings which line the docks. We tried to comfort ourselves with the thought that at least we were spared the Easter hangovers and livers of everyone else on board.

# Byzantine Athens

Another Athens shall arise,
And to remoter time
Bequeath, like sunset to the skies,
The splendour of its prime;

P.B. Shelley, *Hellas*

'This City was the Mother and Well-spring of all literall Arts &
Sciences; & the great Cisterno of Europe whence flowed so many
Conduit pipes of learning all where, but now altogether decayed.'

William Lithgow, *Paineful Peregrinations*

**D**ESMOND stayed forlornly on the dock at Piraeus, buffeted by wind and rain, minding our luggage, while Sue went to look for somewhere to have breakfast. She was so long in returning that – the port of Piraeus being famous for its brothels – Desmond began to fear she might have been kidnapped by white-slavers. Hungry and vile-tempered, we took the underground into Athens.

We had been told to expect a filthy city darkened by fumes and smog. Nothing could have been further from the truth. We found Athens clean and bright in the sunlight which had now returned, infinitely cleaner than Constantinople. While lacking the smart shops of Rome, London or Paris, and despite horrific re-development, it has some attractive squares and public gardens together with pretty streets in Plaka (up the hill beneath the Acropolis). And of course ruins – everywhere one is aware of the Classical past. We found it a most agreeable place, so long as we stayed within what had been the boundaries of the city in the nineteenth century. We were particularly lucky with our hotel, picked entirely by chance out of the many which line Metropoleos Street. For just £10 a night we had clean comfortable rooms with baths complete with plugs, and large balconies looking on to the cathedral and up to the floodlit Acropolis. The hotel's octogenarian manager, a tiny lizard-like creature of great charm and guile – 'I knows everything in Athens' –

claimed they had the best view in the city and that an American professor spending the night in one of them had prolonged his stay to ten weeks to do all his writing on the balcony. The claim seemed far-fetched, delightful as the view is, since only the stone-deaf could contemplate working there.

Our most pressing need, having found a hotel so quickly, was breakfast. Most of the many tavernas in Plaka are open only at night, but luckily we spotted a bar where we could get ouzo – rather early even for us. We definitely needed restoring after our ghastly journey, however, and we were able to buy rolls, cheese and coffee. The bar was full of sailors and also, in consequence, of battered old tarts with slit skirts and crimson lips of the sort so convincingly portrayed by the Greek Minister of Culture thirty years ago, in her film *Never on Sunday*. Apart from the sailors there were very few tourists in Athens, so we could wander round Plaka – usually filled with them – in peace and enjoy its narrow streets, pre-war houses and tiny churches, all of which grew smaller and smaller the higher up the hill one went.

Byzantine Athens was merely a decayed third-rate city, governed from Thebes and not from Constantinople. Every scholar was aware of its glory in Classical times, even knowing the names of a few of its most famous monuments, but otherwise it was totally undistinguished. From the reign of Constantine the Great onward its temples were converted into churches, a process completed by the early fifth century. The Parthenon, formerly the shrine of Pallas Athene (Minerva), became the cathedral of Hagia Sophia, being later re-dedicated to the Virgin of Athens; the Theseion, which had been the shrine of Hephaistos (Vulcan), became the church of St George; the temple of Aesculapius and Hygeia on the slopes of the Acropolis became the church of SS Cosmas and Damian; and the Erechtheion became a church of the Virgin, later of the Trinity. Meanwhile a chapel to St John was built in the temple of Zeus Olympius. Probably some 200 temples were converted or had basilicas built on top of them. The Metropolitan's palace was in the Propylea of the Acropolis, the Pinakothek becoming a chapel of the Archangels Gabriel and Michael, and the reading room of the Emperor Hadrian's library yet another church of Our Lady. Even the Tower of the Winds was turned into a baptistery for the basilica which today lies under the nearby mosque.

At least three Empresses were of Athenian origin. Irene, the wife of

Leo IV and mother of Constantine VI, was the first woman in Byzantine history to be sole ruler of the Empire in her own right – having her son blinded at the age of twenty-seven. Another Athenian was Theophano, the wife of Irene's successor to the throne, Nicephorus I, but we know nothing about her. The most interesting of the three by far was Athenaïs Eudoxia, wife of Theodosius II and daughter of a professor of rhetoric at the pagan Academy of Athens (subsequently closed in 529 by Justinian). She was probably instrumental in bringing Classical learning to Constantinople. During her husband's reign the old university founded by Constantine was expanded to become the most important seat of learning in the Empire, with ten chairs of Greek grammar and ten of Latin grammar, as well as five chairs of Greek rhetoric and three of Latin rhetoric. Eudoxia became a fervent Christian, writing hymns and going on pilgrimage to Jerusalem. She founded churches in the Holy City, returning to Constantinople with precious relics: St Peter's chain, the right arm of St Stephen and, most important of all, the icon reputedly painted by St Luke of the Virgin Hodegetria, which she brought back in 438 as a present for her sister-in-law Pulcheria. The icon is supposed to have survived the Iconoclast period and ended its days at the church of the Chora where it was hacked to pieces by the Turks in the three days of pillage which followed the Fall of Constantinople.

Athens was such a backwater that only two Byzantine Emperors are recorded as having visited it. Constans II, during what Gibbon calls 'his long pilgrimage of disgrace and sacrilegious rapine', spent the winter of 662–3 there on his way to Sicily where he was murdered in his bath. The other Imperial visitor was Basil II. Southern Greece had been invaded by the Slavs, who arrived in the sixth century, devastated by Muslim pirates in the ninth, and then all but conquered by the Bulgars in the tenth. It was Basil II who restored the whole of southern Greece to the Empire. In 1018 he made a ceremonial entry into Ohrid to receive homage from Tsar Samuel's widow. He spent the remainder of that year travelling around his newly acquired territory of Bulgaria, right up to the Danube, before riding down to the Peloponnese. He gave thanks at the church of the Virgin in the Parthenon, presenting it with a wonderful gold dove to hang over the altar, together with gold lamps of superb workmanship; he also had frescoes painted on its walls. Sir George Wheler, describing the church in 1682, does not mention these frescoes but says 'The Roof over the Altar and Quire, added to the Temple by the Greeks, hath the Picture of the Holy Virgin on it, of Mosaic Work, left yet by the Turks; because, as they say, a certain Turk having shot a Musquet at it, his hand presently withered'.

After the annihilation of the Bulgars there was a spate of church building in and around Athens, which included the monastery of Daphni some six miles west of the city. Many of perhaps 200 churches built between 1000 and 1200 still remain but, in keeping with the lowly status of Athens at that time, are all small and lacking in good frescoes or mosaics. Most are built of stone and brick, with unusually high drummed domes. For the city was run down and poverty stricken. Not only had it suffered from Slavs, Muslims and Bulgars, but the plague had decimated the population. Its Metropolitan, Michael Akominatos – archbishop there for 35 years and a considerable scholar who had studied at Constantinople – compared life in Athens to life in Hell. 'Living for years in Athens I too have fallen into barbarism,' he writes. He tells of a generation 'poor in body and soul' and sheds tears over the city's ruined walls and empty streets, its ragged, famished population. The sole industries appear to have been soap boiling and weaving monks' habits. Akominatos complains that the local wine (obviously retsina) is so dreadful 'as to seem pressed from the juice of the pine instead of the grape'.

Athens had hitherto escaped the attention of invaders because of its poverty and sheer insignificance. But in 1205 King Boniface of Thessalonica rode in, his troops sacking the cathedral and destroying Akominatos's precious library. The city became the capital of the Frankish Lordship – later Duchy – of 'Satines', which included Attica, Boeotia, the Megarid and parts of Locris. It was lost to the Emperors for ever. Gothic churches and chapels, castles and palaces, were built, Cistercian monks installed at Daphni, outlandish coins known as *tournesia* were struck, bearing lilies and Western crosses. The thirteenth-century court of Athens was compared to Camelot by contemporaries. The Franks intermarried with the '*Griffons*' (as they called the Greeks), becoming *Gasmoules*, or half-castes whose first language was Greek. In consequence, by the time the Duchy of Athens fell to the Turks in 1456 it had for long been very much part of the Byzantine world, even if never reconquered by the Emperors and if its Catholic Dukes were of Latin origin. It stayed in Turkish hands until 1821, a squalid, miserably poor little provincial town, completely overshadowed by the neighbouring town of Corinth. Many were surprised when, in 1834, it was chosen to be the capital of the new Kingdom of Greece.

Byzantine Athens is confined to churches and museums. There is a fine example of the former in the Agora, Hagioi Apostoli, an eleventh-century cross-in-square edifice, brilliantly restored in 1954. The fourteenth-century frescoes in the main body of the church are original, having spent centuries under plaster. Those of later date in the narthex come from the demolished church of Hagios Spiridion close by. Near the Agora is Hagios Soter (the only church built at Athens during Frankish rule), whose bricked-up door was ordered by King Otto (1832–62) to remain blocked until Greece has recovered Constantinople.

Apart from Hagioi Apostoli none of the Athenian churches have Byzantine frescoes and all of them have rather disappointing interiors. At first we found it most frustrating to find so many shut but later, having talked to Dr Baltoyiannis at the Byzantine Museum, we realized that we were missing nothing and that their charm lies in their attractive exteriors. All these city churches are within easy walking distance of each other, scattered around Plaka and Ermou Street. What we liked particularly about these little buildings was the way one comes upon them so unexpectedly. They are hidden by the modern blocks of flats which surround them – even those among the older houses in Plaka up the northern slope of the Acropolis seem like children with grown-ups. The most perfect example of this is our favourite church, the enchanting twelfth-century Panagia Goepoepicoos or Little Cathedral in Metropoleos Square, which is dwarfed by the quite handsome houses round the square while the dreadful nineteenth-century cathedral towers over it. The church's exterior is a fascinating jumble of bits and pieces – antique friezes, Byzantine peacocks from a much earlier church (possibly founded by the Empress Irene), and Frankish coats of arms added when the Villehardouin and de La Roche families ruled Athens. The entire church appears to be constructed out of marble from old buildings and is unlike anything else in the city. Another church, of which we became very fond, was Hagia Dynami (Holy Strength) near our hotel in Metropoleos Street. It is not truly Byzantine, having been built in the seventeenth century when the Turks insisted that churches must be smaller than mosques. No Turk could possibly have taken exception to Hagia Dynami. It is so minute that an office block has been built over it, the ground-floor ceilings being higher than the church which nestles among the pillars supporting the first floor. Mass is celebrated here every morning, and it is filled with people on their way to work who come to light a candle and say a prayer. Here we heard once again *Kyrie eleison, Christe eleison*, the only Greek words in the Latin Mass, banished from its vernacular versions by scholar poets who nonetheless protest that they seek unity between Catholics and Orthodox. (Later an Athenian told us that in former years the interior had been festooned with ex-votos from married ladies in thanksgiving for the return of errant lovers from other arms.)

We noticed throughout our travels in Greece how much a part of everyday life the Orthodox Church still is, for Greeks of all ages. It was after all the one thing which sustained them during centuries of Turkish oppression. As Clark says in his *Peloponnesus*: 'It was for ages the sole bond of union among them – the only national institution which remained to remind them that they had once been free. So they clung to the Church and its usage in spite of the most grinding tyranny; for in it they saw not only all their hopes hereafter, but their single chance of ultimate deliverance on earth.'

The largest collections of Byzantine works of art in the world are to be found in Athens – in the Byzantine Museum, the Benaki Museum, and the Paul and Alexandra Canellopoulos Museum. We started with the first as being the only one open on a Tuesday. The former palace of the Duchesse de Plaisance, the widow of Napoleon's arch-treasurer, it is in Kephissia Street opposite the British Embassy, and built in the style of an Italian villa of the Renaissance – a most successful pastiche with enormous charm. It contains almost too much, although everything is arranged and displayed with skill and sensitivity. One room is a convincing reconstruction of the heart of a fifth- to seventh-century basilica, using original pieces from various sites; it has a low marble iconostasis with an entrance arch raised to the height of a priest, a bishop's throne behind the altar, and a pulpit. Another room simulates the interior of a domed cross-in-square church, with a polychrome floor which came from a Christian church on the Acropolis. There are two rooms full of rescued fragments of frescoes, and room after room of superb panel paintings, among which are not only Greek icons from the twelfth to nineteenth centuries but an almost Byzantine crucifixion by Paolo Veneziano and two fine works by the seventeenth-century Cretan Manuel Tsanes (whom some consider to be the last icon painter of authentic genius). There is a magnificent fourteenth-century crucifixion which was stolen from Monemvasia in the 1970s; when it was recovered after three months in the hands of thieves it had been broken into five pieces to facilitate concealment, but it has been brilliantly restored by the craftsmen of the museum's workshops, and is now one of the finest things in the collection. There are many fine illuminated Gospels from the Comnenan and Palaeologan periods, and a superb chrysobull of the Emperor Andronicus II dated 1301, which shows the Basileus, crowned and in purple robes, standing with Christ against a gold background; at the end is the Imperial signature in red – 'Andronicus in Christ God Faithful King and Emperor of the Romans Palaeologus'. ('Chrysobull' was the name given to Imperial edicts which were always partly in gold.)

Desmond, a little overwhelmed by such a wealth of exhibits, was gazing somewhat vaguely at a small icon when his eye was caught by the name of the artist printed underneath. It was perhaps the most exciting object in the entire museum, if not the most attractive – one of the only four known icons by Domenico Theotocopoulos, El Greco. It was discovered as recently as 1985 by a young archaeologist, Georgios Mastoropoulos, who was examining the icons in a church on the little Aegean island of Syros when his incredulous eyes suddenly saw the signature of El Greco. He telephoned the Greek Ministry of Culture, who flew a party of experts out to Syros the same afternoon. Restoration revealed a good deal about the master's decidedly idiosyncratic approach to icon painting. He was clearly an experimenter, using both traditional and completely new Western techniques side by side with those of Byzantium. In this panel of the Dormition of the Virgin Christ wears yellow robes – an exceptionally rare colour – while a candlestick by the Virgin's head supported by three naked nymphs is like something by Benvenuto Cellini. As well as lying on the bier Our Lady is shown in Heaven, which is most unusual in Byzantine art. It is known that after studying under the great traditionalist icon painter Michael Damaskinos on Crete, El Greco went to Venice, where his brother was what would nowadays be called secretary of the Greek seamen's union, before ultimately settling in Spain. It is hard to believe that this little painting is by the master of 'The Burial of Count Orgaz'. (A wish to discover what inspired El Greco's extraordinary originality had much to do with the revival of interest in Byzantine art.) Nevertheless it enabled experts to establish beyond doubt the attribution of two icons in the Benaki Museum, only one of which is signed – 'Domenico', without the 'Theotocopoulos'.

However, on reflection we thought that probably the most illuminating items in the Byzantine Museum were on a wall of one of the rooms near the entrance. They were a few fragments of Frankish-Byzantine reliefs in stone, dating from the thirteenth century, which were completely Gothic in feeling. Nothing else could convey quite so vividly the shattering impact of Frankish colonization upon Byzantium.

Afterward we spoke to the curator, Dr Chrysanthe Baltoyiannis, a shy, pleasant, dedicated scholar. She showed us her impressive new book – an illustrated study of one of the most important collections of Greek icons still in private hands. It was she who told us the story of the El Greco icon's discovery. She also told us about important new advances in the study of Byzantine iconography. Many icons are much earlier than hitherto thought; an entire school of painting formerly attributed to the eighteenth century has been re-attributed to the fifteenth, while some Virgins with Western faces formerly considered to be seventeenth-century Cretan work heavily influenced by the West are now believed to have been painted on Crete during the 1400s. Separate schools have been identified, belonging respectively to Constantinople, Thrace, Thessalonica, Kastoria and Mount Athos. During the fifteenth century an atelier on Mount Athos literally mass-produced icons, and until the Turkish conquest of 1669 Crete annually exported thousands of icons to Venice and southern Italy.

The Benaki Museum being shut we had to contain our impatience to see the other El Greco icons till the following day. We made a detour on our way back to the hotel to look at Hagioi Theodori in Klauthmonos Square, one of the prettiest of the eleventh-century churches, and its contemporary the Kapnikarea (or 'tax collector') which has a many gabled exo-narthex. The latter, one of the best preserved, is built on the site of the church founded by Athenaïs Eudoxia, and starts on an island in the extremely busy Ermou Street. In the interests of research we risked life and limb, braving the onslaught of wild Athenian taxi-drivers, to visit the interior; we were disappointed to find the frescoes modern.

After ordering a bottle of Evian water at the hotel we noticed that its cap was unfastened. Insisting sternly on a sealed bottle we fancied that our ancient manager blushed, or at least turned a deeper shade of yellow, his eyes growing even more Saurian. Plainly he made a small fortune by filling empty Evian bottles from the tap in the hotel kitchen.

The Benaki Museum is in the Benaki family mansion, one of the few neo-classical houses to survive in central Athens and gives some idea of what the city must have looked like before World War II and the unfortunate 'redevelopment' which followed. The collections are the work of one man, Anthony Benaki (1873–1954), a member of an immensely rich family of Alexandrian Greeks. It is a superb example of what can be achieved by private wealth handled responsibly. Although not primarily a Byzantine museum, the Benaki's Byzantine collection is of the utmost importance. The ceramics are especially good; outstanding are a large red-brown bowl with cream griffins, a small yellow bowl with a sgraffito drawing of a dove, and a pale grey-green bowl with sgraffito spirals. There is a magnificent silver dish from the sixth century, absolutely classical in style, and a processional cross from Hagia Sophia at Constantinople. Among the icons are two fine Tsanes (one of St Mark with the Venetian lion, his symbol) and some by Michael Damaskinos, the teacher of El Greco.

Having been told by Dr Baltoyiannis that there were two El Greco icons, we were disappointed to find that the better of the two – that of The Adoration of the Magi – had been removed for restoration. Painted after the artist had left Crete for Venice, it is completely Western in colour and feeling. Nor is it Byzantine in composition, being almost identical with that on the same subject by the Venetian Schiavone. The Virgin, in a pink robe, holds the naked Child, who leans forward to accept a gift from a kneeling magus. We found the dilapidated icon of St Luke painting his icon of the Virgin Hodegetria (executed in Crete when El Greco was still in his teens) much more interesting. The Evangelist is shown seated at an easel on which sits the icon brought back to Constantinople by the Empress Eudoxia. Unfortunately the panel is in dreadful condition, in far greater need of restoration than The Adoration of the Magi.

It is not too much to say that the Benaki's illuminated manuscripts, from the eleventh and twelfth centuries, are exquisite. However what genuinely thrilled us was an argyrobull (a silver bull to distinguish it from the golden Imperial variety) dated 1456 and signed in red 'Demetrius the Porphyrogenitus Despot of Mistra Palaeologus'.

In the basement was a collection described unpromisingly as 'Handicraft of the Greek Islands'. On inspection, it proved fascinating, consisting of folk costumes of extraordinary richness and beauty. Some obviously retained vivid echoes of the Byzantine world, especially those from Crete, the Dodecanese and Cyprus, which resisted the Turks longest. There were some lovely dresses, which we had expected to see in country districts – as we had those in Yugoslavia – but sadly the Greeks of the mainland do not appear to wear them any longer, only producing them for folk-dancing exhibitions. In the remote mountain villages of the Pindus some Vlachs still wear their distinctive costume, but they are not true Greeks.

For the moment we had had a surfeit of museum gazing and were suffering from cultural indigestion – there had been too many good things to see. So we took a bus, as hot as an oven, into the suburbs to Daphni, marvelling en route at the friendliness of our fellow passengers and the laxity with which fares were collected. We alighted in a main road hellishly full of fast and merciless traffic and went into the park next to the monastery. It stands on the site of a temple dedicated to the nymph Daphne. (The daughter of a river god, she caught Apollo's roving eye but escaped through being changed into a laurel bush.) There was a fortified basilica here as early as the fifth century, but the present monastery dates from 1100, the church of the Dormition being an octagon supporting a dome, with a long narrow narthex of two stories on the west. Some 30 years later an exo-narthex was added, open on three sides with arches resting on antique Ionic columns – which presumably came from the temple. (All except one of these columns were acquired by Lord Elgin and taken to London).

The monastery's first hundred years were peaceful enough, but after the Frankish conquest it saw unending troubles. In 1207 the 'Megaskyr' Odo de La Roche drove out the Orthodox monks and replaced them by French Cistercians, who occupied it for over two centuries, during which time it was for long the only house of their order in Greece, and a mausoleum for the Dukes of Athens; among others Duke Guy II (1287–1308) was buried here, last of the House of

La Roche. The monastery was constantly attacked by the Byzantines. In the fourteenth century the Cistercians demolished the upper floor of the narthex, which was once either the library or the abbot's lodging, and used its stones to build fortifications. The Cistercians were expelled in their turn when Athens fell to the Turks in 1455. Orthodox monks returned at the beginning of the sixteenth century and remained here until the Greek War of Independence. The Turks drove the community out for a second time for harbouring fugitive patriots, and it was successively a barracks, an arsenal and a mental hospital before passing into the hands of an archaeological society in 1888. Since then a painstaking programme of conservation and restoration has been carried out by both private foundations and the state.

The mosaics are Daphni's real glory, equal to anything we had seen at Ravenna or Constantinople. The most famous is of course the terrifyingly stern Christos Pantocrator in the dome. Among other superb mosaics we ourselves were particularly struck by the Kiss of Judas, in which Peter is cutting off the ear of Malchus – in this case a young boy – with a knife instead of the usual sword. There is another, not unusual, touch in the Harrowing of Hell where Christ tramples on the body of the fettered Lord of Hades. The Crucifixion is especially poignant, and in its tender compassion reminded us of the Pietà at Nerezi, painted sixty years later. Among the many saints scattered around the church we were interested to see Sergius and Bacchus, since these are peculiarly Eastern saints who are seldom found west of Constantinople. Possibly the unknown founder of the church came from the East, perhaps even from the martyrs' native Syria.

On our return from Daphni we made our way to a neo-classical mansion high on the northern slope of the Acropolis. The Paul and Alexandra Canellopoulos Museum is much smaller than either the Benaki or the Byzantine but, much to the surprise of both of us, we enjoyed it even more. The jewellery here is a glittering testimony to the truth of the claim made by the great Byzantinist Orlandos that the very word Byzantium was synonymous with luxury – wonderful crosses, pendants, earrings and rings. There are marvellous coins, including solidi of the Iconoclast Emperors bearing plain crosses, and Coptic textiles from Byzantine Egypt. The icons are equally distinguished, ranging from a sixth-century Virgin from St Catherine's monastery (a rare survivor from before Iconoclast destruction) to sixteenth- and seventeenth-century Cretan examples by Michael Damaskinos and Manuel Tsanes. One of our favourites was a charming icon of three very ladylike female saints who look not only pious, but elegant as well.

As we emerged from the museum a very tall old man wearing very dark glasses and extremely handsome shoes came up and asked if we were English. He had the rosette of an officer of the Legion d'honneur in his button-hole and was clearly very distinguished. He was Paul Canellopoulos, creator of the museum, a lifelong collector of both ancient and Byzantine art who has used his great fortune to wonderful effect. He had served with the British forces at El Alamein, where he lost an eye, had hidden Harold Macmillan in his flat in Athens in 1945 when the latter was investigating the political situation, and had fought at the side of General Scobie against the Greek Communists during the Greek civil war of 1945–7. Tragically, he lost almost the entire sight of his remaining eye in 1983 and can no longer see the museum which he and his wife have created. Nevertheless he knows where everything is and insisted on showing us around for a second time. Among the Byzantine pieces of which he is especially proud are the wax on wood icons from Mount Sinai (where he worked for a year), a thirteenth-century panel of St Michael thrusting the Devil down to Hell, and an icon showing the discovery of the True Cross at Jerusalem by the Empress Helena which depicts the excavation and the actual moment of finding. He told us that iconography recognizes no fewer than 1068 types of Virgin, of which 100 are represented in his museum. (This we found puzzling as Denis of Fourna states there are only sixteen.) He showed us an icon by Theophanes the Greek, the teacher of the great Russian fifteenth-century master Andrei Rublev, a Venetian-Cretan icon of circa 1500 of Christ and the Samaritan woman at the well with the roofs of Jerusalem in the background – reminiscent of a hill town in Tuscany – and a post-Byzantine icon of the Empress Eudoxia (wife of Arcadius) being turned away from Hagia Sophia by St John Chrysostom. He whispered 'She had many friends, you know'. Other treasures included a gold bracelet which had belonged to the Empress Anna, a huge lapis lazuli seal depicting the Empress Theodora, and a head of the Emperor Galerius – builder of the Rotunda at Thessalonica.

Mr Canellopoulos darted from object to object, talking at great speed 'Look at this! Look at this! Only the Greeks could make such beautiful things!' He went on so fast that it was impossible to take in much of what he said, but his enthusiasm was infectious and his collection magnificent. When we had done a lightning tour of the Byzantine rooms we were rushed upstairs to see the Antiquities. 'I never buy anything which is not beautiful,' he said, which was quite obvious. His Tanagraean figurines were enchanting, as were his kraters (the scene on one of which was considered totally unsuitable for female eyes). Then we were whisked away in his car to his flat, where he kept his favourite things. Over the fireplace hung a portrait of his wife painted by Annigoni, beneath it the head of a Venus from Milos – 'To show how beautiful my wife is'. She certainly seemed to fit in very well with his collection. Almost incredibly, he produced the fourth El Greco icon, a Nativity which he had found in Crete. He allowed us to handle a superb triptych by Manuel Tsanes with a portrait of the donor, a Cretan sea-captain wearing seventeenth-century Western dress like his Venetian masters, black with a huge white turndown collar, reminding one of an English Puritan. Even more striking in its own way was a Pietà of circa 1250 in the 'Byzantine-Gothic' style. When we left him we took with us a sense of outrage that such a man of all people should have been deprived of his sight.

Elated by our encounter, we hurried to the Acropolis. En route we looked for the cave, high on the south side of the hill, which housed the church of the Virgin of the Grotto. With binoculars we could just make out a hole but, the enclosure of the theatre of Dionysius being shut, we were unable to get any nearer than the main road. From Wheler's description we did not miss too much. 'This Grotto is a pretty large Place within, and hath two Cells, one above another'. What is remarkable is the fact that he visited it at all – clearly contempt for all things Byzantine did not become fashionable until the eighteenth century.

The Parthenon, it must be admitted, was disappointing, so much of it having been closed to the public. We found ourselves lamenting that all vestiges of Byzantine churches had been removed. We are unquestionably Philhellenes but for us Hellas is also Byzantium, the Greece of Emperors and Patriarch, not just the Greece of Olympian gods and philosophers.

We agreed that it was time we left the metropolis. Desmond was peculiarly anxious to do so after an encounter during the previous night. It had been his first meeting with a real live bedbug, the most bloodthirsty member of the insect creation, which had drunk a great deal before being caught and killed. We did not complain. Otherwise the hotel was spotlessly clean and we had grown too fond of its wily old manager to wish to upset him. In any case he might have replied as a Calabrian hotelier did long ago, when Norman Douglas complained he had found bedbugs in his sheets: 'What do you expect to find? Humming-birds?'

# Hosios Loukas and the rock monasteries of The Meteora

'Most of the population of Mezzovo turned out to see the procession
of the Milordos Inglesis'

The Hon Robert Curzon, *Visits to Monasteries in the Levant*

'Remember, O Lord, those in deserts, and monasteries, and dens,
and caves of the earth.'

*The Liturgy of St Basil the Great*

OUR NEW hired car was an un-
lovely object, a prematurely
aged white Nissan Cherry which bore the scars of what had all too
plainly been a very nasty accident indeed. It already had one hundred
thousand miles on the clock, although the man at the rental office
assured us they only kept their cars for eighteen months. It was not
the car we had ordered and we disliked it on sight. It was unwieldy,
uncomfortable and had a fiendish self-locking boot which was going
to be a cause of sorrow.

We drove gingerly out of Athens, north-west through Attica and
over the watershed into Boeotia. Our route followed the old road
taken by all those making the pilgrimage to the shrine at Delphi until
its closure by the Emperor Theodosius in 388. The country in Attica
was dull but bleak – low hills covered with sage and coggyria, and
endless flocks of sheep and goats. We had expected the scenery to be
more majestic but, until we were well past Thebes and had joined the
new main road, we were not conscious of the great bulk of Parnassus
rising before us.

By the eleventh century Thebes was the third city of Byzantine
Greece and the centre of the silk industry, with a large Jewish
population. It is a good indication of how insignificant Athens had

become, despite all its new churches, that Thebes, set in an unhealthy and mosquito-ridden plain, should be preferred as the residence of the Duke of Athens when the Franks conquered the country in 1205. Nothing remains from Imperial times though the squat Santamari – the corner tower of a Frankish palace famed throughout medieval Europe for its size and luxury – survives forlornly.

Our plan was to visit the monastery of Hosios Loukas and then spend the night at Delphi, a village overflowing with hotels where accommodation would be no problem. Once there it would be a simple task to convince the strict Byzantinist of the party that the shrine must be visited: after all, the Temple of Apollo had been turned into a church dedicated to Profitas Elias – Sir George Wheler saw it in 1682. All trace of the church has been obliterated by the archaeologists.

We made a short detour to Skripou, the ancient Orchomenos, to see the church of the Dormition which, dating from 874, is the oldest cross in square church in Greece. The road ran through cotton fields intersected by canals, across the plain where, in 1377, the Catalans defeated the Duke of Athens to gain control of Boeotia. The church, founded by the Protospatharios Leo Strategos of the Theme of Hellas, is a remarkable building constructed, as is so often the case, out of material taken from the Hellenic theatre and from the Temple of the Graces on whose site it stands. The pillars from the temple have been cut into discs which, with dressed stone of great antiquity, have been incorporated into the west wall. The east end is covered with reliefs of fabulous beasts, leopards and boars and on the south wall two peacocks strut beneath a sundial. The exterior is far more interesting than the gloomy interior, where the only things of note are the courses of carved reliefs.

We were glad to come out into the sun and sit in the ruins of the little theatre opposite the churchyard. A large and exquisite butterfly alighted on a stone beside us – an Idas Blue according to the book – and we wondered if it were named after the Idas who was Apollo's successful rival in love and who, like the god, rode in a winged chariot. The peace of the theatre was shattered by the arrival of some gypsy children who, having spotted our car, had come to beg. Their shrill cries reminded us of the touts in Constantinople.

Instead of going back to the main road, we turned right towards Lamia, passing on our way the strange Lion of Chaeroneia who guards the final resting place of the Theban Sacred Band. The troops of Alexander the Great massacred all the two hundred and fifty four members of this crack regiment, who stood their ground till the last man died. The lion, immensely tall and thin, sits on his haunches on a pedestal erected over the ossuary in a cypress grove by the side of the road.

Soon we turned left out of the plain and climbed the slopes and spurs of Parnassus. At one stage we were surrounded by an enormous flock of the most handsome goats we had ever seen, red and black with long, shaggy coats and horns like handlebars. After negotiating numerous hairpin bends on our tortuous descent, we arrived at the bottom of the Cleft Way at the spot where Oedipus met and slew his father before going on to marry his mother. It is still a remote and beautiful spot, dominated by the mighty heights of Parnassus.

We reached the monastery of Hosios Loukas at mid-day – impeccable timing as three coach loads of tourists were toiling up the steps to the car park in search of their vehicles and lunch. Set on the side of the bowl of a fertile valley and sheltered by the foothills of Helicon, the monastery has one of the most delightful positions of any in Greece. In antiquity this was the village of Steiros and the two churches in the courtyard, built on the site of the Temple of Demeter, are to a great extent constructed from the ancient stones.

Hosios Loukas (896–953) became a monk and a hermit at the age of fourteen. After many wanderings he settled in Steiros, where a community gathered around and the present monastery arose. The word Hosios means Holy Man, and even in his lifetime 'Holy Luke' worked many miracles, and still more after his death. He had an impressive gift of second sight, foreseeing a Bulgar invasion and the liberation of Crete from the Arabs by a man named Romanus. When Crete fell to the troops of Romanus II twenty years later the prophecy was recalled and, according to legend, by order of the Emperor a suitably splendid shrine began to be erected here in honour of the holy man. What makes Loukas so appealing a saint is his genuine liking for his fellow human beings without any exception. So widespread was his fame as a wonderworker that for centuries his shrine attracted rich bequests. In the 1200s it was plundered by the Franks who stole his relics – one of them is still at the Vatican. The monastery has suffered from looting and devastation over the centuries, especially during the War of Independence when the Greek flag was hoisted by the abbot to summon the men of Boeotia to rise against the Turks. In recent years, however, it has been the object of truly inspired restoration.

For anyone like us, who is disheartened by Hagia Sophia's wretchedly dilapidated state, the larger of the two churches here is the perfect tonic. The design is similar to that of the church at Daphni (which may well derive from it) but more mosaic has survived while the walls are still sheathed in gleaming marble panels, and the polychrome floor of *opus Alexandrinum* remains intact. As Wheler said in 1682, 'And truly, this is the finest church I saw in all Greece, next to Santa Sophia at Constantinople; notwithstanding it is old, and hath suffered very much by earthquakes, and Time'. It gives the most convincing picture of ecclesiastical splendour at the height of the Eastern Empire.

Although badly damaged by earthquakes in 1593 and again in 1659 – those in the dome being replaced with frescoes in the seventeenth century – the mosaics are the most numerous and important in Greece. The monks insist the church was founded by Romanus, but if this were so all work on the building would have ceased during the reign of his successor, Nicephorus Phocas, a grizzled old soldier who forbade all building of new churches, prefering to repair those already in existence. The church was finished by the Abbot Philotheos and it is almost certain that the mosaics were commissioned by the Emperor Basil II during his triumphal tour of the Balkans in 1018; Sir Steven Runciman considers they reflect the austere taste of the Emperor. Certainly they lack the delicacy and feeling of those at Daphni, but the effect of the tall marble clad walls, surmounted by these simple figures against a glittering gold background, is awe-inspiring. Not all the ceilings are decorated with mosaics, the side chapels being covered with frescoes from the eleventh century. The most interesting is that of Joshua in full Byzantine battle dress which, although it appears to have been painted on the north-east wall of the interior of Hosios Loukas, is in fact on the exterior of the narthex of the church of the Virgin next door, the two churches sharing a common wall at this point.

Apart from the usual scenes from the Life and Passion of Christ and the Life of the Virgin, in the squinches and the narthex, the church is filled with a veritable army of saints. Some full length, others in medallions, they appear in the dome, the cross vaults and even on the intrados of the arches. There are over one hundred and fifty of them; warrior saints in abundance, as befitting what had been a border district, female saints with our old friends Constantine and Helena, monks and martyrs. Hosios Loukas is there, his hands raised in prayer in a particularly striking mosaic. As well as these are holy men from the Old Testament – the three companions of Daniel, Shadrach, Meshach and Abednego, who, thanks to their belief in their God, survived the fiery furnace – and Daniel himself with two lions, as small as spaniels, licking his feet. In the narthex the Apostles, strange squat figures with large heads, seemed vaguely familiar. It was not until we consulted our books on our return to England that we realized they bore a strong resemblance to those in St Mark's.

Beneath the church lies the crypt dedicated to St Barbara which, until ransacked by the Franks, housed the mortal remains of Hosios Loukas. The entire ceiling is covered with frescoed medallions of saints set against a patterned background. On the walls the rather crude and much damaged scenes from the Passion have been likened to those in the rock-churches of Cappadocia. Abbot Philotheos appears with his monks and there are two portraits of Hosios Loukas himself. But nothing can compare with the splendour of the church above.

Back in the courtyard, the smaller church, dedicated to the Virgin, was begun in Hosios Loukas's lifetime in 946 with financial help from the Strategos Krenites of Thebes and completed in 955. It is cruciform in design, with a dome. Only a few frescoes have survived, eleventh- or twelfth-century portraits of saints, though much of the fine marble floor is in good condition.

The monk's refectory has also been restored, a two-storey building with traces of fresco work. The brethren ate in the upper storey, housing their wine and olive presses in the lower. Next door there is an eleventh-century cistern. Some of the cells have been restored and others are currently being refurbished. The present community consists of fewer than a dozen monks, who live in the wisteria-clad inner courtyard. Although the Divine Liturgy is celebrated and the Office sung – in the smaller church – Hosios Loukas has become more of a museum than a monastery and even has a restaurant.

At Arachova, famous for its rugs – hung out at every shop to attract the coach loads of tourists on their way to Delphi – the dry red wine was quite good. With that and cold roast lamb we had a passable lunch at a table overlooking the great valley beneath us. No doubt such wine, famous for miles around, was drunk at Hosios Loukas in the days of its prosperity long ago and offered to visiting Imperial dignitaries. We were still in Paschal week, and lamb was the only thing on the menu in this simple restaurant, but it was pink and tender and surprisingly good. The view from Arachova (it is amazing how many Slav place names still exist), clinging to the side of Parnassus at three thousand feet, was spectacular.

After lunch we drove westwards, came round a corner and there, suddenly, was Delphi. Unfortunately the building which first catches the eye is not the Temple of Apollo but the hideous modern museum at the bottom of the Sacred Way. The medieval village of Kastri, built on the ruins of the holy places, was demolished at the end of the last century and the inhabitants rehoused at modern Delphi half a mile away and, by design, out of sight of the shrine. Although the place was full of coaches we had no difficulty in finding a cheap hotel with a magical view down to the olive groves of the Sacred Plain. At dinner in a simple taverna at the top of the village – our choice after a lengthy inspection of every restaurant in Delphi, most of which had identical food to the one before – we struck another new wine, an excellent pink retsina from Distomo, the scene of savage Nazi reprisals in the last war and the neighbour of Hosios Loukas. We decided the Byzantines must have drunk this too.

Next morning we made a point of rising early and being at the great shrine by eight o'clock since we guessed, correctly as it turned out, that by ten it would be swarming with other tourists. In fact there were probably far fewer than usual, and no Americans at all, because of fears of terrorism and nervousness about possible radiation from Chernobyl. Nevertheless there were Germans in abundance, brutally shepherded by ferocious mädchen with dog whistles.

From Mycenean times until the demise of paganism Delphi was the holiest place in Greece. Strabo (who was born about 64 BC) tells us that in his day it was believed to possess the most truthful oracle in the world. Legend claimed that a great snake, the Python, once inhabited the caves of Mount Parnassus but was slain by Apollo, to whom a temple was built. From a chasm in the centre of the temple emerged strange and intoxicating vapours, enabling the attendant priestess – known as the Pythia – to foretell the future.

Sir George Wheler was the first traveller to discover ancient Delphi. When he visited it a monastery stood in the gymnasium and a chapel dedicated to St John occupied the shrine at the Castelian Spring. Of the Temple of Apollo there was no trace, but Sir George rightly assumed it must have been where, in his day, stood a church dedicated to Profitas Elias. Reading these accounts of the early travellers, one realizes how lucky one is today that so many of the ancient monuments have been restored to something of their former glory. Wheler, and after him Col. Leake, armed with their copies of Strabo and Pausanias, could, for the most part, only see these glories in their imagination. But it was largely thanks to them that eventually so many of the sites have been identified and resurrected.

Even hordes of tourists cannot stop Delphi being beautiful (though industrialists are planning to build factories in the plain below). One can well understand why the ancient Greeks set up shrines here. Something unmistakably numinous still lingers, a species of pagan holiness. Keeping ahead of the German tourists we walked briskly up the Sacred Way which curls up the hillside to the highest point of the ancient site, the Stadium. Allowing ourselves only three hours in which to explore, we could not hope to see everything in detail, but at least we could get an impression of what is probably the most beautiful shrine in Greece. The Stadium, vast and impressive with a rather ugly Roman triumphal arch and seats for seven thousand spectators, was completely empty. Not a single fellow-tourist arrived to detract from the atmosphere. In our imagination athletes still ran races as they had when the Pythian Games were inaugurated in honour of Apollo. Occasionally we could hear the dog-whistle far below, but it was almost drowned by the twittering of birds in the pines. At a great height above us flew griffon vultures, hunting the slopes of Parnassus.

We went down the hill, past the theatre to the Temple of Apollo (restored only in 1939, not long before the German invasion) and the Altar of Apollo, presented by Chians as a thanks offering for their part in the victory over the Persians at Plataea. From below, we could see the terrace on which stood the Serpent Column, now at Constantinople, and possibly the quadriga (the experts are not agreed on this) whose four horses now adorn St Mark's. We passed the Athenian Treasury, sole survivor of the many treasuries belonging to the towns and islands and which held their votive offerings, into the museum.

We hurried through with unseemly haste, pausing only to see the bronze charioteer whose almond eyes stare in eternal victory. In the Agora we found Early Christian and Byzantine stonework piled in the booths where votive offerings to Apollo or the oracle could once be purchased. Capitals and broken columns with the odd cross or chi-rho and slabs inscribed in Greek. The pair of us lamented our lack of a proper classical education. Both of us had been taught Latin but neither had learnt any Greek. For people attracted by Classical Greece, or indeed by Byzantium, this is a wretched handicap.

From Delphi we drove to Lamia, stopping at Amphissa on our way. A few medieval battlements still surmount huge blocks of archaic masonry on an acropolis which was sacked by Philip of Macedon. Once it was among the most formidable Frankish strongholds in Greece, with three rows of curtain walls, glaring down from its crag onto the olive groves of the Krissaean plain far below. Salona – as the Franks called it – was a fief of the Duchy of Athens, its mighty keep being built in 1205 by the Picard family of Autremencourt. Eventually it passed to the Fadrique, a bastard branch of the royal house of Aragon. Its last count, Louis Fadrique, died in 1382 leaving it in the hands of his widow, Helena Cantacuzene, a cousin of the Despot of Mistra and a grandchild of the Emperor John VI. She soon installed a Greek bishop – the castle contains the ruins (both barely recognizable) of a Catholic and an Orthodox church – while postponing the marriage of her only child, the Countess Maria, who was rightful heiress of Salona. Helena took as a lover a villainous priest whom she allowed to govern for her. Besides imposing extortionate taxes, being not content with his noble mistress, the man debauched the girls of the entire neighbourhood – among them the new bishop's niece, whom he carried off to the castle. When Sultan Bayezid invaded northern Greece in 1395 the outraged prelate invited him to occupy Salona. The priest promptly killed the girl and prepared to defend the castle, but was murdered in his turn by one of the garrison, who took both his head and the castle keys to Bayezid. The Sultan sent the Countess Maria back to his harem, where he is said to have afterwards murdered her. He handed Helena to his troops to serve as a whore.

Amid cypress trees and olives not far from the castle is the attractive little Byzantine church of Hagios Sotirios, dating from the twelfth century, with notably fine brickwork decoration on its exterior. Sadly it was locked. Unable to discover who held the key, we consoled ourselves by taking turns on a swing, which rather surprisingly hung from a branch of the enormous plane tree in the churchyard; the tree also served as a belfry, the bell hanging from another branch. From the terrace we could see the southern entrance to the pass of Gravia. The Bulgars swept through in the tenth century and destroyed the Byzantine castle. Hagios Sotirios was built in the time of prosperity after Basil the Bulgar Slayer had defeated Samuel and brought peace to a long troubled area.

The Lamia road winds up to Gravia in a series of hairpin bends, passes through Brallos, and down by a most tortuous route to the plain. On the bends we often came across shrines, a really bad bend having as many as three, each a sad reminder of a fatal accident. The weather, which all morning had been perfect, started to deteriorate and by four o'clock the storm broke – thunder, lighting and torrential rain. The wonderful views we had been expecting to see were hidden by the downpour, which only abated as we reached Lamia. This storm set the pattern for days to come. With great regularity between four and five the sky would darken and down would come the rain. We tried to plan our church visiting accordingly but on many occasions missed seeing what must have been very beautiful country.

We spent the night at Lamia. Apart from the vast Frankish kastro – built on the site of a Byzantine fortress – on the hill above it there is little of interest in that pleasant town. We had an unusually good meal of grilled prawns and excellent retsina from the barrel, however, in an unpretentious bar not far from the main square.

Next day our route took us north through the Othrys Mountains with, at Domokos, a splendid medieval castle on a rocky eminence, and down to the exceedingly depressing plain of Thessaly – mile upon mile of arable with not even one of the famous Thessalian horses to enliven the landscape. The roofs of Karditsa are supposed to provide homes for hundreds of storks, but we saw none. Bored with this dreary road we decided to make a detour to the west and were rewarded at Phanari by the sight of a large castle perched upon the hill. We parked the car in the village and clambered up the grassy slope, surveyed by a grazing donkey who voiced his hideous displeasure at our arrival, to the battered but still menacing towers which even now dominate the plain of Thessaly. Once Phanari was a bone of contention between Franks and Byzantines, the Despots of Epirus being particularly anxious to regain it from the detested invaders. Here we saw many butterflies including swallowtails of the ordinary and kite variety, but were unable to find any trace of the Byzantine church we were sure had once been in the fortress.

We had heard vaguely that there was an interesting church at Pili, just off the road we were now following, so stopping only at Mavromati for an early mezze and the best ouzo of our entire trip, we continued to Pili. We accosted a priest, a tough unsmiling little man with a grey beard who spoke some German, who got into our car and guided us over the river Portaikos and up the far bank to the Porta Panagia. Set beneath oak-covered crags at the mouth of one of the ancient passes into Epirus, the church stands on the river bank, surrounded by cypress trees. It is a thirteenth-century basilica with three semi-hexagonal apses and a huge cupola, to which a domed narthex was added later. It was built in 1283 by John Ducas, Duke of Neopatras, a bastard cousin of the Despots of Epirus; constantly at war with both Franks and Byzantines he survived only with the help of the Vlachs, marrying one of their chieftain's daughters. His tomb is here, and above it there is a fresco which portrays him with the Virgin and an angel. Other good frescoes of the same date are very badly damaged. What astonished us was to find two full-length mosaic portraits of Christ and the Virgin, also from the thirteenth century, in marble frames with polychrome decoration on either side of the iconostasis. These were of fine quality and most unusual for such a late date – in the provinces frescoes, being so much cheaper than mosaic, were generally preferred. We took the priest back to the café, where he refused to accept the slightest contribution towards his own church.

We joined the main road at Trikkala. Above us loomed the ruins of another Byzantine fortress but, eager to reach Kalambaka before the storm clouds gathered, we did not stop. From afar we could see the rocks of the Meteora. Quite unlike anything we had met before, they reminded us most forcibly of a great cluster of stalagmites, so thin and tall were the fingers stretching up from the plain. It was only when we were in their shadow at Kalambaka that we realized quite how high they were – some being over 1,500 feet above the plain. Hermits settled here in caves and on pinnacles perhaps as long ago as a thousand years; but communities of monks – all hesychasts who required silence – established themselves only in the fourteenth century. Until the 1920s their monasteries could not be reached by any means other than a series of wooden ladders or, still more terrifying, in a net, drawn up by a rope, which would revolve at great speed. Col. Leake, who visited it twice between 1806 and 1809, advises keeping the eyes shut for the ascent to prevent dizziness; but as the ghastly experience lasted for all of half an hour, nothing would have induced either of us to set foot on the Meteora by such means. Fortunately ramps, bridges and flights of stairs cut in the rock now provide comparatively easy if tiring access. A price has of course to be paid in tourists. For the independent traveller, however, these are not too much of a distraction since they tend to come in parties whose leaders seldom allow them to stay more than three minutes in any one building. A number wait miserably outside, either because they have been refused admittance for wearing shorts or sleeveless dresses, or because they are septuaginarians who fear with justice that all the stairs will bring on a coronary.

Once there were twenty-four monasteries on the Meteora. Today six remain, and of these we were only able to visit four. Until quite recently the monks had dwindled to fewer than a score, and it seemed as though the monastic life of the Meteora was doomed to extinction. Thirty years ago an architectural historian, Cecil Stewart, wrote with gloomy prescience:

> Now all is past. There are no Serbians at Meteora today (in 1957), and only a few Greeks. Almost everything portable that was of value, vestments and plate, ikons and reliquaries, was pillaged during the last war, first by the Italians and later by Communists. Only the buildings remain. For a few more years, until the last monk dies, they will preserve the traditions of their royal founders. Then they will be deserted except for the birds; and nature, already at work on the frescoes, and no longer checked by man, will resume control. Like Dušan's empire, Meteora, the Monasteries of the Air, will become the stuff of history.

Fortunately this prophecy has not been fulfilled. As on Mount Athos, since the 1960s the communities here have been attracting recruits, and today there are a reasonable number of young monks.

None of the monasteries still standing was built while Thessaly was part of the Byzantine Empire. The earliest, Hagios Stefanos, a foundation of Anthony Cantacuzenus, dates from the beginning of the fourteenth century when the Meteora belonged to Epirus. It became part of Byzantium once more in 1333 under the Emperor Andronicus III, who visited it that year. Of the other five still in existence the monastery of Barlaam and the monastery of the Transfiguration of the Great Meteoron were built under Serbian rule and the remaining three under Turkish.

On 16 April 1346 Stephen Dušan, ruler of the Serbs, was crowned Emperor of the Serbs and Greeks by the Serbian patriarch at Skopje. Two years later he added Thessaly to his Macedonian conquests and, although the Serbian Empire began to break up on his death in 1355, Thessaly never returned to Byzantium. These changes cannot have really effected the lives of ordinary Thessalonians. Less than forty years after the death of Dušan, the Ottoman general Evrenoz Bey conquered Thessaly, yet all the frescoes of the various churches date from after this period. Perhaps this explains the particularly horrible tortures and martyrdoms in every narthex, which may have been a reminder that the early Christians had had to suffer even greater torments than they were likely to experience.

Having found rooms at the Odyssion hotel facing the smooth rock of the Meteora, we drove through the village of Kastraki and started up the road to the top. The first monastery on the way up is that of Hagios Nikolaos tou Anapavsa, built in 1527 on the site of one founded during Serbian rule. Its principal attraction is its little chapel, whose frescoes were painted that year by a certain Theophanes the Cretan. In recent years they have been beautifully restored and, because the chapel is so tiny, are unusually easy to see. Although painted so late we found them charming – our favourite being that of Adam naming the animals in which, among the normal elephant, snake and deer in the Garden of Eden, an enchanting pink dragon breathes fire at a surprised lion. A young monk told us, in excellent English, that his community consisted of four professed monks together with five novices, all of them young men, and that there was a considerable revival of monastic life in modern Greece. He was clearly pleased by our interest, pressing Turkish Delight on us while ignoring the coach load of fellow-tourists who were trying to gain admittance. As we left we noticed ravens flying about the crag of Roussanou and white butterflies – black-veined whites which have been extinct in England since 1925 – in the tiny vineyard at the foot of the rock which provides wine for the monastery.

We went on to the convent of Hagios Stephanos, said to have been founded in 1300. The Emperor Andronicus III Palaeologus spent some time here in 1333 and in consequence the monastery acquired the rank of an Imperial and Patriarchal foundation, being at one time the richest house on the Meteora because of lavish Imperial endowments. It is now inhabited by a small community of nuns. There are two churches, one, with very damaged frescoes, built in the mid-fourteenth century, and the other in 1798. Frankly, Hagios Stephanos is a little boring when compared to the other monasteries here. Its museum does contain, however, a glorious icon of the Deposition of Christ painted by Manuel Tsanes in 1680.

Hagios Stephanos is the easiest of the Meteora's monasteries to reach, with access across a wide wooden bridge. Unluckily on leaving it we took a wrong turning, to find ourselves on the most alarming road we had so far met – with at one point a sheer drop of several hundred feet on both sides. During the descent to Kalambaka the road – and the yawning abyss – was obscured by 'the post-meridian showers which characterize the Grecian spring'.

Kalambaka boasts a church far older than anything on the Meteora. Built originally in the seventh century on the site of a temple dedicated to Apollo, the present church of the Dormition was founded in the twelfth by the Emperor Manuel I Comnenus, thus making it the only truly Byzantine church in the immediate vicinity. A basilica with three aisles, it has been altered over the centuries, but retains some fourteenth-century frescoes near the sanctuary as well as the original marble seating for the bishop and his priests at the end of the apse, and a magnificent marble ambo with seven steps each side. (The priest told us in Italian that the number represented the Seven Sacraments of the Orthodox Church.) The majority of the frescoes date from the sixteenth century, the most memorable being a splendid Elijah ascending into heaven in his fiery chariot, and the very colourful and crowded scenes from the Passion. In the narthex is painted the text of a chrysobull of Andronicus III defining the rights and boundaries of the diocese of Stagi (the medieval name for Kalambaka) – presumably drawn up while he visited the Meteora in 1333. At the door we were delighted to see a genuinely medieval notice in English reading 'Please Drop Your Obolus in the Box'.

For some reason the road did not seem so daunting next morning. Sue, who had spent a sleepless night in anticipation of the horrors to come, drove first to the Great Meteoron, largest of the monasteries.

One has to be fit to climb all the many, many flights of stairs cut in the rock, though they are perfectly safe. The hermit Athenasius appears to have reached a cave half way up the rock by a succession of scaling ladders in 1344. By 1362, when he was granted the privileges for a monastic house by the Serbian 'Emperor' Simeon Uroš (Dušan's bastard brother, who had set himself up at Trikkala) he had established a community on the Broad Rock, fifteen hundred feet above the valley. The next head of the monastery was Uroš's son John, who as a monk took the name Ioasaph. His sister Maria Angelina married the Serbian Lord of Ioannina, Thomas Preljubo-vić, and endowed her brother's monastery so munificently that he was able to rebuild its church in 1387. This was again rebuilt in the sixteenth century, and is most elaborate, with a great twelve-sided central dome and a smaller dome over the sanctuary. Its frescoes date from 1541–2 and although sufficiently restored are a little too bright and unsubtle to satisfy everyone. We were surprised to see among the usual Byzantine saints that very Western figure, St Sebastian, full of arrows. The narthex, painted by another artist, concentrates on various horrible martyrdoms – saints being flayed alive, boiled alive, roasted alive, fried alive, buried alive and so on. The museum, in what was once the monk's refectory, has some interesting things though badly presented. There is a fifteenth-century Byzantine musical score, book bindings inlaid with repoussé decorations on silver or brass plates, and some outstanding fourteenth-century icons – notably a diptych of the Mourning Virgin and the Dead Christ which is thought to have been painted by an artist who worked in the church of the Peribleptos at Mistra. Equally interesting is the icon of Doubting Thomas with portraits of Maria Angelina and Thomas Preljubović dating from the same period. It is fortunate that any of the manuscripts literary or musical, still survive. Robert Curzon in 1859 attempted to buy some, unsuccessfully, and found them in a dreadful state from the ravages of mice and mildew. Less scrupulous abbots in the past were presumably persuaded to sell their treasures. Equally fortunate is the preservation of some very beautiful embroideries from the fourteenth and fifteenth centuries – an epitaphios with the symbols of the evangelists in the corners, and a collection of stoles.

The monastery of Barlaam is not far from the Great Meteoron as the crow flies but is separated by an immense abyss. It too was founded in the fourteenth century but was then deserted for many years before being refounded in the early sixteenth. Its chapel, which dates from 1518, has been perhaps a little too enthusiastically restored. The frescoes were painted in 1548 by the Cretan Frangos Catalanos, save for those in the narthex, which were done in 1566 by two monks from Thebes, the brothers Dicotaris. We were fortunate in that an aged, white bearded monk who had been dozing in the church suddenly woke up and told us all we wanted to know; indeed he would not stop, save for moments when he broke into chanting. To the right of the altar the Empress Irene is shown presenting an icon, while on the left the Feast of the Holy Cross is depicted – a bishop holds up a cross while beneath are some Byzantine magnates. There is a Pentecost over the iconostasis. The narthex contains martyrdoms of the same horrible sort as in the exonarthex at the Great Meteoron, but at the right and left of the main door there are two most interesting frescoes of Byzantine Emperors presiding over Ecumenical Councils, in their capacity as Thirteenth Apostle. Also here was our old friend St Onuphrius, as usual clad only in his long white beard.

The museum had some marvellous things. There are chrysobulls of Andronicus III and one, deliberately phrased in the Byzantine style, bears the signature of Dušan's son, 'Stephen Uroš in Christ God Faithful King and Emperor of the Romans, Serbians and every Albanian'. There are good examples of fifteenth-century embroidery and silver and, most precious of all, a Gospel of 960 in a tiny hand, inscribed by the Emperor Constantine Porphyrogenitus himself. Other items of interest at Barlaam include a sixteenth-century wine barrel with a capacity of 12,000 litres (one wonders how many monks fell, inebriated to their deaths from the pinnacle) and a gruesome 'Tower of the Ascent', whence miserable visitors were winched up in a large net from the ground far below.

The next stage of our journey, a long haul up through the Pindus range, took us over the Katara Pass, at 5,600 ft, the highest in Greece. It was this route, in reverse, that Julius Caesar took when he marched from Illyria (modern Albania) to meet the forces of Domitius at Kalambaka. Domitius, coming from Heraclea Lyncestis near Bitola, joined Caesar to defeat Pompey at Farsala. Seeing these places, ancient history began to come alive for us.

The mountains were as beautiful as anything we had seen in

Yugoslavia and the road vastly superior. Snow still lingered near the top which, unlike the razor back of the Čakor Pass in Serbia, stretches for some distance in a plateau before descending to the little capital of the Pindus, Metsovo. We were distressed by the sight of pine trees disfigured by the larva of the pine moth whose communal cocoons, often as big as footballs, clung to every branch. Alpine swifts swooped and glided above the trees, but we were disappointed to find very few interesting flowers. Coming down to Metsovo the view was outstanding. Range upon snow-capped range of the Pindus stretched for miles in every direction. The sun, which so often eluded us when we were driving, shone and the air was crisp and cold.

Metsovo, where we stopped for a late lunch, is, despite its remoteness and height, very much a tourist centre. The shops were filled with rugs, less gaudy than those at Arachova, and old copper and tin cooking utensils, identical to those we had seen in Turkey. There were even lunch tins with four compartments like those belonging to the shepherd in the fresco at Kurbinovo – how little has life changed since Imperial times! Metsovo was the only place in Greece where we saw a distinctive folk costume. The men wore homespun and the women velvet dresses with cuffs flaring from the elbow, embroidered waistcoats and aprons. During lunch at a pavement café we suddenly heard a language which to Desmond (who had spent part of his childhood in Bucharest) sounded very like Romanian. We realized it must be Vlach, a tongue believed to be a descendant of the Latin spoken by the Roman colonists of Dacia in what is now Romania. According to Edward Lear, in his *Journal of a Landscape Painter in Albania*, when writing of the Vlachs at Metsovo: 'Many of the men emigrate as labourers, artizans etc. to Germany, Hungary, Russia, etc., and return only in the summer to their families. They retain their language.' Metsovo is the Greek capital of this shepherd race, a people who roam all over the Balkan countries. They were well known to the Byzantines, who regarded them as an unmitigated nuisance. After the Empire's temporary collapse in 1204 the Vlachs even set up their own kingdom of Great Wallachia.

We pressed on to Ioannina. The pines had given way to beeches, at this height barely in leaf, but lower down we came across walnuts and mulberries. In Byzantine days, silk veils were sent to Constantinople from Ioannina. At four o'clock, right on time, the heavens opened and our first view of the town was through a curtain of rain.

# The despots of
# Epirus–Ioannina and Arta

'Morn dawns; and with it stern Albania's hills,
Dark Suli's rocks, and Pindus' inland peak,
Robed half in mist, bedewed with snowy rills,
Arrayed in many a dun and purple streak,
Arise; and, as the clouds along them break,
Disclose the dwelling of the mountaineer:
Here roams the wolf – the eagle whets his beak –
        Birds – beasts of prey – and wilder men appear.'

Lord Byron, *Childe Harold's Pilgrimage*

WE HAD read so much about this city which thrilled Regency England that, as we drove down from the mountains towards Ioannina, our expectations were a little too high. They were buoyed up by the dramatic spectacle of the great lake below which suddenly appeared out of the mist. In the event we were to be somewhat disappointed. Yet the place has a remarkable history.

Byzantine Ioannina was occupied by the Norman Bohemond of Taranto in 1082. When the Emperor Alexius I attempted to retake the city he was defeated and, according to his loyal daughter Anna Comnena in her fascinating biography the Alexiad, 'came to the conclusion that he must save himself in order to fight again', fleeing ignominiously over the mountains to Ohrid. The ruler of the principality of Epirus, Michael I, made it his first capital, rebuilding its walls, before settling at Arta instead. In the following century it fell into Serbian hands and Simeon Uroš, the self-styled 'Emperor of the Greeks and Serbs', who ruled at Trikkala, installed his son-in-law Thomas Preljubović at Ioannina in 1367. He looted and taxed his subjects mercilessly, and indulged in 'unnatural vices'. The Chronicle of Epirus informs us that 'all wickedness is small compared with the wickedness of Thomas'. (Among his wickedness was blinding the Prior of Metsovo – after accepting payment to spare his eyes – and increasing his revenues by licensing brothels.) Eventually Thomas was murdered by his bodyguards in 1385. His widow Maria Angelina married a Florentine adventurer Esau Buondelmonti, who ruled wisely and benevolently. The Turks took the city in 1430 and remained there until 1912.

Ioannina first became widely known in the West from the Second Canto of Lord Byron's *Childe Harold*, published in 1812 after the poet's visit to that unspeakable Albanian, Ali Pasha, the 'Lion of Ioannina'. Ali Pasha was an appalling figure, treacherous, ferocious and vicious, noted for parsimony and dirtiness, who tortured and massacred his subjects by the thousand, raped his own daughter-in-law, kept a seraglio of boys and schemed constantly against his over-lord the Sultan. He nevertheless had great charm and could behave with courtesy when it suited him. His court was thronged with Greek men of letters and Greek nationalists, the Schools of Ioannina being the most famous in the country. Admittedly many of the scholars were virtual prisoners, kept as surety for the good behaviour of their relatives in other parts of Epirus, but certainly learning was less actively repressed than in the islands off the west coast under Venetian rule. Ali Pasha's avaricious disposition allowed him to throw nothing away. The passages leading to his apartments were hung with rusting scabbards, broken pistols and damaged utensils; broken furniture made access difficult, while it appears from Leake's account that the servants were unable to clean the rooms. 'His great apartment covered with a Gobelin carpet, surrounded with the most costly sofas, musical clocks and mirrors is defended by cross iron bars, rougher than would be considered tolerable in the streets of London. They are intended to prevent his servants from passing through the windows when the chamber is locked'. In 1822 the Sultan, alarmed by the rise of what was effectively an independent state, sent an army against Ioannina and had its Pasha murdered at the age of 82. Byron, who met him in October 1809, writes that in 'that aged venerable face' one could see no hint of 'The deeds that lurk beneath'.

Today Ioannina is a busy, bustling place, though its beauty has been spoilt since Byron's time. Ribbon development around part of the lake, petrol stations and blocks of offices and flats are a poor substitute for the romantic lattice balconies of Turkish houses and fields of corn sweeping down to the reedy, bird-haunted shores. One long narrow street remains to remind one of the past. Crammed from end to end with the workshops of the silversmiths, it cannot have changed since the days of Turkish rule. The citadel still retains buildings used by Ali Pasha and traces of Byzantine walls, but the Schools perished in the fires of 1820.

At the offices of the Department of Byzantine Antiquities in the centre of Ioannina we met Barbara Papadopoulos, an engaging young woman who quickly won our hearts by her enthusiasm. Her responsibilities included the care and supervision of all Byzantine monuments over an enormous area from the Albanian border to the Gulf of Corinth. Although she obviously had more than enough to do she seemed pleased to meet two people who shared her interests, telling us where to go in Epirus and, equally important, where to get the best food in the town. Rather to our disappointment she advised us against taking a boat trip to the island in the lake. None of the five Byzantine churches has frescoes dating from before the Fall of Constantinople, and she suggested it would be preferable to visit either a village miles away right on the Albanian border (where the church might well be closed) or Kastaniani, a hamlet near Dodona, where she could leave a message for the priest to meet us. We had been looking forward to visiting the island and to eating at one of the fish restaurants which line the shore but, on her recommendation, compromised by having an early lunch at the Nautical Club of Ioannina, a reasonable restaurant overlooking the lake, where we tasted the intriguing wine from Zitsa.

Col. Leake, who was at Zitsa in April 1809, says that it was rumoured to make the best wine in Epirus, though in his experience only that produced by the monastery of Profitas Elias was drinkable, that made by the peasants being an inferior retsina. Today the wine, no doubt like that of Leake's monks, is un-resinated (aretsina), a pale russet in colour and very slightly sparkling. We found it pleasant enough even if it did bear a resemblance to Mateus rosé. There is also a white – untried by us – which is said to be good. Both are often bottled in champagne-type bottles with thick gold foil round the necks, giving the horrific impression that the wine is a Greek imitation of Asti Spumante.

Our appointment with the priest at Kastaniani not being till mid-afternoon, we drove to Dodona, the shrine of the oldest oracle in Greece, and only a few miles from the church we had arranged to see. Wild roses in great profusion and campanulas grew beside the narrow, twisting road which snaked up the hills towards Mt Tomaron Col. Leake, who, whilst British Resident at Ioannina, explored the surrounding countryside for classical remains, decided Tomaron must be Mt Mitsikeli, the great hill facing Ioannina across the lake. He was convinced, against all evidence to the contrary, that Dodona lay beneath Ali Pasha's palace in the citadel of Ioannina; his explanation of the lack of ancient stones was that they had been used as building material elsewhere. The actual site, fourteen miles south-west of the town, was identified only in 1873.

With our usual good luck, we arrived at Dodona just as two coach loads of tourists were leaving. The only sounds as we wandered around the solemn shrine were the mellow jangling of sheep bells and the fiddling of innumerable crickets. The oak trees – quercus ilex – whose rustling leaves inspired the priestess of the oracle – have all gone but, as at its younger rival Delphi, at Dodona there is a strong feeling of being in an ancient and holy spot. In its days as famous as Delphi, it too was consulted by Croesus while he was deciding whether to attack the Persians. Unfortunately there is no record of the advice given at Dodona, but he chose to listen to the oracle at Delphi, little realizing that the prophecy 'If you attack the Persians you will destroy a great empire' meant his own.

According to Herodotus the first priestess at Dodona was a woman carried off by the Phoenicians from the Theban Temple of Zeus in Egypt and sold into slavery in Greece. He discounts the old tradition that a black bird with the gift of speech showed the local inhabitants where to erect the shrine. Bronze tripods dating from the eighth century BC have been discovered at the site of the oracle, but after the sack of Dodona and the burning of the Sacred Grove by the Aetolian army in 219 BC, nothing remains of the ancient sanctuary.

> Oh! Where, Dodona! is thine agéd Grove,
> Prophetic Fount, and Oracle Divine?
> What valley echoed the response of Jove?
> What trace remaineth of the Thunderer's shrine?
> All, all forgotten.

Thus wrote Byron, who in 1809 thought he had visited the site. As his guide was Col. Leake he is undoubtedly talking about Ioannina, so it comes as no surprise that all is forgotten. While there is nothing left of the original shrine, there is plenty to see from the time of Pyrrhus. It was then that the theatre and the temples to Zeus and Herakles were built to glorify the sanctuary. These were restored and embellished by Philip of Macedon after the burning of the grove. An Ionic portico surrounded the oracle, the columns of which were later used for the Christian basilica built on the site of the Temple of Herakles after the Emperor Theodosius abolished the pagan oracles. The basilica, the cathedral of the diocese of Dodona, was abandoned after the invasion of the Slavs. Long grass and wild flowers filled the foundations of the apse and, loosely coiled on a slab of marble fallen from the iconostasis, lay a most evil-smelling dead snake. Leaving the rotting corpse, we climbed to the top of the beautifully restored theatre. The fertile valley stretched before us to the gentle slopes of Mt Tomaron (reminding us of the setting of Hosios Loukas) and the stones of the theatre were warm to the touch. It was tempting to doze among the crickets and the Idas Blue butterflies, but it was time to leave for Kastaniani and a later world.

At Kastaniani a rough road zig-zagged up the hillside until it petered out beside a few houses and the tiny church of the Taxiarchs. The priest not having returned from the fields, we settled down to wait under a tree, a donkey and a very shy pointer bitch for company. Just as, with a lot of persuasion, she was plucking up enough courage to approach us, a surly man appeared and gave her a savage kick, whereupon she slank off into the undergrowth and we saw no more of her. The sky grew darker as thunder clouds massed above Tomaron, but the rain held off until the priest arrived. Under the usual stovepipe hat and great black beard he wore a grey cassock showing that he belonged to the 'white clergy'. These marry before being ordained deacons; clerics who are already deacons may not take wives. Their highest rank is archpriest, since bishops have nearly always been monks. To us this seemed an admirable arrangements, particularly for a priest in a remote parish who needs the companionship of a wife and children and who probably does not aspire to the highest ranks in the Church. Equally a bishop, with the responsibilities of that office, does not want the encumbrance of a family.

The little church, with frescoes of the Taxiarchs on the exterior, squatted beside the ruins of an earlier building. Owing to the difficulties of communication, we were unable to discover their date. Nor were the frescoes inside much help as they were so filthy. Saints peered from blackened walls. In the barrel vault, Christ could be made out with the Twelve Apostles, but we could only guess at their date – possibly fourteenth century. While Desmond was taken to look at the sanctuary – an area banned to women – Sue climbed some scaffolding to try to get a closer look, but it was impossible to decipher more than vague shapes in the gloom. Chalk marks and gauze stuck to various sections indicated they were about to undergo restoration, as did the presence of scaffolding.

The rain, 'the usual post-meridian rain' which we later discovered had so inconvenienced Leake on his mounted travels in Greece, now came down in stair-rods, soaking us before we even reached the car. Any fine views – and surely there must be many – between Kastaniani and Arta were completely hidden until we had almost reached our destination, the capital of the Despotate of Epirus.

The Despotate of Epirus, though fluctuating in size, at its most powerful stretched from the Gulf of Corinth in the south to Dyrrachium (Durrës) in what is now Albania. When Constantinople fell to the Crusaders in 1204 this area became part of the spoils of Venice, but the Serenissima renounced her claim, prefering to concentrate on a collection of ports and islands giving her control of the sea route to Constantinople and the Eastern Mediterranean. Epirus became one of the Byzantine 'successor states' under Michael Angelus Comnenus Ducas, a bastard first cousin of the Emperor Isaac II. Refugees flocked to him from all over the Empire. As Ostrogorsky says of Epirus, 'it became a centre of Byzantine cultural traditions and a political rallying point'. The new capital Arta became the most important Greek city in Greece, now that Thessalonica and Constantinople were under alien rule, and moreover a city whose prosperity rivalled that of Thessalonica.

Michael and Theodore, the first rulers of Epirus, did not take the title of Despot. This was given to Michael II when, having been defeated by John Vatatzes, he recognized the suzerainty of Nicaea. At the same time his son Nicephorus, kept at Nicaea as a hostage for his father's good behaviour, on his betrothal to the Emperor's granddaughter Maria also received the title. Strictly speaking the Despotate came into being only in 1250, but most modern writers call it by this name from the beginning.

Michael built up a formidable army of Epirots, refugees, Albanians, Vlachs and mercenaries which, together with the area's grim terrain, discouraged any Frankish thoughts of conquest. His methods – murder, massacre and torture supplementing aggressive warfare and diplomacy of the most ruthless and cynical sort – were considered savage even by his own less squeamish age. Pope Innocent III claimed that he crucified Frankish knights, testimony which has to be taken seriously. Michael came to a sticky end in 1214. As he lay in bed while on campaign he was murdered by a slave who was rumoured to be a papal spy.

Michael was succeeded as ruler of Epirus by his half-brother Theodore, an even more formidable figure who, after a long seige, captured Thessalonica from the Franks. He had himself crowned there as Emperor of the Romaioi by the Archbishop of Ohrid in 1224, reviving all the pomp and ceremony of the old Imperial court. There were two other successor states, one at Nicaea and the other at Trebizond on the Black Sea. Trebizond, isolated from the rest of the Empire even before 1204 (although it hung on for a few years after the Fall of Constantinople) had no further part to play in the history of Byzantium. Nicaea's ruler, however, was acknowledged by most Byzantines as the real Emperor, since he had been crowned by the Ecumenical Patriarch, who had translated his seat from Constantinople to Nicaea. In consequence there was bitter rivalry between the two Emperors.

Theodore, intensely ambitious, was determined to take Constantinople and restore the Empire. His ally against the Franks had been John Asen II of Bulgaria, who also had designs on Constantinople. Rashly Theodore declared war on Asen but in 1230 was defeated, captured and blinded. Eventually he was succeeded by his incapable sons. Then in 1246 Nicaea annexed Thessalonica and Theodore, who had been sent home from Bulgaria to his family, was given an estate at Vodena. Still ambitious as ever, he could not accept a life of retirement.

Michael II Angelus, a bastard son of Michael I, had installed himself at Epirus, taking the title Despot of Hellas. He married one of his daughters to King Manfred of Sicily and another to William of Villehardouin, Duke of Achaia. Egged on by the blind Theodore, this triple alliance marched against the new Emperor of Nicaea, Michael VIII Palaeologus, only to be defeated by the Nicaean army at

Pelagonia in 1259. His imperial ambitions finally dashed, Michael again recognized the suzerainty of Nicaea. Theodore ended his days in a Nicaean prison.

The last Angelus to rule Epirus, the Despot Thomas, was assassinated in 1318 by his Italian nephew Nicholas Orsini, Count of Cephalonia, who ruled as Despot for five years before being murdered by his brother John II. The new Despot turned Orthodox and married a scion of the reigning Imperial family Anna Palaeologina, who poisoned him in 1335 through fear for her own life. Epirus and Arta were briefly recovered by Andronicus III for the Empire but within a decade were conquered by Tsar Dušan. After him the 'Emperor' Simeon Uroš ruled it from 1357 to 1367, when he handed it over to the Albanian clan of Liosa, who soon lost it to the Boua, a much more formidable tribe. Their redoubtable chief Ghin Boua Spata was widely feared. He captured the Grand Master of the Knights of Rhodes, Fra Juan Fernandez de Heredia, whom he sold to the Turks, and beseiged his neighbour Thomas Preljubović in Ioannina. Byron's verdict that 'No nation is so detested and dreaded by their neighbours as the Albanese' seems to have been the case in Byzantine times. The Spata clan continued to hold Arta until 1417, when it was restored to the Despotate by the new ruler Carlo Tocco II, Count of Cephalonia.

Today Arta is an undistinguished if pleasant and friendly little place. Far from prosperous, its only products are orange juice and tinned pork. Horrifying though Chernobyl and the shelling of Tripoli might be they certainly made our search for accommodation much easier wherever we went. The Xenia hotel in Arta is usually fully booked for months in advance and we had resigned ourselves to staying at one of the noisy establishments in the main square. On applying for rooms at the Xenia, however, we were delighted to find it half empty, so we booked ourselves in for two nights. The hotel is set in the middle of a thirteenth-century Byzantine castle – of which only the external walls remain – itself built on the foundations of King Pyrrhus's citadel of Ambracia. Our rooms overlooked groves of citrus fruit where nightingales sang in competition with the frogs croaking in the reed beds of the river Aracthus, whose sluggish waters made a loop round three sides of the town. We had crossed the river to enter Arta and had noticed on our left the very beautiful old bridge, begun by the Romans, improved by the Byzantines and completed by the

Turks, which spans the river parallel with the new one. In one of its piers is reputedly immured the wife of the master mason responsible for its construction in the seventeenth century. Legend has it that during the building of the bridge, the central pier was swept away every night until a bird told the mason the only thing that could ensure its stability was the body of his wife. The river god seems to have accepted the sacrifice, since the bridge still stands. As we were assured by the Arta tourist guide, this story has been the subject of no fewer than six plays and two operas.

Apart from our perfectly adequate if rather dull mezze, the following day there seemed to be nothing worth eating in the entire town. All we could find that evening were sausages, liver and the nastiest bottled retsina we came across anywhere. Our meal ended with a power cut which plunged the town into darkness. We could not hope to return to the hotel without assistance, so we went into a crowded candlelit bar for help. A friendly young man jumped up as soon as we had made ourselves understood, abandoned his Metaxa brandy, and guided us back through the intense gloom, chattering all the way with commendable civic pride about the beauties of Arta.

Next morning we searched in vain for the Tourist Police. We found what we thought was a police station, but as we were trying to explain that we wanted a map showing the churches in and around Arta, it suddenly dawned on us that we were talking to the head Fire Officer, and not the Tourist Police at all. Greatly embarrassed at our mistake we slunk off to try the Council offices. Much to our amazement we were received with open arms by the Mayor, a cheerful figure with a heavy grey moustache and wearing a brown leather bomber jacket, who, on hearing what we wanted, whisked us upstairs to his office. Here, seated on uncomfortable 'French' chairs, we drank tiny cups of coffee while, sitting at his desk beneath the arms of Greece and a huge painting of Christ, Christos Papageorgiou explained why he was so glad to see us. The municipality, keen to attract tourists, wished to promote its Byzantine churches and build a conference centre for Byzantinists when, by some miracle, money became available. The Greek Minister for Culture being more interested in the Elgin Marbles than Byzantine frescoes, we were the answer to his prayer – the chance of free publicity abroad on the delights of Arta. He called in his public relations officer, Georgios Botetsios, a man with a sad drooping black moustache who spoke reasonable English

(learnt during an unforgettable month at Hove some years previously). He offered to accompany us to all the churches in the vicinity.

   He took us first to the church which, from it foundation in about
1290, had been that of the court, the Parigoritissa – also known as the
Evangelistra. Sir George Wheler, while travelling in Epirus, met 'a
Signior Manno Mannea, a rich merchant of that place [who] told me,
that the Cathedral Church of this place, called Evangelistra, that is,
the Annunciation, is a great Building, that hath as many doors and
windows as there are days in the year, and that it is sustained by
above Two hundred Marble Pillars'. If Sir George had been able to
visit Arta himself, he would have realized this description was the
product of civic pride and grossly exaggerated. Yet another example
of this came from our charming and enthusiastic companion, who
announced that the Parigoritissa was second only to Hagia Sophia.
Edward Lear – who might have given us a more entertaining
description – merely says it is 'very curious', and we found no reason
to disagree with him. Faintly reminiscent of the Fethiye Camii in
Constantinople, but totally lacking in grace, it was quite the ugliest
large church we had encountered in all our travels. Inside it is
different from any other Byzantine church; its construction is extraordinary, an eccentric combination of double columns, one on top of
the other, in three tiers, supporting squinches arranged in an octagon
on which rests the drum of the main dome. The intention was clearly
to produce an impression of soaring height, but the overall effect is
not only clumsy and awkward but also alarming – the dome looks as
though it might come crashing down at any moment.

   The founder of the Parigoritissa, Nicephorus, had been a hostage
at Nicaea during the struggle for power between his father Michael II
and the Emperor John III Vatatzes. He married as his first wife
Maria, grand-daughter of Vatatzes, then on her death he took as his
second wife Anna, niece of the Emperor Michael VIII Palaeologus.
Together they founded the church. With their background one would
have expected a finer building. Originally the box-shaped church was
surrounded on three sides by a wooden porch, which explains why
the exterior below the first row of windows is of plain, rough brick
whereas above this the brick is laid in tidy patterns. Presumably these
lower walls were plastered and covered with frescoes but, with the
porch, they have disappeared. So, too, have the original frescoes
inside, the earliest (decorating the sanctuary), having been painted by

the monk Athanasius in the sixteenth century. In the dome the enormous mosaic of Christos Pantocrator is contemporary with the church, but so crude and provincial that it is difficult to believe it dates from the same period as the Deesis in Hagia Sophia. The marble pillars with their capitals are a strange mixture of different eras. Taken from the ruins of Nicopolis, some are antique while others are early Christian. The carvings round the arches – the most interesting decorations in the building – are a medley of Byzantine and southern Italian.

From having been the church of the court before the fall of Arta to the Turks, in 1448 the Parigoritissa, stripped of its marble panels and iconostasis, became for eighty years a cattle byre and stable. The marbles embellished a Muslim school of religion, and the paved floor was destroyed. Then at the beginning of the sixteenth century that enlightened Sultan, Bayezid II (travelling incognito dressed as a dervish), received such hospitality at the monastery of Kato Panagia that he presented the Abbot with the Parigoritissa, with permission for it to be used again for services. Reconsecrated in 1530 by the Patriarch Jeremias of Constantinople, the missing iconostasis was replaced with one of solid masonry covered with frescoes – a fashion much followed in Greece, as we were to discover as we journeyed south. During the War of Independence the Parigoritissa suffered greatly. For three years the Turks used it as a fortress. When Urquardt visited it in 1838 he found Albanian troops bivouacked and the windows walled up. By the Treaty of Berlin in 1881 Arta became nominally part of Greece, but the Turks did not finally leave for another thirty years.

Between the Parigoritissa and the castle lies the church of Hagios Vasilios with, a few yards away, the ruins of the church of Hagios Loukas, a tiny chapel which may have been superseded by its slightly larger neighbour. Hagios Vasilios, a two-aisled basilica dating from the thirteenth century, has most unusual decorations on the exterior. Two large polychrome tiles of faience flank the window above the apse; the left-hand one depicts Christ Crucified with the Virgin and St John, while that on the right shows SS Vasilios, Gregory and John Chrysostom. These are surely the result of Italian influence, as must be the sea-green, ochre, white and terra-cotta coloured diamond-shaped tiles in rows between the more obviously Byzantine brick banding. We realized later that these tiled decorations are a common enough sight in the district. Inside are some sadly faded yet still interesting frescoes, notable for their competent draughtmanship, with two rows of saints on each side and a Christ who, most unusually, stands on a rock in the Jordan for His baptism.

Having collected our car from the hotel, we drove out of Arta along the tree-lined bank of the Aracthus to the monastery of Kato Panagia. Founded by Michael II in atonement for his treatment of his saintly Despina, once it housed a community of three hundred monks owning vast estates (including the Parigoritissa); but today there are only twenty-five nuns, who support themselves by rug making and embroidery. A nun took us round the church. Its greatest treasure is a carved wooden iconostasis whose Holy Doors – those in the centre – are surmounted by a group symbolizing the Trinity. The nun assured us these doors dated from the church's foundation in the thirteenth century, though we, as amateurs, could find little difference in style between these and the eighteenth- and nineteenth-century work we had seen elsewhere. A few of the frescoes in the sanctuary date from the foundation, but the majority are eighteenth century and almost hidden under two hundred years of candle smoke. The whole interior is exceptionally gloomy, very far from the Byzantine ideal of beauty and splendour, yet we felt that with cleaning, even the mud-coloured antique columns with their blackened capitals might come alive. This sooty grime seems to be a feature of Epirot churches. At first we thought there must be great treasures, if only one could see them, but then we realized that these frescoes are very late works which, like a fading beauty, might benefit from a discreet veil. On the exterior of the narthex, as in Moldavian churches, between rows of saints are scenes from the Creation. In one the Almighty, wearing a most Byzantine crown, breathes life into Adam while a unicorn trots by in the Garden of Eden. The nun took us to her garden, a delightful spot filled with orange, olive and oleander trees, where we were seated in the shade and given cumquats in syrup before our departure. She blessed us as we left, saying, 'May the Panagia go with you'.

George Botetsios then having an appointment, we returned to Arta and agreed to meet him at three, when he would be free to take us to other churches just outside the town. This gave us time for a mezze of gigantic proportions (but indifferent quality) and an extra slug of ouzo, as well as a visit to the remaining church in the town.

The fourteenth-century church of Hagia Theodora lay across the street from the bar where we had lunch. To reach it, we walked under an arch and across a school playground, empty at this hour. The church is a basilica with a domed narthex and the semi-hexagonal apse which seems to be typical of Epirus. Its fine antique columns and elaborate capitals are said to have come from an early Christian basilica at the ancient city of Nicopolis nearby. There is also an odd exo-narthex at the south side, with almost Western vaulting, which serves as both a cloister and a porch. The external brickwork is especially intricate, with varied bands of many patterns, cartwheels, herring-bone and dogtooth predominating, while two polychrome faience tiles flank the window above the apse. Inside there are some fine marble carpet-like patterns on the floor, with porphyry surrounds, and a rebuilt tomb, reputedly that of the foundress herself. Among the smoke-blackened frescoes with late, fussy scenes was an old friend – St Luke painting the icon of the Virgin Hodegetria.

The foundress, the Blessed Theodora, had an unusually colourful career, even by the criteria of medieval Orthodox saints. A princess of Frankish blood, daughter of John Petraleiphas, lord of the Mountain of Agrapha, she was married to the Despot Michael II Angelus, who grew bored by her piety. He fell in love with a beautiful Greek enchantress, the Lady Gangrene, who so bewitched him that he not only turned Theodora out of her palace but banished her to the wilderness. Here she lived in the mountains existing on herbs, roots and berries (apparently after the fashion of the Naked Grazing Monks), occasionally being succoured by hermits or taking shelter in a monastery. Then Christ came to the Despot in a terrifying dream, threatening him with destruction by thunder and lightning unless he repented of his treatment of his consort, explaining that the Lady Gangrene was acting under Satan's orders. Next morning Michael rushed out of his palace and searched the hills until he found Theodora, bringing her home with abject apologies. She was magnaminous enough to rescue Gangrene, about to be paraded for stoning by a jeering crowd. Theodora took advantage of her rehabilitation to found this church. Some years later she took the veil at Kato Panagia; where she remained until her death.

Having picked up Georgios from his office, we set off for the monastery of Blachernae. It soon became apparent that our companion was an extremely nervous passenger. Mutters of 'Very dangerous road, Greeks very bad drivers' forced our pace down to that of a snail.

(It was only when we returned to England that we discovered that Greeks do not take a driving test.) We arrived at the Blachernae without incident to find it the most interesting church in Epirus. Founded in the twelfth century, it was considerably altered by Michael II, who hired artists from Constantinople. The building itself is rather a muddle – the three apses do not match and there have been further alterations since Michael's day – but it contains some interesting tombs and a series of frescoes superior to anything in Arta. Michael and two of his sons, John and Demetrius, lie buried here, as does Anna Palaeologina Comnena Ducaena, wife of his youngest son, Nicephorus. The original iconostasis has been destroyed, but fragments from it are set in the exterior of the narthex, used as lintels for the doorways lowered in Ottoman times to prevent the Turks from riding into the church. The Archangel Michael guards the west wall and on the north two peacocks, with necks entwined, stand in frozen embrace above the doorway. Under the wooden planks protecting the inlaid marble floor are roundels of Byzantine eagles while, above them, the post-Byzantine fresco of the Pantocrator in the dome is riddled with Turkish bullets.

In 1976 a fresco of the greatest historical importance was discovered under the Turkish plaster of the narthex. Dating from the fourteenth century, its shows the Litany of the Icon of the Virgin Hodegetria, which took place every Tuesday in a square in Constantinople. By tradition this litany was inaugurated by the Empress Pulcheria, for whom her sister-in-law Eudoxia Athenaïs had brought back the icon from the Holy Land. What makes this fresco so important is that it shows scenes of everyday Byzantine life portrayed nowhere else and only known from the accounts of travellers to Constantinople. A confraternity of twenty strong men, each wearing a long rufous grown, took it in turns to carry the icon which, according to these accounts, was made of stone set with jewels and pearls. The fresco is very badly damaged, but when the protective gauze was briefly raised for our inspection, it was possible to make out various scenes of men and women selling fruit and drinks, beautifully apparelled ladies watching the procession from colonnaded balconies, the clergy following the icon and laymen clad in their best. Nowhere else had we seen women dressed as they are here. Instead of the traditional Imperial head-dresses we found in sacred art, these ladies wore fringed long scarves wound round their heads and necks, very similar to those of modern Turkish peasants. We wondered whether the fresco was painted during the period from 1340 when Epirus returned to the Byzantine Empire and 1348 when Tsar Dušan made it part of Serbia, or if it were done during the rule of the Despots. If the latter, it demonstrates the closeness of Epirus's ties with Constantinople.

We visited two more churches that afternoon, both well worth seeing. At Hagios Nikolaos tis Rodias (St Nicholas of the Pomegranate) thirteenth-century frescoes are gradually being uncovered. Byzantine eagles decorate the capitals of the heavy, squat pillars and the exterior is unusually elaborate for such a small church. Without our guide we would have experienced great difficulty in finding both this church and that of Hagios Demetrios Katsouris. These tiny churches, set among the groves of oranges, are invisible from a distance, and one is unlikely to come upon them by chance. Hagios Demetrios is a small but massive building dating from the ninth or tenth century but rebuilt as a cruciform church by the Despots; if a stone inscription has been interpreted correctly, the foundation date was 818 – in the reign of Leo V, the iconoclast emperor murdered in front of the High Altar of Hagia Sophia on Christmas Day 820. Abandoned in the eighteenth century it has recently been taken back as a place of worship. The post-Byzantine frescoes hide those from the days of the Despots, but there are still some fine early ones dating from the twelfth century in the sanctuary. Probably because the church was closed in the period when wooden iconastases became fashionable, Hagios Demetrios has managed to retain most of its original marble templon, on which appear two sphinx and an eagle catching a hare.

Georgios being without a car we took him back to his village of Kolomboti, to which he had returned after several gloomy years spent working in the Piraeus. His wife Ioanna was the local schoolmistress, a pretty, cheerful young woman with two children – six-year-old Ianni and four-year-old Artemis. The village was completely modern, the old houses having been abandoned some years before after an earthquake. We found the children watching that popular television series of the 1970s *Catweasel*, dubbed in Greek. We went next door to meet Georgios's parents. Despite the suburban setting the old people kept all the charm, friendliness and dignity of the Greek countryside, making us welcome in the warmest way. So too did their son and daughter-in-law. They invited us to have supper with them at a restaurant in the village square, where we ate souvlaki, liver and chips with an unresinated white wine which was opened with pride. A travelling fair had set up its stalls in the square, and Ianni and Artemis spent a great deal of time, between hastily snatched mouthfuls of food, in the dodgem cars and on the merry-go-round. The village with its enormous square seemed (apart from the music blaring forth from the fair) peaceful and prosperous, though bitter memories of the Turkish occupation still linger. Pointing to the village church Georgios recounted how when it was being built in 1741 the local Pasha told the villagers that they must complete it in forty days or else he would have it demolished. Fortunately they finished in time.

Next morning we had to say goodbye to Arta. We were unaccountably sad at leaving, perhaps influenced by our sojourn in a Byzantine castle. Nevertheless we realized that though Epirus had once been a powerful state, and if Arta had briefly rivalled Thessalonica, even during the great days of the Despots it had never been more than a provincial backwater. This was more forcefully brought home to us when, on our way to the Peloponnese, we climbed the steep hill to Angelokastro, once the second capital of the Despots. The citadel, with its ruined tower and small church (much altered), is tiny, and the village it guards can never have been very much bigger than it is now. We began to wonder if we were ever going to find Byzantium. Far from feeling that we were getting nearer and nearer, the glory we had imagined seemed to be receding from our grasp the further we travelled. It began to rain; not the dramatic storm we had come to expect every afternoon but a very English drizzle which blotted out what was probably very dull countryside. The promise of a fifteenth-century church with wall paintings drew us to Aitoliko, a small town on an island in the lagoon north of Missolonghi. The church of the Panagia in the middle of the town of a later date and with modern wall paintings cannot have been the one the author of the Blue Guide had in mind, but extensive enquiries revealed no alternative. The only thing of note – pointed out with great pride by an old woman cleaning the church – was an elaborately worked epitaphios hanging in a glass case on the south wall.

En route we passed Missolonghi. One cannot help feeling immensely sad that Byron, Philhellene that he was, should have chosen such a depressing place to die. Even allowing for the rain, it must at all times be one of the few ugly corners of the whole of Greece, desolate flat and muddy, the lagoon the perfect breeding ground for the malaria which killed him. In sober mood we boarded the ferry at Andirrion and left Epirus behind us.

# The Byzantine Peloponnese

'With a prosperous wind we compassed a part of Morea; more
famous by the name of Peloponnessus; shaped like a plantaine leafe,
and imbraced almost by the Corinthian & Saronian armes of the
Mediterraneum.'

George Sandys, *A relation of a journey begun in An. Dom 1610*

'Morea . . . is at this day the most fertile and best inhabited Province
of all the Empyre of Greece.'

William Lithgow, *Paineful Peregrinations*

THE Peloponnese (or the Morea as it was usually called before the fall of Constantinople) was where the last revival and cultural renaissance of Byzantium took place in the fourteenth and fifteenth centuries. For hundreds of years it had suffered from invasion by the Slavs, Avars and Bulgars, and it became finally part of the Empire only in the eleventh century under Basil II the Bulgar-Slayer. Converted from paganism to Christianity during the reign of Basil I, in the hills it retained pockets of an earlier faith. In the thirteenth century it was conquered by the Franks, whose rule extended over the entire peninsula, apart from the ports of Methone and Coron which belonged to Venice. As Nikos Kazantsakis puts it, however: 'Little by little the natives regained their courage and began to assume foreign traits, eating, singing, waging war like the Franks.' Then the 'blond dragons mingled with the women and forgot their homeland. They had children, the Gasmouli. The children emulated their mothers, they spoke the mother's tongue and became Greeks.' Above all, the Greeks learnt to beat the Franks at their own game of fighting. Eventually a new Byzantine state emerged, governed by a Despot who was always the brother or son of the Emperor at Constantinople. From 1262 until the beginning of the fifteenth century the principality covered only Laconia. The Despot held the wild Mani from his stronghold of Maina; his seaport was Monemvasia and his capital

Mistra. By 1460, Byzantium had regained all her lands lost to the Franks.

Although from 1262 the Empire owned Laconia, it had great trouble in keeping it – six thousand mounted troops were needed to ensure its safety, mercenaries which Byzantium could ill afford. Each governor was appointed only for a year, and it was not until 1348 that this system was changed. From this time on the governor was always a member of the Imperial family and the appointment was for life or until elevation to the purple. While the principal foe in the thirteenth century had been the Frank, by the end of the following century it was the Turk. In 1395, the Despot Theodore I, defeated by Evrenoz Bey at Corinth, was forced to acknowledge the suzerainty of the Turk. Two years later Athens was temporarily occupied by the Ottomans, and the Morea ravaged as far as the south coast. The defeat of the Turkish army at Ankara by Tamerlane in 1402 gave Byzantium a breathing space, but the Morea became a vassal state again in 1423 and remained so until the end. In 1446 the Turks destroyed the Hexamilion, the great wall built by Manuel II to guard Corinth, and took sixty thousand prisoners in the Morea. The days of the Despots were numbered, yet it was during these troubled times that the final flowering of Byzantine art took place.

After the travelling of the past five weeks Sue in particular was tired. Unable to face driving the two hundred and fifty miles from Arta to Sparta on roads which, judging by the map, looked fairly alarming, she insisted on spending the night at Patras. A mistake. Medieval Patras was destroyed by the Turks in 1821 and the modern city, built on a grid pattern, is noisy, dirty and totally lacking in charm. We had difficulty finding rooms, ending up in the central but comfortless El Greco. Walking out to dinner we expected rats to emerge from the pavements – we were not far from the docks. Before the War of Independence (and possibly afterward as well) Patras had been the centre of the slave trade. In *The Modern Traveller* – published in 1826 – Mr. Swan records: 'Black slaves are more numerous at Patra than any other part of Greece; after having faithfully served their masters a certain number of years, they obtain their freedom and marry.' Looking around the streets we were almost disappointed to discover no one of noticeably negroid descent. We dined – perhaps supped would be more accurate – at a workman's cafe down a side street near the hotel. We had a cheerful meal surrounded by dockers and a few tables of foreigners waiting to catch the ferry to Brindisi.

The drive to Sparta was lovely. Well rested after an early night, we could appreciate the green hills with fine oak and walnut trees which gradually gave way to mountains covered with the yellow blossoms of sage. There was very little traffic, and few villages. At Tripotama we were in Arcady and the land of the centaurs. Mountainous and dramatic, the Peloponnese in spring is also much greener than the country north of the Gulf of Corinth. We found it as beautiful as Serbia – or what we remembered of Serbia. Already days, churches and scenes had begun to merge into one another.

Tripolis has little to offer. Like Patras it was destroyed during the War of Independence. Once the fortified capital of the Pasha of the Morea, it was taken by Kolokotronis and his Maniot followers in 1821. Six thousand Turks were tortured and slaughtered, two thousand Jews stripped naked, driven out of the town and then killed, their bodies left unburied to spread the plague which raged throughout the war. 'Every corner was ransacked to discover new victims', wrote Gordon, 'and the unhappy Jewish population (even more than the Turks objects of fanatical hatred) expired amongst torments which we dare not describe'. He goes on to claim (most unjustly) in his *History of the Greek Revolution*, that the Jews had always supported the Turks in their suppression of the Greeks, and that only recently they had murdered the Patriarch at Constantinople, and dragged his mutilated body through the streets 'with foul indignities'.

The Albanian inhabitants of Tripolis – Leake says one fifth of the population of Greece was Albanian – were escorted by Kolokotronis's men to the other side of the Gulf of Corinth where, once free, they committed atrocities. These Albanian settlers had been introduced into the Morea as early as the eighth century by the iconoclast Emperor Constantine V and on a much greater scale in the late fourteenth century by the Despot Theodore. In a funeral oration delivered at Mistra in 1415 his brother, the Emperor Manuel II, warmly applauds Theodore's efforts to colonize the Peloponnese. (A third of the population had, as in other European countries, perished from the Black Death in 1348.) We began to wonder how many of the present-day Greeks can claim pure descent from the Hellenes. Slavs, Avars, Bulgarians, Franks, Turks, Goths and Albanians all must have left their marks, while the Venetians held Coron, Methone and

Monemvasia and negro slaves married at Patras. More Albanians were imported in 1770, this time by the Turks, who sent for them as mercenaries against the rising fomented by Prince Orloff. Fifteen thousand Albanians arrived, including women and children, and the Turks had great trouble in getting rid of them after the rising was suppressed. Hassan Bey finally defeated them outside Tripolis, where he made a pyramid of their heads – a favourite Turkish pastime. By the beginning of the last century it was becoming fashionable for Turks to dress their children in Albanian clothes, though 'it would not comport with their own dignity and prejudices to adopt it themselves'. Clark, writing fifty years after Leake, says: 'The conspicuously gallant part, however, which they played in the War of Liberation has obliterated all recollections of old grievances, and the adoption of the Albanian as the national costume of regenerate and re-christened Hellas is an official mark of complete reconciliation.' Not only have they left a legacy of costume but the dance for men called the Tzamikos is of Albanian origin.

We paused in Tripolis for lunch but, anxious to get to Sparta and Mistra, did not linger. We had read descriptions of the road from Tripolis to Sparta, yet the first view of Taygetos from the top of the Kleisoura Pass still took us by surprise. It was a constant source of wonder to us that the earth could throw up, seemingly from nowhere, quite such a spectacular range of mountains. With no foothills to speak of they rise out of the Laconian plain from seven hundred feet above sea level to nearly eight thousand feet at the top of Mt Taygetos. Clark's description is the best. 'We have before us a wide prospect of mountain scenery – a panorama on a scale of magnificence which, except among the high Alps, cannot be paralleled in Europe . . . From the main chain, here visible almost from one end to the other, huge masses project at regular intervals, descending by a succession of precipices to the plain – like a great Titanic wall flanked with buttresses and cumbered about its base with immemorial ruin.' Among this 'immemorial ruin' lay Mistra.

Sparta, built in 1834 to rehouse the inhabitants of Mistra after Ibrahim Pasha on his flight south in 1825 had left it in flames, is a dull but not unpleasant little town well supplied with hotels. We ignored them at first, preferring to stay at Mistra, but on finding the only hotel in the village fully booked by a German coach tour, changed our plans. We booked rooms for a couple of nights four days

ahead and drove up to the gates to try to see as much as possible while
we were there. Unluckily the opening times have altered since the
Blue Guide was published, and far from closing at dusk, it now shuts
at three o'clock; we were too late. But that glimpse from below
excited us more than anything in Greece so far. The castle, appearing
out of low clouds on its crag and lit by a shaft of light, was almost a
vision of the past; the old town below, hidden from view by the
swirling mist, must surely be filled with brightly decked citizens, if
only we could see them. Not daring to break the spell, we drove back
to Sparta and found rooms at the Apollon, an adequate if character-
less hotel on the Tripolis road.

It now seemed sensible to us to leave Mistra till last. In denying us
rooms at the Byzantion Hotel, Fate had taken a hand and we were
willing to allow her to guide our path. Our glimpse of the capital of
the Despots of the Morea had shown us that the Grail was within our
grasp, that Mistra would be a fitting end to our journey, the
culmination of all our hopes.

The part of Greece, and indeed the Morea, we both wanted to see
was the Deep Mani – the Land of Evil Counsel. The name alone was
enough to draw us there, but a further enticement was the quantity of
Byzantine churches which litter the peninsula. We had been given an
introduction to the greatest living authority on the Mani and king of
travel writers, Patrick Leigh Fermor. He and his wife Joan first saw
the site of their house at Kardamyli from the mountain tops when
walking over the Taygetos a quarter of a century ago. Some years
later they bought some land above a small bay outside the village,
built an extremely pretty house – designed by them – and have lived
there ever since. Bidden to lunch, next morning we set off south from
Sparta. The route over the Taygetos and via Kalamata would have
been much more exciting, but we were anxious to find somewhere to
stay near the land of Evil Counsel, and our experience at Mistra had
made us see the advisability of booking rooms before mid-day.

The Mani is divided into two districts. Inner or Messenian Mani
runs between the Taygetos and the sea to Kalamata, while Deep
Mani ends at Cape Matapan – the most southerly point in Europe
save for Tarifa in Spain. The dividing line is the natural barrier of the
Ravine of Milolanghado at Vitylo. We turned northwards at Areopo-
lis for Kardamyli in Messenian Mani. The road curled round the bay
of Vitylo past a new hotel on the beach into which we promptly

booked ourselves for two nights. Inner Mani is very pretty with gentle, fertile country stretching up the slopes of Pentadaktylos – one of the last strongholds of the Slavs when Basil had cleared them from the rest of the Peloponnese – and filled with sleepy villages and lovely coves. Kardamyli has always been the most important of these villages, its name unchanged since the days of Agamemnon. It is mentioned in the Ninth Book of the Iliad as being one of the cities offered by the king (together with the choice of one of his daughters) to Achilles as a bribe to continue the war against Troy.

When the Leigh Fermors settled here, theirs was the only car in the Mani. Now Kardamyli has boutiques and a discotheque is being built. At lunch on a shady terrace we mentioned our discovery of the wine of Chios whereupon our host quoted a line from 'The Isles of Greece' in Byron's *Don Juan*, 'And shed the blood of Scio's vine'. Patrick Leigh Fermor has been described (by the late Sir Iain Moncreiffe) as 'a Byronic figure whose creative power is used to the full in splashing on to the canvas of his time the everyday colour of his own real life'. A handsome black-haired man, he looked no more than fifty, yet we knew that his travels had begun in the 1930s. An illness had delayed the second volume of his saga of walking across Europe to Constantinople before the War, but now it was about to be torn from him and sent to his publisher, plainly a harrowing moment for such a perfectionist. He told us how it had been made possible by the miraculous return of diaries which he had left in Romania long ago, and that he would reach Constantinople in the third volume. (Since our visit the second volume – *Between the Woods and the Water* – has appeared and has been recognized as a masterpiece.)

He is also famous for those two enchanting books, *Mani* and *Roumeli*. These tell in vivid, lapidary prose of his roamings through the southern Peloponnese and remote areas of northern Greece. Filled with strange adventures, memorable meetings, arcane knowledge and wild, haunted landscape, they are a poignant lament for the passing of the old life of the Greek countryside, of customs largely unchanged since Homeric times. No-one could be more loyal to the memory of Byzantium. In *Mani* he has written of his instinctive hatred of Frankish ruins in Greece, how he is unmoved by 'distant echoes of horns and Burgundian hounds along the ravines of Achaia'.

Before lunch we caught a tantalising glimpse of a library which included – besides many, many volumes of the Classics and a mouth-watering study of Greek birds – numerous books on Crete. We told our host we had read *Ill Met By Moonlight* by Stanley Moss, an account of the kidnapping of General Kreipe (the German commander in Crete) in 1943, in which he played a key role. By pure coincidence, after our return to England we were to meet (on a London to Brighton train) Colonel Schooling, the British Intelligence officer who had charge of the General after his arrival at Mersa Matruh en route for a prisoner-of-war camp. 'I do feel an old fool,' a gloomy Kreipe had confided to him. 'Here I am as the result of what can only be described as a schoolboy prank.' Far from being a 'prank', it was an exploit which lifted the spirits of everyone serving in North Africa. Even the General admitted that he had been treated by Moss and Leigh Fermor – the raid's two leaders – with 'chivalry and courtesy'. Elsewhere, the latter has recounted how when, gazing over the mountains at dawn, the General began to recite quietly an ode of Horace, he finished it for him – a moment transcending the animosity of war. He spent no less than two years in German-occupied Crete, disguised as a shepherd.

The Leigh Fermors advised us to stop at Kambinari on our way back to Vitylo, to see the church of Hagios Nikolaos. It has an unusual Christos Pantocrator and an interesting St Nicholas cycle painted when the tenth-century basilica was restored by a local nobleman in 1348.

Just as we were coming down to the great horseshoe bay of Vitylo, a Golden Oriole flew across the road – a streak of yellow against the blue of the sea. It disappeared from view in the direction of the Land of Evil Counsel, and following its line we noticed on the other side of the Ravine of Milolanghado the glowering fortress of Kelefa, guarding the entrance to the Deep Mani.

Our hotel on the beach proved to be a cheerful establishment, where people from the neighbouring villages came to dine or drink the local wine. The owner who did the cooking was a hoarse-voiced, weather-beaten, jovial figure said to have begun his career selling newspapers in Athens, and bursting with pride in his property. He had a good deal to worry him, since there were so few foreigners on account of Chernobyl. We enjoyed his excellent grilled fish and a bottle of the strong unresinated local wine. As we drank our coffee we were joined by a middle-aged Greek who, unlike our host, spoke English. On hearing that we were interested in frescoes, he advised us to go to a church we had seen on the hill above the hotel. The priest of Dekoulou was sitting in his stovepipe hat at the next table with his wife and four children. Our new friend rushed across and on enquiry discovered that the following day was special, the saint's day of the church. On no account should we miss this festival.

Next morning, on reaching the village of Vitylo, there was no sign of life. We parked the car then wandered around trying to get our bearings. At last, as though guided by some invisible hand, we followed a path between the houses which led to a platform overlooking the valley. The monastery lay below us to our right. Then we saw groups of people converging on it from various paths which crisscrossed the southern slope of Pentadaktylos. We turned back and managed to join one of these cobbled paths, which took us downhill and past a twelfth-century church with a pile of skulls outside. This must have been the one Mr Marriott of Rokeby visited in 1795. He found 'a beautiful fluted Ionic column supporting a beam at one end of the aisle, three or four Ionic capitals in the wall of the church, and on the outside of the church the foundations of a temple'. He thought it was the temple of Serapis. We were unable to enter the building to check the capitals, but the stone platform on which it was resting looked to be of great antiquity and a suitable site for a temple.

Ahead of us on the track the villagers were gathering, drawing in ever more people from all directions. Some of the women carried a few roses, others covered baskets of cakes, while one or two of the men came with a bottle of wine. On arriving at the monastery of Dekoulou (of which only the church remains in use, the monastic cells and outhouses having fallen into decay), these provisions were left outside, the roses being taken in to decorate the icons. The Liturgy had already begun, but worshippers in an Orthodox church move about freely during the service, treating the building as a loved and familiar place. Each woman lit a candle, placed it before an icon which she then adorned with roses, adding to those brought by earlier arrivals. More and more people came into the church, and with each newly lit candle we began to see more of the dim interior. Apart from the candles, the only light came from two tiny windows, one in the apse and one in the south wall by the lectern. None of this was strong enough to illuminate the frescoed dome, which stretched up in eerie blackness above our heads. On a table in front of the Holy Door lay five round loaves, nearly two feet in diameter, one on top of the other, with five lighted candles – representing the five wounds of Christ – stuck in the topmost.

The priest we had seen at the hotel the previous night was the celebrant. In emerald green vestments, a man of about thirty-five with the horny hands of a peasant, he possessed a strong and resonant voice and great natural dignity, someone whose devotion was almost tangible. But this devotion was immensely powerful, never sentimental, a driving force within him, which stirred us to the soul. The top loaf was removed from the table by the server, one of his sons. The Holy Door being open, we could see the priest, silhouetted against the shaft of sunlight coming through the window of the sanctuary, consecrating the bread and wine at a canopied altar. He raised a cloth (known as a ripidion) and gently fanned the elements to symbolize the fluttering wings of the descending Holy Ghost. The bearded young cantor at the lectern had the face of a painted saint. The air was heavy with incense, smoke from the burning candles, and the scent of roses. For all the crudeness of the eighteenth-century frescoes, in the faint light they were indistinguishable from master-pieces. The atmosphere was mysterious, moving, truly numinous – we were never to feel nearer Byzantium. A group of children now went up the steps to the Holy Door, where they were given the wine and the bread mixed together in a chalice, from a gilded spoon. At the end of the Liturgy the rest of the congregation filed up to kiss the priest's hand while receiving the antidoron, a piece of the blessed but unconsecrated bread. We were surprised to see such young children taking communion, but later discovered that they are chrismated (confirmed) immediately after being baptised.

Throughout our journey we were struck by the Orthodox approach to God through beauty. In our own century the Russian theologian Bulgakov wrote: 'Orthodoxy is first of all the love of beauty. It must be inspired by the vision of heavenly glory, and this contemplation is the essence of Orthodoxy.' Long before him, the fourteenth century Byzantine Nicholas Cabasilas claimed that 'Christ by his beauty overcame the world.' We were also impressed by the sense of mystery which we experienced at services. These approaches, through beauty and the numinous, were shared until recently by the Western Church which will pay – is already paying – a ruinous price for abandoning them.

One should never forget that when in the presence of mosaics, frescoes or icons, Byzantines believed – as do modern Orthodox – that they were being watched closely by the saints portrayed, however obscured the likenesses might be by centuries of candle smoke. They were keenly aware of the nearness of the next world; as St John Damascene writes, man 'is the connecting link between visible and invisible nature'. In the West the vision of some of the seventeenth-century mystics who had read the Greek Fathers was surprisingly similar. For the poet Thomas Traherne (c1637–74) Heaven was close in much the same way. In *Shadows in the Water* he wrote:

> Thus did I by the Water's brink
> Another world beneath me think
> . . .O Ye that stand upon the Brink
> Whom I so near me through the Chink
> With Wonder See: What Faces there,
> Whose Feet, whose Bodies, do ye wear?

and elsewhere writes 'A Film kept off that stood between'. Nowhere did the Byzantines feel this film to be thinner or more transparent than when in the presence of sacred paintings in their churches.

We had not been able to make out if the prayer for the King was said. Until recently this was done at every Liturgy in Greece by the priests, just as their predecessors had prayed for the Byzantine Basileus. Staunchly conservative and monarchist, the Maniots would certainly resent the prayer's omission; to a man – and woman – they remain loyal to King Constantine.

After the service we all filed out and sat on a low wall at the back of the monastery, where we were plied with sweet bread and almond and chocolate cakes – there was no sign of the wine. A member of the congregation who spoke a little English told us that the monastery was the benefice of a local family still living in the village. We longed to question her about traditions in the Orthodox church, but her English would not have been up to any complicated answers. One tradition which may have died out is noted in *Voyage to the Levant*, published in 1718 by an anonymous author, and concerns the bread. 'The Man or Woman that kneads the Bread design'd for Consecration, must be pure; that is to say, the Man must not have known his Wife, nor the Woman her Husband, the Eve of the Day on which the Bread is made.' But we could hardly have questioned her about that.

After Mass we drove into the Deep Mani, the Land of Evil Counsel. Far from being the treasure trove of Byzantine remains we had expected, with a tiny church around every corner, it turned out to be a nightmare of frustration. None of our books was of any help. What we needed, and found only after our return to England, was Peter Greenhalgh's extremely readable paperback, *Deep into Mani*, which has minutely detailed instructions on how to find Maniot churches. We can only say that we had always thought we would be very unlikely to have time to see the Mani properly, travelling against time as we were, not daring to believe that our journey would go so smoothly as it did. The omission of this particular paperback wrecked the entire day.

More by good luck than good management, at Gerolomin, a small fishing port in the south, we found a priest who advised us to go to Hagios Petros at Kiparisso, the only old church he knew. The name rang a bell – it was at Kyparisso that Col. Leake spent an unforgettable night in 1805. Because the incumbent was unable to offer him and his servants accommodation in his own small hut, Leake's party was invited to use 'the church of the Panayia where the eating of a meat supper in the church during the most rigid of Greek fasts, seems to shock the liberal Macarius himself, and we are duly punished by myriads of fleas, which prevented all possibility of sleeping'. We settled down at a café on the quay to a glass of ouzo and a plate of mezze. A mongrel covered with the most repulsive sores ambled over and sat beside us, and we were beseiged by an army of emaciated cats who took no notice of the dog – obviously there were more tourists in the Mani than we had thought. Our priest sat at the next table playing cards with a group of tough fishermen; savage-eyed and voluble, he seemed more like a pirate than a cleric. But this was to be expected. The Maniots – men, women and priests alike – have always been 'peculiarly addicted to assassination', even more so than the Albanians, according to Leake who knew both districts well. 'Next to the captains the priests are the chief men in the Maniate wars, both in council and field; and in the quarrels which so frequently occur between separate villages or families, they are generally the promotors and leaders of the strike.' They may have calmed down since 1805, and of course there are far fewer of them, judging by the number of churches which are now in ruins, but we certainly got the impression that if trouble were ever to flare up again this priest would be in the thick of it. We hoped he no longer considered it necessary to carry a loaded pistol under his grey cassock. In the old days it was not unknown for there to be a shoot-out in church – always after the consecration of the sacrament – the priests keeping their pistols behind the altar during the Liturgy.

The last Byzantines had done their best to improve the Maniots. In 1415 Manuel II marched from Mistra to the Deep Mani, the first Emperor to do so since the Bulgar Slayer. He demolished a substantial number of the chieftains' fortified towers (most of which must have been rebuilt to judge by the quantities that still remain) from which they waged clan feuds of unrelenting ferocity. Isidore of Monemvasia tells us that in addition the Emperor outlawed a social custom of immemorial antiquity; at feasts the Maniots were accustomed to dip fingers or toes cut from slain enemies in their goblets before drinking a friend's health. This was plainly considered bad form in the politer society of Constantinople and Mistra.

The Land of Evil Counsel slumbered in the early afternoon heat. Stony and inhospitable, no trees breaking up the endless narrow terraces and walls built to clear the land, the last finger of Taygetos rose above us. On the low ground grew olives, prickly pear and tiny patches of cereal, but it was difficult to see how the inhabitants – of whom there was now no sign – could exist in this barren land. Leake had trouble getting food – even oil being scarce and bread, wine and vinegar almost unobtainable. Later we learned from Haris Calligas at Monemvasia that when she had stayed in the Mani while doing her thesis twenty years ago, bread was scarce even then.

So far we had seen no female Maniots, not even at Gerolomin. This was a grave disappointment since we had built up a fanciful impression of the Mani, completely unrelated to modern life. Lord Charlemont in 1749 says of Maniots: 'They are governed by their own peculiar laws which appear to be of the true Lycurgian cast, if we may be allowed to judge from one which is in force amongst them. If it is proved of a woman that she is a prostitute, the penalty is that her nose shall be cut off, and one of her ears; and this they exercise with a view, as they say, of encouraging matrimony.' We were unable to learn whether this still holds good. At Kiparisso the only human being we found braving the sun was an old lady of obvious virtue (complete with nose and both ears) tending a vegetable patch near the beach. She escorted us through tiny fields with immensely high walls, all that was left of the houses which once surrounded Hagios Petros. The church itself is no more than a ruin, only the lower parts of the walls still standing, with fragments of marble littering the ground. An inscribed pair of stelae formed the door posts. One was dedicated to Julia Domna, the second wife of Septimus Severus and an educated woman who was a well-known philosopher. Slightly disappointed at first with Hagios Petros – we had hoped to be shown a church with frescoes – we then realized how fortunate we were. Constantine VII Porphyrogenitus avers that Maniots only became Christian in the ninth century, but here was a church of a much earlier date, late fifth or early sixth century, anticipating the Emperor's missionaries by nearly four hundred years. Kiparissos with its safe harbour had always been important. It was in this bay that Belisarius sought shelter for his fleet when on his way to North Africa to regain Carthage for the Empire. Here also the Vandal King Genseric had been repelled by the Maniots when attempting to take the Peloponnese. Ancient stones litter the headland above Hagios Petros. We tried to explore, but without proper shoes walking in the Mani is unbearable torture. Thorny bushes and jagged stones formed a well-nigh impenetrable barrier, and we soon gave up. In any case our search was for churches, not classical remains.

We drove south, hoping to come across other churches, but saw none. Our route took us over the shoulder of Taygetos, and there on the hill in front of us were the towers of Vathia. The Deep Mani is full of these tower villages, houses built higher and higher to give their occupants an advantage over their neighbours in the endless feuds. Seen from below, Vathia is a particularly striking example; doubtless there are larger communities of tower houses – Kitta springs to mind – but against the stony landscape they are difficult to spot. The road climbed higher and became increasingly alarming. On the right there seemed to be nothing between us and the sea, hundreds of feet below. Then it turned east over the isthmus; now on our right the long finger of Cape Matapan pointed to Libya. Although still in the Deep Mani we had left the Land of Evil Counsel and were now on the east side of the peninsula at Porto Kayio. Black-eared wheatears flitted from stone to stone, though there was no sign of the quails migrating from Africa which used to darken the sky on their journey north and to whom Porto Kayio owes its name. Unprepared to walk to Cape Matapan, we retraced our route to Vathia, the Land of Evil Counsel and the dozens of churches hidden in the Deep Mani.

Yet hidden they remained. We saw, from a distance, what we

imagined to be Tourloti, but found no road leading to it. We pressed on, sure of finding a side road eventually – which indeed we did – though our struggles along dusty unsurfaced lanes produced nothing recognisably Byzantine. Soon we started quarrelling, one of us eager to continue the search, the other fed up with a wasted day and the appalling tracks. We returned to the main road and then, as a last resort, turned off into the Cavo Grosso, the large headland half way down the west coast from which protrudes the Tigani – Frying Pan – a peninsula with a narrow, impossibly stony neck (the handle of the frying pan) on whose summit stands the ruined castle of Maina.

Almost immediately we came across a Byzantine church. This turned out to be that of Hagios Sotiros at Gardenitsa, an eleventh-century building with an unusual domed porch – one of only two in the Mani – and stone-work which is (according to Peter Greenhalgh) typical of the area. We even succeeded, on enquiring of a man sitting beside the road, in finding the key hidden on a ledge in the porch. Sadly, once inside, there was little to see. We had found one of the churches without frescoes. Many of the Maniot churches possess good, if rather provincial, frescoes dating from the tenth to fourteenth centuries. Notable among these (if they have not turned to dust with neglect) are those of Hagios Stratiyos at Boularii and the twelfth-century church of Episkopi overlooking Mezapos Bay.

From Hagia Kyriaki, where we went next in search of another church, we could make out the ruins of Castle Maina. The walls are seven hundred and fifty metres in circumference and contain the remains not only of defensive towers but of houses and a large Byzantine church, part of which dates from the ninth century. It seems likely that this was both the acropolis of Messe in Homeric times and the site of the Imperial stronghold of Kastro Maina. That mine of information, the Emperor Constantine VII Porphyrogenitus, tells us that 'The inhabitants of the city of Maina are not of the race of the aforesaid Slavs, but of the ancient Romans . . . and became Christians in the reign of the glorious Basil. The place where they live is waterless and inaccessible but bears the olive, whence their comfort is.' If this were really Kastro Maina, which now seems almost certain, then the church was the bishop's cathedral. This must also be the site of Le Grant Maigne, the great castle built – or rather rebuilt – by William de Villehardouin, Duke of Achaia and son-in-law of the Despot Michael II of Epirus. With Monemvasia and Mistra, this formed the third great link in a triangle to guard the southern Peloponnese. A Frankish community as big as a town lived here, complete with a Catholic bishop of Maina. The prelate found life so uncomfortable and dangerous that after a few years he was allowed to return to Italy. But neither did the Duke of Achaia live there or own it for long. Captured at Pelagonia in 1259 by the Nicaean Emperor Michael VIII, William was forced to relinquish his three castles to obtain his release. They returned to Byzantium in 1262 and the castle remained the seat of a Byzantine governor until the fall of Mistra in 1460.

We were taken aback at the hotel that evening when our Greek friend of the night before came up and asked: 'How is Wittgenstein regarded at Cambridge these days?' We were ashamed to confess we didn't know and had no acquaintance with philosophy or philosophers. While plainly disappointed, he was a tolerant man who turned out to be most interesting on a variety of subjects. Knowing our obsession with the past he talked about the Mani at the beginning of the last century. Napoleon anchored in the Bay of Vitylo on his way to Egypt in the summer of 1798, having been offered the use of all the harbours in the Mani by the Bey of Githion, Zanetos Grigorakis. Bonaparte had become the great hope of liberation from the Turkish oppressors. A few years later the Bishop of Korytza (then in Macedonia but now Korçe in Albania) considered the Emperor 'deficient in policy, in having gone to Egypt instead of coming here [Albania], where the consequences would have been much more important, and from whence he could not have been driven out'. Another admirer was Petrobey Mavromichalis, who lived at Limeni, the tiny port in the bay of Vitylo a few hundred yards from the hotel. We had noticed his restored tower house on our way back from the Deep Mani. In 1821 Mavromichalis, a week before the official rising by the Archbishop of Patras at Kalavrita, raised the Mani in the revolt which spread over the entire Peloponnese and eventually ended in the Liberation of Greece. Napoleon has a further connection with Vitylo. Leake was assured that his family came from here and, on emigrating to Corsica, translated their Greek name of Kalomeros into the Italian Buonaparte. A story to which Leake gives no credence. Our Greek friend went on to talk about the present. He had known Cavafy and Kazantsakis, and also the director Kakoyannis, whose best film he considered was *A Woman in Black*. But he spent most of the evening lamenting the decline of the Greek language.

Our journey from Vitylo to Monemvasia began well. We took the road to Githion, passing the remains of Castle Passava, a Frankish stronghold built by Jean de Nivelet to guard the Mani, and stopped at Githion for a cup of coffee (it being too early for ouzo). The pretty little port was for us one of the most attractive towns in Greece – and one of the most romantic. In the bay, and joined to the town by a causeway, is the island of Kranai. In the Third Book of the Iliad Paris reminds Helen how he took her from 'lovely Lacedaemon in my sea-going ships and we spent the night on the isle of Cranae in each other's arms, never till now have I been so much in love with you or felt such sweet desire'. This was the lovers' first night together – they would not have spared a thought for what chaos might ensue.

We lunched at Molaoi, drawn there by the promise of the remnant of a fortress and a Byzantine church. It was unclear from the Blue Guide whether the church as well as the fortress was only a remnant. In any case we found nothing of interest although the village, set on the east slope of a three thousand foot hill, was a pleasant place for ouzo and mezze. Our road wandered through gentle country, well planted with olives. We passed the turning to Velies, the main food-producing area for medieval Monemvasia, and arrived in sight of the Rock in the early afternoon.

Monemvasia was the seaport of the Despots of the Morea. The city was founded by the Emperor Maurice in 583, and by 746 was the most important on the east coast of the Peloponnese, guarding as it did the great trade route from the West to Constantinople and the Levant. The following year the plague decimated the population (brought by cargo ships from the East) and the hated Emperor Constantine V sent Slav and Albanian colonists to replace inhabitants who had perished. Over the years it successfully resisted Arab and Norman attacks, but in 1249, after a three-year seige, it fell to the Franks, who with the aid of the Venetians had starved the city into submission. Within thirteen years they were forced to return Monemvasia to the Emperor as part of William of Villehardouin's ransom. Long ago its great families had developed a way of life half mercantile and half piratical, which they continued under the Franks. Michael VIII Palaeologus, keenly aware of the city's strategic importance, freed its merchants from taxation throughout the Empire and gave it an Orthodox Metropolitan. A chrysobull of

Andronicus II dated 1301 (of which the original is in the British Museum and a copy in Athens) lists the Metropolitan's estates and privileges. One of these privileges was to assume the place of the Patriarch of Jerusalem in the synod when the latter happened to be absent, therefore taking precedence over the Patriarchs of Alexandria and Antioch.

The period under the Despots was Monemvasia's golden age, the summit of its commercial importance, a time during which it contained forty monasteries and churches together with many schools and libraries and a population of between forty and fifty thousand. In 1450 the Despot Demetrius described its community as one of the most useful and important in his domains. When the Morea fell to the Turks in 1460 Monemvasia, undefeated, placed itself under the rule of the Pope; but the Papacy was too weak to defend the city, and interfered with its clergy. After four years its citizens turned to Venice. Commerce flourished and the Venetians restored many of the churches. Unfortunately, when Suleiman the Magnificent beat the West at Preveza, the Venetians left Monemvasia to the Turks, the Podestà fleeing with the cannon and the bells. Under Turkish rule the city declined, and by the end of the eighteenth century the only export was red dye for fezzes in Alexandria. Only three hundred families lived on the rock, of which half were Greek. The Turks were expelled after a four-month seige in 1821 – the first stronghold to capitulate to the patriots in the War of Independence.

Standing as it does on a great rock, the city is often compared to Gibraltar. When wet its stone is like porphyry, and the Turkish name for Monemvasia was the 'Violet Rock'. It may be approached only by a causeway – *monem basia*, or single entrance in medieval Greek – and, since its buildings are on the seaward side, is invisible from the shore. In its day it was impregnable, its cannon commanding from the frowning heights the compact lower town and the road up to the citadel. On the other side its guns covered the causeway to the mainland as well as the harbours. The only way it ever fell was from being starved into submission. All food came from the mainland, where the citizens owned large estates round Velies. Here too were some of the vineyards for the famous wine of Monemvasia, so prized in Venice, from which Malmsey derives its name; when the Turks came the growers uprooted their vines and left for Madeira. Their wine is said to have resembled the sweet amber wine produced today on the island of Santorini. In fact much of the wine called Malmsey was grown on the islands and merely exported from Monemvasia.

A shopkeeper whom we asked for advice told us to go and see Alexander and Haris Calligas. They are architects who have lived on Monemvasia since 1966 and have devoted their lives to inspiring and guiding its restoration in the most sensitive way possible. Unfortunately, during the week it is almost a ghost town, the restored houses being almost exclusively bought by Athenian week-enders. Eighty families lived on the rock in 1945, and now only ten do so. Nevertheless it is an enchanting place whose atmosphere of history makes it irresistible. Although the upper town in the citadel on the rock is now deserted (the last inhabitant left in 1911) and the houses are mere heaps of rubble, the lower town has survived. The houses have been rebuilt over the centuries, extending over the streets owing to lack of space, but the general plan is that of Byzantine days.

We climbed a steep path which zig-zagged up the cliff face to a massive citadel with a crooked tunnel leading to the town, then picked our way through the ruins and scrub to a terrace from where there is a sheer drop of eight hundred feet to the sea below. On the very edge of the cliff, beside the crumbling bastions and curtain wall of the citadel, stands the church of Hagia Sophia, founded by the Emperor Andronicus I Comnenus at the end of the twelfth century and later extended by the Emperor Andronicus II Palaeologus. Then it was a monastic foundation, though all the cells have long since crumbled to dust. In the church there is some fine carving and fragments of frescoes, but its oddest feature is the sixteenth-century exo-narthex, built like a loggia, which was added when the Venetians restored the church.

The sky beginning to darken with storm clouds, we decided to cut short our visit to the upper town. In any case this was in such a state of disrepair that it was hard to imagine the strange skyscrapers with spires which (if a seventeenth-century drawing be accurate) once graced the area round Hagia Sophia. The mighty cisterns which supplied the citizens with water throughout the weary sieges are still just recognizable. The view of the lower town is well worth the climb to the citadel; from the portal a toy village was laid out at our feet. Domes and tiled roofs, gardens – a surprising amount of tiny gardens – and squares nestled in the protection of the crenellated walls surrounding three sides of the town. We reached the safety of a café before it rained, and by the time we had finished our ice-creams the sun had come out. We wandered through the steaming narrow streets, sometimes disappearing under houses, to appear in a square or at the top of a flight of stairs. Hottentot fig, valerian and horned poppies grew in profusion amongst the houses awaiting restoration and on the waste ground at the far end of the town. We found ourselves outside the church of Panagia Chrysaphitissa, an early eighteenth-century building which replaced an earlier one destroyed by Morosini in 1690. We were fascinated to see votive offerings hanging in a case containing an icon of the Virgin. Gold arms, legs and noses dangled beside watches and rings. The festival of the Panagia Chrysaphitissa on 2 May is second only in importance to Easter in Monemvasia.

That evening the Calligas asked us for a drink at their sixteenth-century house. They were a couple as likeable as they were learned, very encouraging about our search for Byzantium. They gave us some excellent wine, unresinated, dry but full, brownish-coloured and above all grown at Velies – though it cannot have been the same as the old Malmsey, which was sweet. They also introduced us to the most handsome and prosperous cat and dog we met throughout our entire journey, one a chocolate point Siamese, the other a glossy coated Irish setter; they both walked into the room as thought they owned the house, prodding us firmly with smooth paws whenever they thought we were not paying them sufficient attention. To listen to their owners was to gain some idea of how rich and splendid Monemvasia must have been in its days of Byzantine opulence.

The next morning being Sunday, we attended the Liturgy in the church of Christos Elkomenos in the lower town. We were surprised to find only three others in the congregation. Later we discovered that the main Liturgy in the Greek Orthodox Church may take place on Saturday night instead of Sunday morning. After the beautiful and very moving service at Dekoulou, this Liturgy with its tiny congregation came as an anti-climax, the young priest, in his sky blue vestments trimmed with cloth of silver, lacking the sheer charisma of his brother at Dekoulou. In a glass case we noticed a copy of the icon, stolen from the church, now in the Byzantine Museum in Athens. The icon, believed to be inspired by the Byzantine Passion Play *Christ Suffering*, may have been painted by the artist who worked on the

decoration in the Peribleptos at Mistra. It is sad to see all the
treasures of Monemvasia scattered round the world, but they are
undoubtedly safer in museums. Other icons were stolen from the
church and have not been recovered, and the icon of Christ Suffering
was broken into five pieces by the thieves. Apart from this icon in
Athens and the chrysobull of Andronicus II at the British Museum,
the Victoria and Albert Museum possesses a very fine epitaphios
dating from 1407 which also came from Monemvasia.

Col. Leake visited Monemvasia (of course) in 1805, almost certainly staying at the Stellakis house down by the sea. He visited a
monastery said to have been founded by Andronicus Comnenus, but
it is not clear whether he means Hagia Sophia or Christos
Elkomenos. Knowing his passion for classical remains he is likely to
have climbed to the acropolis, so one must assume he is describing
Hagia Sophia, which was definitely a monastic foundation. And yet
the description fits Christos Elkomenos even better. It is larger than
most Greek churches, having been considerably altered by the
Venetians, and there are the remains of two Byzantine thrones. 'The
church is one of the largest in Greece, but is maintained in a state fit
for the church service towards the altar only; of the rest of the
building nothing is left but the bare walls; at the end opposite to the
altar are the remains of two thrones, which were destroyed by the
Turks after the Russian invasion.'

On the advice of the Calligas we went to Geraki from Monemvasia,
since they told us it had many churches with frescoes which had been
discovered and restored in the last fifteen years. Its name is the Greek
word for falcon, and the great bare hill broods over the Laconian
plain like some bird of prey. Guarding the north-eastern flank of La
Cremonie, it was of vital strategic importance in the Frankish
conquest of the Peloponnese, and given to Guy de Nivelet as a barony
with six lesser lordships. Here Guy's son Jean built the great fortress,
parts of which still guard the remains of the medieval village.

We lunched at a large and starkly decorated restaurant in the
modern village built on the site of a Mycenaean acropolis. The view
over the plain was breathtaking. We could make out small towers,
some of which may well have been built as Frankish manor houses.
In the far distance rose the dizzy snow-covered heights of Taygetos.
The restaurant was fairly full, and we were interested to see men with
very different features from those of Sparta. We wondered if they

could be the descendants of the Slavs who still inhabited the hills of Lacedaemon and Pentadaktylos in Constantine Porphyrogenitus's day. The Slav place names were still in use before the War of Independence, as Leake's map proves, Mt Parnon then being called Mt Malevo. Modern Geraki lies on one ridge of Parnon and the medieval town on another to the south east of the village.

A reasonable road took us half way up the hill and then we were forced to toil the rest of the way on foot. The world 'toil' is justified, since not only was the ascent to this imposing eyrie on a stronghold extremely steep, but the wind was so powerful that it nearly blew Sue off the summit. On the slope below the citadel are the remains of several churches and chapels, those with roofs being locked. Peering through the unglazed windows of a dark little chapel we could just make out a fresco of the Nativity. On the right sat Joseph with his back to the Mother and Child, disclaiming responsibility for the Son of God. Beside him a woman languidly drew her hand through the water in the bath to check its temperature. It suddenly (and belatedly – we had after all been looking at scenes of the Nativity for six weeks) occurred to us that in Western art the Baby is rarely washed (an exception being the Nativities of Giotto and his followers). Was this an example of the better hygiene of Byzantium, or was it purely the symbolic preparation for baptism? The largest church of Frankish Geraki lies just inside the portal. Over the door is an heraldic shield bearing a plain chequy coat-of-arms – perhaps that of the Nivelets – while inside a small carved shrine with a Gothic arch has another shield which is lozengy. No doubt this wild place saw tournaments at which both coats were worn with pride. (Although scarcely on the same scale as that great tournament at Corinth, where all the Latin Chivalry met after the Nivelets had lost Geraki to Byzantium.)

On that windswept, exhilarating hillside we felt a sudden surge of sympathy with the Franks, fellow Westerners. They may have been adventurers, but like us they were lured by Byzantium. Nikos Kazantsakis, of all unlikely people, succumbed to the lingering spell of the Franks when he visited Geraki: 'As I passed through the narrow, open fortress gate, crossed the devasted Gothic chambers and grass-choked courtyards, and, scaling a wild fig tree, reached the upper level and stood atop a rock, I felt like uttering a piercing cry, like a hawk. Sudden joy seized me. In a flash the Franks returned to the Peloponnesos, ravished it, filled it with blonde-headed children, and savage fortresses, and vanished.'

He writes of the Franks with surprising kindness, even admiration: 'They wore iron panoplies and painted shields, they carried huge lances; their Frankish steeds would neigh, and as the poet says, the Greek mares looked on longingly . . . Gourmands, drinkers, libertines, immobile valiants, first in battle, first in wine and with a kiss,' he says of them. 'They brought troubadours with them who sang of love, with strange musical instruments. An unheard of love, romantic, filled with unexpected religious devotion, sensuality and purity.' He continues 'Great bodies, ample souls, thunderous laughter, free opinion and scorn of death. They dressed in variegated colours and sparkled in the sun, and charged, each with a multitude, like natural forces.' Nevertheless the Byzantines proved too much for them in the end.

The last Baron of Geraki, Jean de Nivelet, surrendered his castle to the Emperor's men in 1262. He seems to have been paid handsomely for doing so, for he immediately purchased a magnificent estate on the shores of the Gulf of Corinth.

While the churches on the hill owe a great deal to the West, those on the lower slopes of the modern – and antique – village are purely Byzantine. We found the official custodian by enquiring at the taverna in the village square. An ill-favoured if very friendly barmaid who spoke some French explained what we wanted, but we had no other means of communicating with the surly monoglot guide, who refused to let us take photographs and made us feel thoroughly guilty at wanting to see the churches on a Sunday. Built in the twelfth century, before the coming of the Franks, St John Chrysostom is nothing much to look at from outside – a small, barrel-vaulted, single-aisled basilica; but on entering, one is confronted by a magnificent St George on his white horse and a fine St Demetrius. Above them are roundels in which, alternating with the Virgin and holy women, are delightful little portraits of the Empresses Helena, Irene and Catherine in Byzantine court dress. The prettiest church here is the tiny cross-in-square Evangelistria, which has damaged frescoes of King Solomon and King David; slightly earlier in date, like most of the Geraki churches it incorporates in its walls stones from ancient Gerontai nearby, slabs which seem massive in so minute a building. Our guide showed us two more churches. Hitherto, the names he had given the churches agreed with those in

Dimitriadi's book on the Peloponnese, but he told us that these were dedicated to the Anastasis and to Hagios Sostris. Dimitriadi says they are Hagios Nikolaos and Profitas Elias and Theodore. All the churches on the lower slopes are within a stone's thrown of one another, set in olive groves or small fields. If not of the highest quality, they nonetheless have enormous charm.

Now that we had seen so much of the Morea we were able to appreciate what an exceptionally beautiful principality it must have been. Admittedly we had come across no truly impressive churches, let alone palaces, but we knew that there were many at the capital. We drove as fast as we dared toward Mistra.

# Byzantium discovered–the despots of Mistra

'This extraordinary dead city, set on a steep, sunbaked mountainside
with its vertiginous, crumbling walls, its ruined cisterns and
foundations treacherously masked by thyme and Jerusalem sage,
and its quantity of churches.'

Sir Osbert Lancaster, *Sailing to Byzantium*

'Where'er we tread 'tis haunted holy ground.'

Lord Byron, *Childe Harold*

**A**FTER THE disillusionment of
Constantinople we had always
known that our only real hope of recapturing the atmosphere of
Byzantium would be Mistra. The city gates being shut by the time we
arrived, we wandered round the friendly modern village at the base of
the hill. As at our first brief glimpse, most of the medieval city was
hidden by swirling mist which rolled down from the heights of
Taygetos. There is little to see in the village – the only 'sight' being a
statue of the last Byzantine Emperor Constantine XI, bravest of the
Palaeologi, who died a martyr's death on the walls of Constantinople
– but it was pleasant to stroll wherever our feet led us, with no sense
of urgency. Luckily we had heard of Steven Runciman Street and
that it contained only two houses. Otherwise we might have missed
this tribute to a man who more than anyone has brought Mistra to the
notice of the modern world.

At the taverna opposite our hotel we drank our evening ouzo with
the proprietor, a tough, swarthy man in early middle age who had
worked in America. He told us about Constantine XI: 'He was great
king who could do *nothing*. People of Constantinople all too damn
soft – too much rich, too much drink, too much whore. Real man

though, died fighting.' He added, not altogether accurately, 'Only had 5,000 Greeks against 200,000 Turks.' A keen sportsman, he went on to tell us about Mistra's wildlife. Its game-birds were plagued by foxes, though as many as 2,000, so he claimed, had been shot during the previous winter by the local sporting club. Other unloved canine neighbours included a 'half fox, half dog'. (This must be the rare and graceful golden jackal, which in Europe survives only in the wilder parts of the Balkans.) He was grateful that wolves and bears had died out.

The next morning was so lovely that at 8.00 a.m. we drove up the mountain to see the city of Mistra in sunlight. From half a mile away it seemed as though it must have been immediately recognizable by the last Despot's subjects from the fifteenth century, as if all the roofs were still on, the houses still inhabited. We were unprepared for the sheer drama of its setting. The *Chronicle of the Morea* tells us that William de Villehardouin, who built the castle around which the city grew, 'found a strange hill as though cut off from the mountain', an excellent description even if it omits to mention a background of snowy mountain peaks. Amid many tall dark-green cypress trees the medieval city, containing not only a citadel but the Despot's Palace, a cathedral, monasteries, a dozen churches and the mansions of courtiers with vaulted halls and great balconies, lay before us deserted, ruined yet – cleared of later buildings – totally Byzantine. Although many of the houses and private chapels have disappeared, and although there are great open spaces filled with so many wild flowers that they give the impression the town was an early garden city rather than a thriving, bustling metropolis as crowded as Monemvasia, enough has survived to give a fair idea of Mistra at its prime.

One must not exaggerate the city's splendour. Sir Steven Runciman writes that 'the capital of the Despots of the Morea, though it boasted of a palace and a castle, and several churches, monasteries and schools, was little more than a village'. Nevertheless this small provincial capital demonstrated (to a far greater extent than Arta had ever done), eleven hundred years after Constantine the Great founded New Rome, that Byzantium had lost none of its inspiration or dynamism. A mere quarter of a century before the fall of Constantinople its rulers were capable of conquering the entire Peloponnese, of presiding over a cultural renaissance. For several decades it was one of the intellectual capitals of Europe. The achievement at Mistra proves that, but for an accident of history placing it in the path of the terrible phenomenon of Ottoman expansion, the Eastern Empire had the strength to renew itself yet again.

Mistra's economy was quite unlike that of Constantinople. Its prosperity depended primarily on agriculture, on the fertile farmland in the Plain of Lacedaemonia and on the estates dominated by the modest peel towers of its lords, many of whose ruins survive. There was little in common with that great emporium which had been Constantinople in its days of glory. Olives were grown extensively – every house had a cistern for olive oil as well as for rain water – and the oil was exported from Monemvasia. The most important product was silk; as late as the eighteenth century over sixty tons of silk were exported annually – to Chios, to Ioannina to be made up into lace for Albanian dresses, and to Constantinople to be woven into gauze for mosquito nets. The Orloff rising of 1770 ruined this trade. Although Mistra was liberated for several months the Albanians eventually sacked the town, destroying many of the mulberry trees on which the silk worms fed and killing the larvae. According to Leake, silkworms 'are so delicate that thunder, or even the report of a pistol, will sometimes kill them'. Mistra was ruled by the Albanians for ten years before the Turks regained it.

Ironically, Mistra was founded by the Franks in 1249 to cow not only the Slavs of Taygetos but also the Greeks. In the 13 years that the Franks were there – before it passed to Byzantium in 1262 as part of William de Villehardouin's ransom – they built the citadel and, according to the experts, a palace which later formed the north-east corner of the Palace of the Despots. They must have felt very secure during those 13 years to have built it so far from the citadel. On his release, William, absolved by the Pope from his oath of allegiance to the Emperor Michael VIII, tried to recapture the city. Michael sent an army, however, which included 5,000 Seljuk mercenaries, to drive him off in final retreat.

It was during these troubled times that the inhabitants of Lacedaemonia (as medieval Sparta was called) moved to Mistra and started to build on the hill beneath the citadel, in the area to the south of the road running from the Monemvasia gate to the Nauplia Gate. The city grew so rapidly that houses were built outside the city walls and a second or Lower City came into being. The speed of growth is shown by the fact that, apart from the pre-Frankish chapel in the citadel, the earliest churches at Mistra are all in the Lower City and the Cathedral was almost certainly founded in 1265.

Its emergence as the capital of an autonomous Byzantine state during the fourteenth century was due to able rulers – always Princes of the Imperial House – and to the Empire's parlous condition. Two civil wars, one in the twenties between Andronicus II and his grandson Andronicus III and another twenty years later between John V Palaeologus and John VI Cantcuzenus, were indirectly responsible for the loss of all northern Greece to Tsar Dušan (territory which was not recovered after the Serbian collapse), and for the end of Byzantium as a sea power. Anatolia was overrun by the Turks, who by the close of the century had also conquered Bulgaria and a large part of Serbia, including the erstwhile Byzantine territories of Thessaly, Epirus and Thrace. All that remained to Byzantium by 1400 was the walled city of Thessalonica, Constantinople, Mesembria and Anchialus on the Black Sea, and the Peloponnese. Thessalonica held out till 1423 when the threatened, starving city was handed over to the Venetians by Manuel II's third son the Despot Andronicus Palaeologus. There is nothing in the Serenissima's archives to support the myth that the Despot sold it to the Venetians; the position was so desperate that Andronicus had no other choice. The Venetians promised to defend the city and respect the rights of the citizens, but after seven years, during which the Serenissima had to pay more and more tribute to the Turks, Thessalonica fell to the cannon of Murad II. Meanwhile the Genoese and Venetians had a stranglehold over what was left of Constantinopolitan trade. Only in the Peloponnese were the last, brilliant Palaeologi able to reverse the decline, subduing and assimilating the Franks, establishing a new principality with a sound political and military base (although the use of mercenaries horrified Gemistos Plethon), a state which enjoyed considerable prosperity.

Until 1308 the Byzantine governor of the Morea was changed annually, causing great disruption to the smooth running of the province. From this date the appointment became for a term; indeed the first of these governors, a Cantacuzenus – father of the future Emperor John VI – died in harness in 1316. The first Despot of the Morea, Manuel, was Cantacuzenus' grandson, sent there in 1348 by his father because the Peloponnese was torn by civil war, brigandage and the squabbles of the Franks – whether Gasmoules, Catalans or Italians. John VI, having been deposed by the legitimate Emperor John V Palaeologus, became a monk at Mistra in 1354. Three years later his eldest son Matthew renounced his claim to the throne and joined his father and brother at Mistra where on the death of his brother in 1380, he became Despot. Not only did Manuel's reign bring peace and prosperity but he inaugurated Mistra's career as a cultural centre, building churches, encouraging scholars to settle, founding libraries, patronising scribes and illuminators. In this atmosphere of learning his father wrote his book of homilies and his famous history. Matthew was no less able, but he died after a couple of years, leaving his son Demetrius as Despot.

Constantinople had been content to allow a Cantacuzenus to continue as governor of the Morea, but Demetrius, in trying to secede from the Empire, went too far. John V Palaeologus sent his son Theodore to quash the revolt and rule as Despot; this he did capably enough, despite ill health, until his death in 1407. No intellectual himself, he nonetheless continued to patronize scholars. These were troubled times in the Morea. Although he did a good deal to consolidate Byzantine control in the Peloponnese he was forced to recognize Turkish suzerainty from 1395 when Evrenoz Bey, after successes in Thessaly, occupied the Byzantine fortresses of Akova and Leontari. At one stage Theodore decided to cede Mistra to the Knights of Rhodes; but when they came to claim it in 1402 they were repulsed by the citizens with such fury that the bishop had to intervene to save the knights from being massacred on the spot. Theodore was forced to return his reward and keep Mistra.

We had chosen the loveliest time of the year to visit this best preserved of Byzantine cities. There were wild flowers everywhere on the green hillside; valerian, purple vetch, pink hawksbeard, Tears of the Virgin, convolvulus, phlomis in great profusion and, clinging to the stones and the walls of churches and palaces, the blue trumpets of campanula rupestris. The list is endless; nowhere else had we seen such an extravagance of bloom, and we had the illusion of walking through a palace garden tended by many gardeners. The answer lies in the fencing which keeps out not only tourists but also goats. Apart from a few cats at the Pantanassa the only four-footed beast we saw was a donkey. All this greenery makes a sharp contrast with the sun-parched yellow hill which is Mistra at the end of summer.

We drove up to the car-park at the castle entrance to walk to the citadel, above us on the rocky summit. Probably secure enough when built by William de Villehardouin, it was no match for later artillery, and the town itself was far more vulnerable to attack than Monemvasia. No wonder the last Despot fled when, on looking down from the palace, he saw a great Turkish host winding towards Mistra through the plain below. The citadel could hold a thousand men when it was built, and it was enlarged considerably. The square gate which guards the entrance is on the north-east. At the south there is a round look-out tower, still in reasonable condition, from which defenders had a superb view of the plain of Sparta – and of the approach of an enemy army – with a great vaulted cistern next to it. The citadel and the Upper City relied on cisterns for their water supply, but the Lower City had water piped from a ravine to the north. At the summit is all that is left of the keep, whose plan is roughly oval. Most of the citadel's buildings, destroyed during the Orloff rising in 1770, are no more than grassy heaps of rubble and, in any case, date from the Turkish occupation. Among them, however, is the earliest building in Mistra – a tiny double chapel which pre-dates the citadel. Apart from this chapel there is no evidence of the site having been used before the thirteenth century – ancient stones used in some of the city's churches and houses would have been brought from the plain of Sparta.

On arriving back at the old town after an extremely slippery descent from the citadel we went to see Hagia Sophia. This is the palace chapel, which was, no doubt, why it received a name with Imperial associations. The Despot Manuel built it not long after he became ruler of the Morea, and his monogram may still be seen on the capitals. A small, unpretentious building, architecturally it is notable only for surprising height and an unusually large narthex. Despite heroic attempts at restoration, its frescoes are no more than tattered shadows, but it is still possible to make out many of them. The most interesting, we thought, was the Nativity of the Virgin in which the female attendants wear unusual head-dresses, Phrygian caps with veils hanging from them – like mantillas suspended from their combs. The saddest loss are the portraits of the founder's parents, the Emperor John VI Cantacuzenus and his Empress Irene, which are known to have adorned the wall on either side of the entrance. Its best remaining feature is a splendid polychrome marble 'carpet', the finest in Mistra. There is also a campanile – a sign of Western influence – which was turned into a minaret when, under Turkish rule, the church became a mosque. The church was part of a small monastery, that of the Zoödotes (Life Giver), and the monks' refectory stands near the campanile.

The Despina Cleope, consort of Theodore II Palaeologus, was buried at Hagia Sophia in about 1433. A cousin of Sigismondo Malatesta (despoiler of Sant 'Apollinare in Classe's marbles), she was chosen by Pope Martin V as a bride for the Despot, at the Emperor Manuel's request, in an attempt to forge links between the Catholic and Orthodox worlds. Her husband, a prey to depression and religious mania, did not get on with her at first; no doubt, as a brilliant mathemetician, he resented her interruption of his study of geometry. Yet she too was an intellectual, and a warm patron of scholars. Moreover, much to the Pope's fury, she became an enthusiastic convert to Orthodoxy. Also buried here is the Despina Theodora (born Magdalena), first wife of Constantine XI Palaeologus. After being defeated by Constantine in a naval battle in 1427 her uncle Carlo Tocco, Count of Cephalonia and Lord of Clarenza, gave him Theodora's hand together with Clarenza and the rest of the Tocco possessions in the Peloponnese as a dowry. She died childless after a year of marriage.

Partly Serb – his maternal grandfather Dragaš had been a petty Serbian princeling in Macedonia – Constantine was Manuel's fourth and most formidable son. He ruled only two little towns on the Black Sea in what is now Bulgaria – Mesembria and Anchialus – until in 1427 Theodore, during a fit of melancholy caused by his marriage, offered to abdicate in his favour and become a monk. When Theodore found Cleope more interesting than he had thought and changed his mind he, Constantine and their brother Thomas agreed to rule the Morea as joint Despots. By 1432, when after a long siege Patras fell, largely thanks to Constantine, the entire Peloponnese was once more Byzantine, save for four Venetian ports. By 1443 he had occupied Athens and Thebes, forcing Nerio II Acciajuoli to pay tribute to him instead of to the Turk. He then took Phocis. In happier times so gifted a soldier might well have renewed the Empire. In 1446 Murad II angrily drove him out of these new gains. In 1443 Theodore had exchanged his share of the Morea for Constantine's apanage on the Black Sea and had retired there to await his succession to the Imperial throne when their brother John VIII should die. Ironically he predeceased the Emperor by a few months, both brothers dying in 1448.

From Hagia Sophia we walked gingerly downwards on a steep cobbled lane, very like those at Monemvasia. A cloudburst made it still more slippery. We found shelter under an arch over the road – as at Monemvasia houses were built over the thoroughfares – with a group of Germans who bellowed their disappproval of the weather and scattered orange peel all over the path. Other trippers included Italians and a few French; there were no Americans. The most interesting tourist, so a French girl assured us, was an aged French duke, pointed out by her as a rare beast – he certainly looked like a survivor from before 1789.

As soon as the storm abated we left our fellow-tourists and braved the streets, now turned into rushing torrents, to look for the Palace of the Despots. The L-shaped building is a vast and impressive ruin. The corner of the L is thought to date from Frankish days, in which case the daughter of the Despot Michael II of Epirus must have gazed out of these windows while her husband William de Villehardouin languished in a Byzantine prison. According to the *Chronicle of the Pseudo-Dorotheos* she was 'most beautiful and gracious from her head to her whole body, like a second Helen of Menelaos'. The Palace was enlarged by the Cantacuzene and, on a more magnficient scale, by the Palaeologi. Far from resembling the Venetian palazzi said to be modelled on the great mansions of Constantinople, it has a definitely Florentine air, with windows of the sort from which one might have looked out over the Arno. Theodore I married the daughter of a scion of a family of Florentine merchants, Nerio I Acciajuoli, which may account for the design; but as there are no Palaeologue dwellings (or, if there are, we could not find them) left in Constantinople, it is difficult to say how far the basic eleventh-century pattern had progressed in four hundred years. The throne room of the Palace is 110 feet long and 35 feet wide with two rows of windows – the upper ones being round – and eight fireplaces. It has been suggested that Manuel II – whom Runciman calls 'the most highly respected and most deeply mourned of all the long line of Byzantine emperors' – held his court here in 1407 and again in 1415, when he stayed at Mistra for a year and supervised the rebuilding of the Hexamilion across the Isthmus of Corinth. In 1399 he had made a lengthy tour of Western Europe, begging for help from the Catholic powers against the Turk. He visited the court of Henry IV of England. Dressed always in immaculate white, every inch an emperor, he made a most favourable impression on the whole court, in stark contrast to that to be made a few years later by the Holy Roman Emperor Sigismund, who was notorious for his filth, drunkeness and barbaric behaviour. Manuel, fascinated by the politeness of King Henry, found his host 'smartest in dress and wittiest in wiles'. During sojourns abroad which lasted three years, including two spent at Paris, where he stayed in the Louvre, Manuel left his wife and children at Mistra with his brother Theodore – not trusting his nephew and regent John VII, who was left at Constantinople to rule as Emperor in his absence.

Not far from the Palace – in fact we had passed it on our way down from Hagia Sophia – is the Palataki, built in about 1300 and added to in the following century, the residence of some great Byzantine magnate. There are many houses which were clearly the family mansions of the aristocracy. Yet the court was famed for scholarship rather than luxury. That unhappy couple Theodore and Cleope, serious and austere – he a mathematician, she a keen humanist – welcomed scholars, who loved them both. And no mean scholars came. One was Bessarion, the Orthodox Archbishop of Nicaea, (whose books were to become the foundation of the Marciana Library at Venice), who, after the union of the two churches in 1439, ended his days as a Cardinal in the Church of Rome. Another was Hieronymos Charitonymos, who would be one of the first teachers of Greek in the University of Paris. There was the monk Isidore, a future Metropolitan of Kiev and head of the Russian Church, who eventually became a Cardinal at Rome. His defection so horrified the Russians that they refused to come to the aid of Byzantium in her final, fatal days. The most remarkable of these fifteenth-century scholars was George Gemistos, who took the surname Plethon – Plato.

Plethon was born in Constantinople in the 1360s, settling at Mistra about 1400 where he died at a great age in 1452. As a humanist he attracted many pupils, dominating the city's intellectual life. His reputation was international – Cosimo de' Medici founded the Academy at Florence in his honour. He sent eloquent memoranda to the Despot and the Emperor on how to renew the Empire. 'Do not

forget that neither individuals nor peoples are allowed to lose hope,'
he told them. 'Many thought dead have risen to new life.' But his
solutions did not match his eloquence. Arguing that the Byzantines
were heirs of the ancient Greeks, he proposed social and military
reforms inspired by Plato's *Republic* – reforms which in the late
twentieth century would be recognized as Fascist. (Predictably, in the
1930s his views appealed to Nikos Kazantsakis, who pictured his
angry shade wandering inconsolably, staff in hand, through the ruins
of Mistra, and called him 'The Prophet of Modern Greece'.) His
religious opinions were even odder; he advocated a new creed of his
own, a weird mixture of Platonism and Zoroastrianism, and was
involved with a neo-pagan cell at Mistra, some of whose members
worshipped the Sun God. His fame rested not on his political or
religious ideas, however, but on his genius as a teacher of Platonism.

George Gemistos Plethon was not the only thinker at Mistra to
look back to Antiquity. Bessarion wanted the Basileus to abandon the
title 'King and Emperor of the Romans' and call himself 'King of the
Hellenes' instead, exhorting him to remember the warlike prowess of
the Spartans. The historian Laonicus Chalcocondyles (who on at
least one occasion acted as the Despot Constantine's ambassador)
prophesied that 'a King of the Greeks and his heirs shall one day
restore a realm which the sons of the re-united Hellenes will rule and
of which they shall make a nation'. For the Palaeologan renaissance
which had begun at Constantinople during the previous century, and
which parallelled the Western renaissance, reached its zenith in
fifteenth-century Mistra. This is vividly apparent from the frescoes
here, with their return to Classical forms – so long preserved in
illuminated manuscripts – to human sentiment and drama, their
introduction of movement, and their abandonment of the abstract.

We made our way down the hill and, passing through the well
preserved Monemvasia Gate, came outside the inner walls. A cobbled
road led us across the slope to the monastery (now a convent) of The
All Holy Theotokos 'called Pantanassa', built in 1428 by John
Frangopoulos, Protostrator (Master of the Horse) to Theodore II.
Partly basilical, partly cruciform in plan, with a four-storied belfry
which again must be the result of Western influence, its frescoes are
wonderful – in Runciman's view 'an achievement of supreme beauty'. We were overwhelmed by the glowing fervour in the Raising of
Lazarus and the gentle, clear palette of the Nativity in the gallery

vault. Here the Virgin lies on a Jewish travelling bed at the entrance to a cave, her eyes closed in the exhaustion of childbirth. The frescoes from the gallery upward are all contemporary with the church, but those below were painted in the seventeenth and eighteenth centuries – possibly between 1687, when Morosini took Mistra for Venice, and 1715, when it returned to Ottoman rule. When Leake was here a century later the churches could be restored only on payment of 300 piastres to a mosque at Constantinople. On our way out we passed a number of nuns, attended by suitably ascetic-looking cats, who belong to a tiny community at the Pantanassa comprising the only human beings still to live at Mistra. We were mystified as to how they manage to preserve any vestige of tranquility amid hordes of tourists. Staunchly conservative, they adhere to the old Julian calender, remaining thirteen days behind the rest of us.

The monastery church and refectory of the Perebleptos ('Resplendent One') date from the mid-fourteenth century. A cross-in-square without a narthex, the church is partially built into the hillside, carved out of the rock. Its frescoes, which were probably painted at this time, are generally acknowledged as being among the greatest Byzantine works of art to survive, in particular the Divine Liturgy and the Nativity. Runciman says that the figures in them seem not so much to move as to float, and detects a touch of wistfulness – 'Only the humanity of the faces keeps us from passing into a world of dreams'. This Nativity, very similar to that at the Pantanassa with the Virgin outside a cave in the centre, is more like a large icon than a fresco, and is of a design which later became common for icons of the Nativity in both Greece and Russia. We were surprised to see how small these scenes were, not a bit as we had imagined them. Another scene which became popular in later icons and frescoes – but not as far as we know, in Yugoslavia – is a detail shown here in the Dormition of the Virgin, The fanatical Jew, Athonios, on daring to profane the bier of the Virgin by touching it, is having his hands cut off by an angel.

The gnawing pangs of hunger drove us from the city – breakfast seemed very far away. We also decided we had seen enough for one day; there was almost too much to absorb and we were beginning to suffer from mental indigestion. The following morning would give us time to see the rest. The climb back to the car park was quite sufficient in our under-nourished state. At lunch in the taverna opposite our hotel over souvlaki and pink unresinated wine from the barrel (we felt we deserved more than ouzo and mezze), we agreed, rather nervously since it seemed too good to be true, that we must really be seeing Byzantium. We read in Runciman's *Mistra* of Plethon – 'we picture him, as a philosopher in the old peripatetic tradition, strolling to and fro with his pupils in the great square outside the Despot's Palace, the only level open space in that crowded mountain city'.

Next day we began at the main entrance at the bottom. Here the churches are on roughly the same level, so there was no need to endure all the climbing of the previous day. The Metropolis, the cathedral dedicated to Hagios Demetrios and lowest of the churches, is again basilical below and cruciform above. The cathedral of the Metropolitan of Lacedaemonia, it dates from about 1265, when it was a three-aisled basilica; a narthex was added in 1291, and in the fifteenth century the upper part of the church was destroyed by Bishop Matthew, who added domes and turned it into a cruciform church, decapitating many of the lower frescoes in the process. There is a charming colonnaded courtyard on the north side which, if built in the eighteenth century under the Turkish occupation, somehow *feels* Byzantine. The frescoes, while not of the highest quality and certainly unequal to those at the Perebleptos and the Pantanassa, are interesting in having been painted by at least four different artists during the half century between the earliest in 1270 and the latest (in the narthex) in 1325. Hagios Demetrios as dedicatee features strongly in rather crude and childlike scenes of his life and martyrdom – run through with lances in his prison. Yet in the narthex the dark blue Angel of Judgment in the Second Coming is magnificent, while there is a tremendous Etimasia (preparation of God's throne for the Last Judgment) in the dome, in which stern angels crowd round the menacing, empty throne as they await the coming of the dread Lord of All.

It is odd to reflect that, during the last twenty years of the Despotate, the services here and indeed in all the churches of Mistra, were celebrated by priests of a Church technically re-united with Rome, that prayers were said for the Pope as well as for the Emperor and the Patriarch of Constantinople. In 1439 John VIII and his prelates signed at Florence a document of union between Orthodoxy and Catholicism. Although the vast majority of their subjects refused

to accept what has been irreverently described as 'a shotgun marriage', the last Emperors and Despots all died Papists, even if they
agreed to the union only in the hope that the Papacy might mobilize
the West in a Crusade to save them from the Turks. So anxious was
the Pope, Eugenius IV, that he tolerated the Orthodox practice of
allowing three marriages.

We were deeply moved by a stone slab in the pavement of the
Metropolis on which was carved the Double Eagle – the Imperial
coat-of-arms. Here on 6 January 1449 the Metropolitan placed the
crown on the head of Constantine XI, proclaiming him as 'The in
Christ God Faithful King and Emperor of the Romans . . . Equal to
the Apostles'. If he ruled no more than Constantinople and the
Peloponnese, devout Orthodox nonetheless regarded him as rightful
ruler of the entire created world. Yet, when he sailed away to his once
glorious capital a few weeks later, the Thirteenth Apostle knew very
well that he might be the last Roman Emperor of the East. Neither
Old Rome nor New ever produced a greater hero.

Next to the Metropolis there is a small museum. It contains
fragments of sculpture from Mistra's churches, jewels, pottery and a
few icons. One of them is definitely a bit peculiar, showing St George
leaning from the saddle to kiss St Demetrius on his red horse.

On our way to the monastery of the Brontochion we passed the
pretty little church of the Evangelistria, used for many years as the
ossuary for Mistra. It is believed to date from the beginning of the
fifteenth century but, alone among the churches of Mistra, there are
no documents relating to it. It was firmly locked, much to our
frustration, since we knew that it contains the vestiges of frescoes.

The monastery of the Brontochion, once the richest in the Peloponnese, contains two churches. Hagioi Theodoroi (the Theodores)
was founded about 1295 by Abbot Pachomius, a former official
whose help in governing the Despotate had earned him the warm
gratitude of the Emperor Andronicus II. The other, the Hodegetria-
Afthendiko, was also built by Pachomius, about 15 years later. Both
were in a deplorable condition before inspired restoration by Professor Orlandos in the 1930s. The plan of the former is octagonal with
no narthex and, for the church's size, an enormous dome, while that
of the latter is basilical below and cruciform above. Hagioi Theodoroi's frescoes are too faded to be of much interest, but we could make
out the warrior saint and, in the Dormition, the angel cutting off the

hands of the unfortunate Jew. The frescoes in the Afthendiko are generally thought inferior to those in the Perebleptos and the Pantanassa but we found them very beautiful. In Beckwith's view the Procession of Martyrs 'is painted with a kind of aristocratic finesse, elegant, lofty, and rich in colour'. They hark back to an earlier age, reminding one almost of the mosaics in Ravenna, but the faces of the martyrs are entirely fourteenth century. The frescoes in the narthex would appear to be by another hand. Small crowded scenes of the Life of Christ combine two miracles in one – the Woman of Samaria is jostled by the guests at the Marriage at Cana; the Woman with an Issue of Blood is in the same panel as Christ Healing the Blind Man. All these frescoes benefitted enormously from a brilliant restoration in 1969 which revealed a palette of the utmost delicacy. The majestic portrait of the Just Zacharias, burning eyed and long bearded, is superb. The four walls of the Afthendiko's windowless south chapel are curiously decorated with copies of four chrysobulls of Andronicus II bestowing vast estates, including some still in Frankish hands, on the monastery. In its north chapel is the tomb of Theodore II, who died as a monk five years after his departure from Mistra, where he had ruled as Despot for nearly four decades. Above his tomb a fresco shows him in both roles.

We saw other churches at Mistra, chapels belonging to noble families. All tiny, some shut and others ruined. We saw more than churches. A great deal of the city's fascination is that one can still see the houses of Byzantine noblemen, the outstanding being those of the Lascaris and the Frangopoulos. The first is a two-storied building with a great stable below, the family living on the balconied upper floor. The latter, which belonged to John Frangopoulos (founder of the Pantanassa), dates from the early fifteenth century, and in addition to a balcony has a gabled roof and underground cisterns. The only occupants are some unmistakably patrician lizards, green and bronze, with the most delicate of tails. Had we believed in trans-migration we would have been convinced that they were once Byzantine nobles.

When Constantine XI left Mistra for Constantinople his brothers Thomas and Demetrius ruled the Morea between them, Demetrius at Mistra and Thomas at Clarenza. Here Byzantine civilization lingered for seven years after the fall of Constantinople. But the Despots quarrelled with each other, governed so badly that their subjects rebelled, omitted to pay tribute to the Sultan, and then begged the Pope to send a Crusade to rescue them. At the end of May 1460 a Turkish army appeared before Mistra. Terrified, Demetrius fled with his wife and children to Monemvasia. On the approach of the Turks he again fled, abandoning his family and the town to their fate. Then he threw himself on the mercy of the Sultan, asking the Archon of Monemvasia to deliver his wife and children to the Turk. Treated generously at first by Muhammed II, his goods were later confiscated and he died a monk at Adrianople in 1470. Thomas, Despot of Clarenza, fled to Rome where he died as a pensioner of the Pope in 1465.

A grateful Thomas presented Pius II with a cherished relic, the arm of John the Baptist, now preserved at the cathedral in Siena. In the Piccolomini Library, just off the cathedral, the walls are painted by Pinturicchio with scenes from the life of the Pope (born Aeneas Sylvius Piccolomini) and Thomas, with beard and a green hat, appears in the tenth of these in which the dying Pius sees the Venetian galleys sail into the harbour of Ancona, too late for the Crusade he has called. Thomas also gave one of the most beautiful of all medieval embroideries to his benefactor. The early fourteenth-century cope in the Diocesan Museum of Sacred Art at Pius's birthplace, the Tuscan town of Pienza, was the gift of the Despot although it is not Byzantine work but English.

Since that sad day in May 1460 – a day very probably like the days of our visit – Mistra has been sacked by the Turks, by Sigismondo Malatesta (who also removed the remains of Plethon and took them to his Tempio Malatestiano at Rimini), by the Albanians and by the Egyptians. On 14 September 1825 Mr Swan saw it in flames, left only that morning by Ibrahim Pasha, leader of the Turco-Egyptian army. Yet with all this destruction it remains miraculously intact. Most of the survivors from 1460 either returned to the lowest level – the last thirty families were moved out in 1952 – or settled in the newly founded town of Sparta in 1834. The Upper City has been allowed to crumble in peace. Since the 1930s there has been an unceasing programme of restoration and conservation at what is sometimes called the 'Byzantine Pompeii', though one wishes it could have been on a bigger scale. Many of the frescoes still in existence at the beginning of this century have disappeared.

We genuinely felt that we had found Byzantium here. Perhaps the frescoes have not got quite the beauty of those at the Kariye Camii at Constantinople or at Sopoćani, and certainly no Virgin is as tender as the Virgin of the Annunciation at Mileševa, but only at Mistra does one have an idea of what a Byzantine city really looked like – Monemvasia is too bleak. We believed that we had truly been touched by the spirit of Byzantium on this haunted hill, had done more than catch mere glimpses of Eastern Rome. For all the last great men and women of the Empire rode up and down Mistra's steep and narrow streets, from the beloved Manuel II and the hero Constantine XI to the pagan Plethon, the saintly Gennadius and the delightfully learned Lady Cleope – streets along which they would be able to find their way even today. Only the most poverty stricken imagination could fail to re-people this beautiful little city with the ghosts of the ultimate, doomed Byzantines.

Yet everywhere we had visited in our 50 days – Venice and Ravenna, Serbia and Macedonia (from Manasija to Kurbinovo), Kastoria and Thessalonica, Constantinople, Chios, Athens, Boeotia, the Meteora, Epirus, the Mani and the rest of the Peloponnese – had, if to a lesser degree, lifted the veil of centuries. Someday we shall go back to them all. In the meantime we know beyond question that Byzantium has not vanished like Atlantis, that it is still possible to see its treasures and fall under its spell.

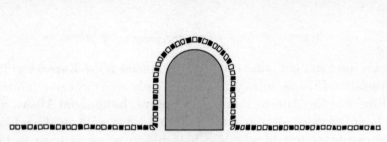

# Appendix
# (Travel, hotels etc.)

**F**EW PEOPLE can spare fifty days as we did, and not many would enjoy the discomfort (a young friend who recently took the train from Thessalonica to Istanbul vowed never to repeat it, preferring to fly home rather than use his Round Europe rail ticket). The ideal solution is to treat Istanbul and Chios as a separate holiday. There are numerous cheap flights to Izmir and to Istanbul, with marvellous things to see between the two towns and round Izmir – Troy, Pergamum, Ephesus and Chios coupled with four or five days in Istanbul make a fascinating holiday. For those who like staying by the sea there are resorts at Çesme and Kuşadasi (the most commercialized) as well as small fishing villages with lovely beaches. The best book on this area is Diana Darke's Guide to Aegean and Mediterranean Turkey. For a list of tourist agencies specializing in Turkey apply to the Turkish Tourist Office, Egyptian House, 170 Piccadilly, London, W.1. Tel: 01–734–8681, who will also provide a list of hotels in Istanbul and elsewhere.

We could very happily have spent a fortnight or longer in Yugoslavia. We saw the most important churches but there are others we would have liked to visit – Staro Nagoricane, Markov Manastir, Kuceviste and Lesnovo, all within striking distance of Skopje; Sv. Naum and Sv. Zaum at Ohrid; Moraca in Montenegro and Arilje west of Kralevo. The cheapest way of doing this is to take a charter flight to Dubrovnik and hire a car there. Three weeks can include Kastoria and Thessalonica. The Yugoslav Travel Club, 98a Garratt

Lane, London S.W.17. Tel: 01–767–3528, offer flights to both Belgrade and Dubrovnik.

Three weeks is more comfortable than two for the Peloponnese and mainland Greece, though days could be saved by missing out the Mani, Kastaniani and some of the difficult-to-find tiny churches round Arta. Numerous charter flights operate to Thessalonica and Athens, while it is possible to include Chios – during the summer there are daily scheduled flights from Athens.

A combination of Yugoslavia and Greece is possible, given the time, but we should point out that to do so we drove 3,000 miles, starting in Belgrade and ending back in Athens after we had left Mistra – not perhaps everybody's idea of a holiday.

We took a two-month excursion ticket to Athens which allowed us to break our journey at one place (in our case Belgrade) on either the way out or the return; it also allowed us to come back when we liked as long as we returned within two months. We booked our car in advance through Pan Adriatic Travel, but discovered at Belgrade that it would have been cheaper to wait until we arrived. This was contrary to the advice given in a couple of guide books, so we may have misunderstood the friendly man at Kompas Hertz in Belgrade. The only hotel we booked in advance was the Kasina in Belgrade, a perfectly adequate B category hotel in the centre, convenient for the National Museum and no great distance from the Fresco Museum.

Hotels in Serbia, the Kosmet and Macedonia, tend to be of a lower standard than those in the rest of Europe although, being fairly modern, all of category A and B have private bathrooms (it is essential to take a bath plug). The Yugoslav National Tourist Office, 143 Regent Street, London, W.l. Tel: 01–734–5243, provides a list with up-to-date prices in dollars, but on the whole sticks to those on the main roads. Nevertheless it can be useful. Apart from the Kasina, none of our hotels cost more than $20 per night for a single room with bath or shower. We stayed at the following:–

Belgrade *Kasina* small rooms central
Kruševac *Rubin* comfortable central
Novi Pazar *Vrbak* comfortable central
Priepolje *Mileševa* comfortable and very cheap outside town
Peć *Metohije* comparatively expensive by river

Prizren   *Theranda*   very drab   central
Skopje   *Táurist*   quiet   central
Ohrid   *Palace*   shabby but comfortable   on lake near the old
town
Bitola   *Epinal*   ' 'orrible 'otel' but supposed to be the best

We liked the look of the hotel at Studenica, a simple establishment in an idyllic setting, but were unable to inspect the rooms; early booking is essential. Apart from the Ohrid Trout we cannot recommend any restaurants. There are plenty of cheap places to eat but for a proper evening meal the safest bet is an hotel. Women do not eat in public anywhere else.

Driving in this part of Yugoslavia is not particularly difficult. One is bound by law to stop and give assistance to anyone involved in an accident but, there being so little traffic, we never had occasion to do so. It is important to buy petrol whenever the opportunity presents itself – filling stations are few and far between. The same applies to money; credit cards are unlikely to be accepted outside large towns, and only certain banks will cash travellers cheques. At the time of writing only 10,000 dinars (about £7) can be taken out of the country, so careful budgeting is advisable.

Because we had hired our car in Yugoslavia we had to leave it there and cross the border by train. It leaves Bitola at about three in the afternoon and arrives in Thessalonica (the first place where there is a national car-hire firm in Greece) at ten. Unwilling to risk arriving so late without booking rooms, we took the branch line to Florina where we stayed the night.

While hotels in Greece are better than those in Serbia or Macedonia, we did not stay in any to which we long to return. To be fair, our aim was to find accommodation to suit our pockets rather than our taste, our only stipulation being that the rooms should be clean and have bathrooms.

Florina   *King Alexander*. Outside town on the way to Kastoria, probably the best in Florina with lovely view.
Kastoria   *Tsamis*. Good rooms with nice position on lake near Dispilio.
Thessalonica   *Rotonda*. Not recommended but, thanks to travel conference the only one with rooms. A good central hotel appears to be the Electra Palace near the waterfront. Avoid

any in Egnatia, Tsimiki or Dhimitriou as being horrendously noisy.

Athens    *Imperial* One of the many in Metropoleos St facing the Cathedral.

Delphi    *Hermes* One of the many on the lower road with uninterrupted views of the plain.

Lamia    *Samaras* fairly quiet with pleasant view

Kalambaka    *Odyssion* quiet but basic

Ioannina    *Xenia* fairly comfortable but not central

Arta    *Xenia* in castle grounds, one of the best we tried

Patras    *El Greco* not recommended. It is better to avoid Patras and stay at Navpaktos on the north side of the Gulf of Corinth and cross by ferry from Andirrion to Rion the following day.

Mistra    *Byzantio* all rooms have views of medieval Mistra-
    booking is essential

Vitylo    *Hotel Itilo* on a shingle beach    small and friendly

Monemvasia    *Monemvasia* is the recommended one here – we stayed at an unpleasant hotel further out on a beach.

Driving outside Athens is no problem, and even the capital itself is less alarming than is sometimes suggested. As Greece is completely geared to the tourist it is easy to get both petrol and money. The only difficulty we had was with opening times of museums – it is advisable to check since hours are not as long as they used to be.

We travelled from Thessalonica by train because it is impossible to fly. There are flights from Athens to Istanbul, but you are not allowed to visit Turkey for more than twelve hours if you have arrived in Greece by charter flight. (Not that this applied to us, but it is worth bearing in mind in case you should wish to combine Greece and Turkey. There are no such restrictions with charter flights to Turkey). WE CANNOT RECOMMEND THE TRAIN JOURNEY.

Hotels in Turkey are very cheap by West European standards. Even in Istanbul it is possible to find a clean, reasonably comfortable room with bathroom for as little as £7 per night. The best hotels – with the exception of the new five-star *Ramada* – are all in the new town. The Turkish Tourist Office's list of hotels is confusing, since the city maps are so bad it is impossible to find most of them. Here the telephone numbers are a help; any hotel with a number beginning with 511, 512, 520, 522, 525, 526, 527 or 528 will be east of

Ataturk Boulevard and within walking distance of Hagia Sophia. Two which have been specially recommended are the *Yesil Konak*, converted from a nineteenth-century house, and the *Kalyon*. Both are near the Blue Mosque and are twice as expensive as the dozens of slightly less central hotels in Laleli.

There are few good restaurants in the Old Town, the best being in *Eminönü* near the Galata Bridge.

Long-distance buses can be thoroughly recommended. Various companies vie with each other to attract custom. We chose Pammukale, booking our tickets at the bus station the night before. Driving is easy on the empty well-paved roads, but one must be particularly careful driving in the dusk as the Turks seem reluctant to use lights until it is pitch dark. In the country tractors drawing trailers full of women returning from working in the fields are a real hazard, since they often pull straight across the road with no lights.

We had enormous difficulty in finding out the ferry timetable from Çeşme to Chios. We enquired at the main office in Istanbul but were given the wrong information. When we were in Turkey there were two sailings a week from Çeşme, on Thursday and Sunday but this could have changed. It may also be possible to sail from Izmir to Chios. Rather surprisingly our one-hour voyage cost as much as the rail fare from Thessalonica to Istanbul.

The best hotel in Chios is the *Chandris Chios* at the end of the harbour. Clean, modern and comfortable it undoubtedly lacks the character of the shabby *Xenia* but is quieter and more central.

# Bibliography

[Books consulted in addition to those in Further Reading]

Baynes, N.H., *Byzantine Studies and other Essays*, London, 1955.

Baynes, N.H., and Ross, H. St. L. B., *Byzantium. An Introduction to East Roman Civilisation*, Oxford, 1948.

Bouras, Charalambos, *Chios*, Athens, 1974.

Bovini, Giuseppe, *Ravenna, its Mosaics and Monuments*, Ravenna, 1978.

Bury, J.B., *History of the Later Roman Empire*, New York, 1969.

Byron, Robert, *The Byzantine Achievement*, London, 1929.

Byron, Robert and Talbot Rice, David, *The Birth of Western Painting*, London, 1930.

*Byzantine and Post-Byzantine Art* (exhibition catalogue), Byzantine Museum, Athens, 1985.

*Cambridge Medieval History*, Vol IV, Cambridge, 1966–7.

Charlemont, Earl of, *Travels of the Earl of Charlmont in Greece and Turkey, 1749*, London, 1984.

Choniates, Nicetas, *L'Histoire de l'Empéreur Jean Comnéne . . .*, Paris, 1672.

*Crusaders as Conquerors, The Chronicle of the Morea*, New York and London, 1948.

Clarke, W.G., *Peleponnesus: Notes of Study and Travel*, London, 1858.

Constantine VII Porphyrogenitus, Emperor, *De administrando imperio* (transl R.J.H. Jenkins), Budapest, 1949.

Coryate, Thomas, *Coryate's Crudities*, London, 1611.

Curzon, Hon. Robert, *Visits to Monasteries in the Levant*, London, 1849.

Diehl, Charles, *Figures Byzantines*, Paris, 1906.

Elliot, W.R., *Monemvasia: The Gibraltar of Greece*, London, 1971.

Every, G., *The Byzantine Patriarchate*, London, 1947.

Foss, A., *Epirus*, London, 1978.

*From Byzantium to El Greco: Greek Frescoes and Icons* (exhibition catalogue), Royal Academy, London, 1987.

Gell, Sir William, *The Itinerary of Greece*, London, 1819.

Gordon, C.B., *The Age of Attila: Fifth-Century Byzantium and the Barbarians*, Michigan, 1960.

Grabar, André, *Christian Iconography*, New York, 1968.

Griffiths, J., *Travels in Europe, Asia Minor and Arabia*, London, 1805.

Haroutunian, Arto der, *Middle-Eastern Cookery*, London, 1982.

Howell, James, *Epistolae Ho-elianae. The Familiar Letters of J. Howell*, London, 1890.

Hussey, J.M., *The Byzantine World*, London, 1957.

*Icons from South Eastern Europe and Syria*, Weitzman K., Chatzidakis M., Miatev K., and Radojević S., London, Belgrade and Sofia, 1968.

Kelly, Laurence, *Istanbul, a Travellers' Companion*, London, 1987.

Kindersley, Anne, *The Mountains of Serbia*, London, 1976.

Krautheimer, R., *Early Christian and Byzantine Architecture*, London, 1965.

Leake, Colonel W.M., *Travels in the Morea*, London, 1830.

Leake, Colonel W.M., *Peloponnesiaca*, London, 1846.

Leake, Colonel W.M., *Travels in Northern Greece*, London, 1835.

Lear, Edward, *Journals of a Landscape Painter in Albania and Illyria*, London, 1851.

Leigh Fermor, Patrick, *Mani*, London 1958.

Leigh Fermor, Patrick, *Roumeli*, London, 1966.

Lithgow, Walter, *Rare Adventures and Painefull Peregrinations*, London, 1632.

Liudprand of Cremona, *The Works of Liudprand of Cremona* (transl F.A. Wright), London, 1930.

Lovizzo, A., *Mosaics of Ravenna*, Ravenna, n.d.

Mackenzie, G. Muir Mackenzie and Irby, A.P., *Travels in the Slavonic Provinces of Turkey-in-Europe*, London, 1867.

Maclagan, M., *The City of Constantinople*, London, 1968.

Miller, W., *The Latins in the Levant*, London, 1908.

Miller, W., *Essays on the Latin Orient*, Cambridge, 1921.

Mont, Sieur du, *A New Voyage to the Levant*, London, 1705.

Mundy, P., *The Travels of Peter Mundy in Europe and Asia, 1608–67*, London, 1907–36.

Nicholl, D.M., *Meteora: The Rock Monasteries of Thessaly*, London, 1975.

Nicholl, D.M., *The Despotate of Epirus*, Oxford, 1958.

Nicholl, D.M., *The Despotate of Epirus 1267–1479*, Cambridge, 1984.

'Odysseus' (Sir Charles Eliot), *Turkey-in-Europe*, London, 1908.

Ouspensky, L., and Lossky, V., *The Meaning of Icons*, Boston, 1952.

Paton, A.A., *Servia or a Residence in Belgrade*, London, 1844.

Pelekanidis, S., and Chatzidakis, M., *Byzantine Art in Greece, Mosaics and Wall Paintings: Kastoria*, Athens, 1985.

Radojević, S., *Yugoslavia: Medieval Frescoes*, London, 1955.

Randolph, Bernard, *The Present State of the Morea*, Oxford, 1986.

Rogan, D.E., *Mani: History and Monuments*, Athens, 1973.

Runciman, Sir Steven, *Byzantine Civilisation*, London, 1933.

Runciman, Sir Steven, *The Eastern Schism*, Oxford, 1955.

Runciman, Sir Steven, *The Emperor Romanus Lecapenus*, Cambridge, 1929.

Sandys, George, *A Relation of a Iourney begun An Dom 1610*, London, 1615.

Sicilianos, D., *Old and New Athens*, London, 1961.

Sutherland, Captain, *A Tour up the Straits from Gibraltar to Constantinople*, London, 1790.

Talbot Rice, David, *The Art of Byzantium*, London, 1951.

Talbot Rice, David, *Byzantine Art*, London, 1961.

Talbot Rice, David, *The Byzantines*, London, 1964.

Talbot Rice, David, *Byzantine Painting. The Last Phase*, London, 1968.

Tournefort, J. Pitton de, *A Voyage into the Levant*, London, 1718.

Townsend, Rev. George Fyler, *A Cruise on the Bosphorus*, London, 1875.

*Treasures of Venice* (Royal Academy exhibition catalogue), London, 1981.

Vasiliev, A.A., *A History of the Byzantine Empire*, Madison, 1928.

Walsh, Rev Robert, *A Residence at Constantinople*, London, 1836.

Wheler, Sir George, *A Journey into Greece*, London, 1682.

# Further reading

[We have listed the most recent and easily accessible editions]

## GENERAL

For the historical background: Edward Gibbon, *The Decline and Fall of the Roman Empire*, Everyman, 1969; Joan Hussey, *The Byzantine World*, London, 1957; Dmitri Obolensky, *The Byzantine Commonwealth*, Weidenfeld, 1971; and George Ostrogorsky, *The History of the Byzantine State*, Blackwell (paperback), 1968.

For art and architecture: John Beckwith, *Early Christian and Byzantine Art*, Harmondsworth, 1970 and *The Art of Constantinople*, London, 1961; André Grabar, *Byzantine Art*, Macmillan, 1979; Gervase Mathew, *Byzantine Aesthetics*, John Murray, 1963; and Sir Steven Runciman, *Byzantine Style and Civilisation*, Penguin (paperback), 1987.

## OTHER USEFUL BOOKS

Cabasilas, N., *Commentary on the Divine Liturgy*, trans. J. M. Hussey and P. A. McNulty, London, 1960.

Comnena, Peter, and Eliopoulos, Edward, *Deep into Mani*, Faber (paperback), 1986.

Lancaster, Sir Osbert, *Sailing to Byzantium*, John Murray, 1969.

Mango, Cyril, *Byzantine Architecture*, Faber (paperback), 1986.

Procopius, *The Secret History*, Penguin (paperback). 1984.

Runciman, Sir Steven, *The Fall of Constantinople*, CUP (paperback), 1987.

Stewart, Cecil, *Serbian Legacy*, George Allen and Unwin, 1959.

Ware, Timothy, *The Orthodox Church*, Penguin (paperback), 1967.

West, Rebecca, *Black Lamb and Grey Falcon*, Macmillan, 1942.

The only readable historical novel about Byzantium is Robert Graves's *Count Belisarius*, Penguin (paperback), 1983. It is based on the life of the Emperor Justinian's great general and his reconquest of North Africa and Italy from the barbarians during the sixth century, much of it derived from the lurid gossip of Procopius.

# Glossary

*Ambo* pulpit
*Augustus, Augusta*, title given to the Emperor and Empress, and occasionally to other members of the Imperial family
*Basileus* King or Emperor
*Bema* chancel
*Catholicon* nave
*Chrysobull* an imperial letter written in gold ink granting privileges
*Ciborium* a free-standing canopy over an altar
*Deesis* Christ between the Virgin and St John the Baptist
*Despot* an independent prince
*Despina* a Despot's consort
*Diaconicon* the southern part of the sanctuary used as a vestry
*Epitaphion* a liturgical cloth used in the ceremonies of Good Friday
*Etimasia* the preparation of the throne of God
*Exarchate* a district presided over by an Imperial governor
*Exedra* open recess
*Exonarthex* outer antechamber of the church's main body
*Ex voto* offering made in pursuance of a vow
*Hodegetria* showing the way
*Hyperagathos* Most Good, Noble
*Iconoclast* a destroyer of images
*Iconodule* a servant of images, in favour of images
*Iconostasis* a screen separating the chancel from the body of the church
*Logothete* Counsellor to the Emperor, sometimes treasurer
*Maphorion* veil
*Martyrium* chapel built over the tomb of a martyr
*Naos* nave, church
*Narthex* antechamber to a church
*Orans* a figure in an attitude of prayer
*Panagia* Most Holy
*Pantocrator* Creator of All
*Paracclesion* side chapel
*Proskynesis* an act of homage before Christ or the Emperor
*Sebastocrator* commander-in-chief
*Skete* a small monestary for two or three monks
*Strategos* a general
*Theotokos* Mother of God
*Župan* Serbian headman or petty ruler

# Index

Abgar, King, 89
Acciajuoli, Nerio I, 231
Acciajuoli, Nerio II, 230
Adolf, King, 25
Akominatos, Michael, 157
Alaric, 25
Albania, 9, 79, 85, 91, 97, 99, 182, 184, 189, 215
Albanians, 50-1, 58, 60-1, 63, 75, 190, 203, 211, 226, 238
Alexander, 127
Alexander the Great, 51, 170
Alexius I Comnenus, 15, 17, 80, 99, 119-20, 126, 136-7, 184
Alexius II Comnenus, 16
Alexius III, 54
Ali Pasha, 185, 187
Amalasuntha, 35
Ambracia, 191
Amphissa, 175
    Hagios Sotirios, 175-6
Anchialus, 227, 230
Andrijevica, 57
Andronicus I Comnenus, 218, 220
Andronicus II Palaeologus, 39, 49, 67, 88, 90, 110, 160, 217, 218, 227, 236
Andronicus III Palaeologus, 108, 179-80, 182, 191, 227
Angelokastro, 199
Angelus, Demetrius, 197
Angelus, John, 197
Angelus, Nicephorus, 197
Ankara, 43, 107, 202
Anna, Empress of Andronicus III, 18, 108, 165
Anthemius of Tralles, 123
Apostolski, Mihailo, 77, 92
Arachova, 172-3, 183
Argentarius, Julian, 28, 36
Arsenius, Archbishop, 54, 64, 80
Arta, 184, 189, 191-3, 197, 199, 202, 225
    Blachernae, 196-7
    Hagia Theodora, 195
    Hagios Demetrios Katsouris, 198
    Hagios Loukas, 194
    Hagios Nikolaos tis Rodias, 198
    Hagios Vasileos, 194
    Kato Panagia, 195-6
    Parigoritissa, 193-5
Asmati, 91
Ataturk, Kemal, 93, 107, 127, 141
Athenaïs Eudoxia, 156, 161-2, 197

Athens, 106, 144, 147, 153-9, 164, 168, 202, 216, 219, 230, 239
    Hagia Dynami, 158
    Hagioi Apostoli, 158
    Hagioi Soter, 158
    Hagioi Theodori, 161
    Hagios Soter, 158
    Hagios Spiridion, 158
    Kapnikarea, 161
    Panagia Goepoepicoos, 158
    Benaki Museum, 159, 161, 164
    Byzantine Museum, 159, 161, 164, 219
    Canellopoulos Museum, 159, 164
Attica, 157, 168

Balabanov, Kosta, 79-80, 90, 92
Balkans, 7-8, 10, 51, 71, 85-6, 112, 127, 171, 225
Baltoyiannis, Dr C., 158, 161-2
Basil I, 201, 206, 214
Basil II Bulgaroctonus, 8, 77, 86, 119, 125, 156, 171, 176, 201
Bayezid I, 9, 43, 61-2, 175
Bayezid II, 194
Bazin, Germain, 53
Beckwith, John, 10, 41, 88, 125, 237
Belgrade, 38-41, 50, 56, 75, 78, 97, 113
    Fresco Museum, 39
    Museum of Orthodox Church, 39, 46
    National Museum, 39
Belisarius, 34-5, 123, 213
Benjamin of Tudela, 136
Bessarion, Ioannes, 14, 232
Bitola, 85, 93, 96, 98, 105, 182
Boeotia, 157, 168-9, 171, 239
Boethius, 33-4
Bogdan, 45
Bohemond of Taranto, 99-100, 184
Boniface of Montferrat, 107, 157
Boninsegna, Gian Paolo, 17
Botetsios, Georgios, 192, 195-6, 198-9
Bulgaria, 56, 78, 86, 156, 190, 227, 230
Bulgarians, 61, 79, 86, 107, 203
Bunyan, John, 77
Buondelmonti, Esau, 185
Bury, J.B., 10
Byron, Lord, 26, 60, 143, 184-5, 191, 199, 206, 224
Byron, Robert, 10

Cabasilas, Nicholas, 209

Čakor Pass, 57-8, 60, 63, 183
Cakoski, Goce, 92-3
Candiano, Doge Pietro IV, 14
Calligas, A. & H., 212, 218, 220
Canellopoulos, Paul, 165-6
Cantacuzene, Helena, 175
Cantacuzenus, Anthony, 178
Cantacuzenus, John, 102, 227
Cantacuzenus, Matthew, 228
Catalanos, Frangos, 182
Çeşme, 140-1
Chaeroneia, 169
Chalcocondyles, Laonicus, 233
Charlemagne, 37, 140
Charitonymous, Hieronymous, 232
Charlemont, Earl of, 145, 148, 152, 212
Charles of Anjou, 78
Chios, 15, 139, 142-52, 206, 226, 239
   Nea Moni, 145-7, 149-50
Christopher the Lombard, 109
Clark, W.G., 148, 150, 153, 159, 204
Classis, 25, 34, 36
Cleope, Despina, 230, 232, 239
Comnena, Anna, 97, 100, 120, 128, 137, 184
Comnenus, Prince Alexius, 80
Comnenus, Prince Isaac, 17, 138
Constans II, 156
Constantine IV, 36
Constantine V, 119, 203
Constantine VI, 156
Constantine VII Porphyrogenitus, 21, 97, 118, 131,
   135-6,182, 213-14, 220
Constantine X Monomachus, 115, 120, 127-8, 145
Constantine XI Palaeologus, 9, 126, 224, 230, 233,
   236-7, 239
Constantine the Great, 7, 16, 39, 53, 89, 103, 111,
   117, 122, 125, 132, 155, 172
Constantinople, 7-10, 13-20, 22-3, 26-7, 29, 32-6,
   39, 41, 46, 49, 53-4, 62, 66, 71-3, 78, 80, 84,
   87-90, 99, 100, 107, 115, 117-22, 124, 126,
   128-34, 136-7, 141, 145-6, 149, 155-8, 161-2,
   164, 171, 174, 183, 189, 190, 193-4, 197-8,
   201, 203, 206, 212, 216, 224-8, 231-7, 239
   Churches:
      Hagia Irene, 136
      Hagia Sophia, 8, 120-3, 125-7, 129-30, 134,
         136-7, 162, 165, 171, 193-4, 198
      Holy Apostles, 13, 15, 18, 129-30
      Fethiye Camii, 129, 137, 193
      Kariye Camii, 137-8, 239
      St John in Studion, 128, 139
      S.S. Sergius & Bacchus, 28, 134
      Archaeological Museum, 130
      Blachernae Palace, 125, 136
      Great Palace, 119, 126, 134-6
      Hippodrome, 16, 29, 117, 119, 123, 131-2, 135
      Mosaic Museum, 130
Constantius, 26
Contarini, Doge Domenico, 15
Corinth, 158, 202, 221
Crete, 19, 24, 160-3, 170, 207
Curzon, Hon. Robert, 168, 181

Dalassena, Anna, 119
Damaskinos, Michael, 160, 162, 165

Dandalo, Anna, 54
Dandolo, Doge Andrea, 17
Dandolo, Doge Enrico, 16, 54, 125
Daphni, 157, 163-4, 171
   Church of the Dormition, 163
Deakin, Sir William , 58
Debar, 76, 81, 85
Dečani, 65-8
Decius, 71
Dekoulou, 208, 219
Delphi, 16, 131, 168-9, 172-5, 187
Demetrius Palaeologus, Despot of Mistra, 163, 217,
   237-8
Demetrius Cantacuzenus, Despot of the Morea, 228
Denis of Fourna, 165
Diehl, Charles, 10
Diocletian, 112
Dispilio, 99
Distomo, 173
Dodona, 186-8
Dragaš, Constantine, 92, 230
Dragutin, 38, 53-4, 71
Dyrrachium, 99, 189

Ecclesius, Bishop, 28, 29
Eliot, Sir Charles, 126
Epirus, 73, 176-8, 184-6, 189-91, 193, 196-200,
   227, 239
Eudocia, sister of Andronicus II, 49
Eudocia, wife of Stephen the First Crowned, 54
Eugenius IV, Pope, 236
Eutychios and Michael, 47, 82, 88
Evrenoz Bey, 179, 202, 228

Fadrique, Louis, 175
Falier, Doge Ordelafo, 17
Florence, 14, 53, 232, 235
Florina, 105-6
Frangopoulos, John, 233, 237
Frederick I Barbarossa, 41
Frederick II Hohenstaufen, 37

Galerius, 109, 111-13, 165
Galla Placidia, 25-7, 33
Gangrene, Lady, 196
Gardenitsa, Hagios Sotiros, 214
Gennadius, Patriarch, 129, 239
Genoese, 143-4, 151, 227
Genseric, 213
George I Terter, 78
Geraki, 220-2
   Anastasis, 222
   Evangelistria, 222
   Hagios Sostris, 222
   Profitas Elias & Theofore, 223
   St John Chrysostom, 222
Gerolomin, 221-2
Gibbon, Edward, 9, 10, 86, 156
Githion, 215-6
Gorgnane: Sv. Nikita, 81-2
Grabar, André, 10, 41, 56, 110, 112, 114
Gracanica, 52, 60, 69, 70, 72, 82
Gravia, 176
Greece, 7, 9, 10, 22, 91, 97, 100, 109, 111, 115, 131,
   139, 143-4, 147, 151, 156, 158-9, 163, 166,

# Index

168-71, 173, 175, 179, 182-3, 187-9, 194, 200, 202-3, 206, 210, 215, 220, 227, 233-4
Greenhalgh, Peter, 211, 214
Gregory, Archbishop, 90, 113
Gregory the Confessor, 14
Grigorakis, Zanetos, 215
Gypsies, 60, 105, 169

Has, 75, 204
Helena, Despina, 46
Helena, Empress, 14, 103, 165, 172
Helena of Bulgaria, 68, 87
Henry IV, Holy Roman Emperor, 99
Henry IV of England, 20, 232
Heraclea Lyncestis, 96, 182
Hexamilion, 202, 231
Honorius, 25-6, 31
Hosios Loukas, 168-73, 188
Howell, James, 22

Ibrahim Pasha, 204, 238
Illyria, 72, 182
Illyrians, 51
Illyricum, 33, 100, 106
Innocent, Pope, 190
Irby, Miss, 65, 69, 70, 107
Irene, Empress, 139, 155-6, 158
Irene, Empress of Alexius I, 17
Irene, Empress of Manuel I, 128
Irene, niece of Michael IX, 14
Ioannina, 99, 181, 183-7, 191, 226
Isaac II Angelus, 54, 77, 120, 189
Isidore of Miletus, 123
Isidore of Monemvasia, 212
Italy, 7, 8, 10, 13, 22, 25-6, 28, 33-5, 41, 100, 111, 122, 161, 215
Ivan Alexander, 68
Ivan Stephen, 68

Jews, 100, 105, 107, 124, 203
Johnson, Hugh, 98
John Asen II of Bulgaria, 190
John Asen III of Bulgaria, 102
John I, Pope, 28
John I Tzimisces, 86
John II Comnenus, 128
John III Vatatzes, 118, 189, 193
John V Palaeologus, 18, 227-8
John VI Cantacuzenus, 74, 111, 126, 175, 227-8
John VII Palaeologus, 232
John VIII Palaeologus, 53, 120, 231, 235
John the Orphanotropus, 127
John Ugleš, Despot, 46
Julian the Apostate, 71
Justin, 29, 122
Justinian I, 8, 29, 30, 32, 78, 111, 118, 122-3, 125, 132, 134, 137, 156
Justinian II, 35-6, 119

Kalambaka, 177, 180, 182
Kalenic, 45-6
Kambinari: Hagios Nikolaos, 207
Karadjordje, 38, 55, 57
Karadjordjević, Peter, 55
Kardamyli, 205-6

Kasia, 119
Kasnitzes, Anna & Nicephorus, 101
Kastaniani, 186, 188-9
  Hagioi Taxiarchis, 188
Kastoria, 92, 97-100, 138, 161, 239
  Hagioi Anrgyroi, 92, 103
  Hagios Athanasios, 101
  Hagios Nikolaos tou Kasnitzi, 101
  Hagios Stephanos, 102
  Panagia Koubelidiki, 102
  Panagia Mavriotissa, 104
  Taxiarches of the Metropolis, 101-2
Katara Pass, 182
Kazantsakis, Nikos, 201, 215, 221, 233
Kiev, Grand Duke of, 115
Kilij Arslan, 132
Kinglake, Alexander, 41, 63
Kiparissos: Hagios Petros, 211-13
Kissas, Stirios, 113-14
Kolokotronis, Patriot, 203
Kosmet, 60-1, 69, 75, 96
Kosovo, 9, 39, 42-3, 46, 60, 70, 78
Kranai, 216
Krenites, Strategus, 172
Krsteski, Djordje, 90
Kruševac, 42, 44, 80
Kurbinovo, 91, 93, 101, 104, 183, 239
  Sv. Djordje, 91, 93

Laconia, 201-2
Lady's Magazine, 129
Lamia, 169, 175-6
Lancaster, Osbert, 224
Larissa, 99-100
La Roche, Guy & Odo de, 163
Lazar, Knez, 42-4, 46, 61-2
Lazar Grebeljanovic, 39
Leake, Col. W.M., 91, 98, 174, 178, 185-8, 189, 203-4, 211-12, 226, 234
Lear, Edward, 86-7, 95, 183, 193
Leigh Fermor, Patrick, 205-7
Lemniotes, Anna, 104
Lemniotes, Theodore, 103
Lemniotes, Theophilus, 104
Leo IV, 156
Leo VI, 18, 119, 124, 127
Leontius, Prefect of Illyricum, 110
Leo, Stategos of Hellas, 169
Lesbos, 15, 140, 145
Lithgow, William, 126, 131, 152, 154, 201
Liudprand of Cremona, 135
Ljubica, Princess, 57
Ljubostina, 46, 62, 83
Lombards, 8, 21, 35-7

Macedonia, 9, 38, 40, 42-3, 50, 71, 77-80, 85, 92, 94, 96, 101, 215, 230, 239
Macmillan, Harold, 165
Maglić, 48
Magnati, Girolamo, 22
Maina, 201, 214-5
Malatesta, Sigismondo, 37, 230, 238
Manasija, 41-5, 47, 53, 67, 239
Mandeville, Sir John, 132
Manfred, King of Sicily, 78, 190

# Index

Mani, 201, 205, 207, 210-16, 239
Manuel I Comnenus, 15, 16, 128, 136, 180
Manuel II Palaeologus, 18, 38, 92, 202, 212, 227, 230-1, 239
Manuel, Despot of the Morea, 227-9
Manzikert, 8
Maria of Antioch, 16, 120
Maria of Epirus, 189, 193
Maria of Trebizond, 120
Marko Kralevic, 92
Marriott of Rokeby, 208
Martin V, Pope, 230
Mastropoulos, Georgios, 160
Matka: Sv. Andrija, 83-4
Matthew, Despot of the Morea, 228
Maurice, 217
Mavromichalis, Petrobey, 215
Maximian, Bishop, 28, 32
Maximian, Emperor, 110, 134
Mehmet II, 9, 117, 129-30
Mesembria, 227, 230
Mesta, 146-8
Meteora, 168, 177-80, 239
  Barlaam, 179, 181-2
  Great Meteoron, 179, 180-2
  Hagios Nikolaos tou Anapavsa, 179
  Hagios Stephanos, 178, 179
Metsovo, 168, 183
Michael III, 85
Michael IV, 127-8
Michael V, 128
Michael I, Despot of Epirus, 184, 189-90
Michael II, Despot of Epirus, 189-90, 193, 195-7, 214, 231
Michael VIII Palaeologus, 54, 78, 104, 126, 136, 190, 193, 215-16, 226
Michael IX Palaeologus, 14
Michael Šišman, 68
Mileševa, 54-5, 113, 239
Milicia, 44, 46, 61-2, 69
Milutin, 39, 46, 49, 51, 54, 64, 66, 68, 70-2, 74, 78, 82, 90, 113
Miševski, Dušan, 80-1, 98
Missolonghi, 199
Mistra, 9, 14, 52, 181, 202, 204-5, 212, 214-15, 220, 223-59
  Churches:
    Brontochion, 236
    Evangelistria, 236
    Hagia Sophia, 229-32
    Hagioi Theodori, 236
    Hodegetria Afthendiko, 236-7
    Metropolis, (Hagios Demetrios), 235
    Pantanassa, 228, 233-5, 237
  Despot's Palace, 225-6, 232, 234
  Palataki, 232
Moncreiffe, Sir Iain of that Ilk, 206
Monemvasia, 160, 201, 204, 212, 214-20, 226, 229, 231, 238
  Christos Elkomenos, 219-30
  Hagia Sophia, 218, 220
  Panagia Chrysaphitissa, 219
Montenegro, 51, 54, 58
Morris, Jan, 106
Moscow, Grand Duke of, 126

Morea, 201-3, 205, 216-17, 223, 227-30
Moss, Stanley, 207
Mount Athos, 42-3, 47-8, 53, 106, 161, 178
Moussakes, Stoias & Theodore, 101
Muhammed II, 238
Muir Mackenzie, Miss, 65, 69, 70, 167
Mundy, Peter, 62
Murad I, 61
Murad II, 43, 140, 227, 230
Murano, 22-3
  Santi Maria e Donato, 23

Napoleon Bonaparte, 16, 159, 215
Nemanja, Constantine, 67
Neon, Bishop, 31-3
Nerezi, 80-1, 85, 92, 164
  Sv. Pantaleimon, 80
Nicaea, 8, 14, 53-4, 90, 189-91
Nicephorus I, 156
Nicephorus I, Despot of Epirus, 189
Nicopolis, 194, 196
Nikolovski, Zoran, 81
Niš, 39, 41
Nivelet, Guy de, 220
Nivelet, Jean de, 216, 220-2
Normans, 8, 99-100, 107, 141
Novi Pazar, 50-1, 54
  Sv. Petar, 51

Obilić, Milos, 61
Odoacer, 33
Ohrid, 54, 78, 82, 84-7, 90-1, 93, 113, 156, 184
  Sv. Jovan Kaneo, 87, 90
  Sv. Kliment, 88, 90
  Sv. Naum, 91
  Sv. Nikola Bolnicki, 87
  Sv. Sofije, 88, 90
Orlandos, Prof., 236
Orloff, Prince, 204, 226, 229
Orseolo, Doge Pietro, 17
Orsini, John & Nicholas, 191
Ostrogorsky, George, 128, 189

Pachomius, Abbot, 236
Palaeologina, Anna, 191, 193, 197
Palaeologina, Irene, 102
Palaeologina, Maria, 137
Palaeologina, Maria, wife of Uroš III, 79
Palaeologus, Andronicus, Depot, 227
Papadopoulos, Barbara, 186
Papageorgiou, Christos, 192
Paton, A.A., 44
Patras, 202-4, 230
Peć, 47, 57, 59, 63-5, 69, 76, 80,
  Holy Apostles, 63
  Sv. Demetrius, 64
  St. Nicholas, 64
  Virgin Hodegetria, 64
Pelagonia, 191, 215
Peloponnese, 9, 10, 102, 148, 156, 199, 203, 206, 213, 215-16, 220-2, 225, 227-8, 230, 236, 239
Pepcal, George, 68
Peter III of Aragon, 78
Petraleiphas, John, 196

# Index

Phanari, 176
Philip of Courtenay, 71
Philip of Macedon, 96, 188
Philotheos, Abbot, 171-2
Phocis, 230
Piero della Francesca, 53
Pili, 177
Pius II, Pope, 238
Plethon, George Gemistos, 227, 235, 239
Pollington, Lord, 41
Porto Kayio, 213
Preljubović, Maria Angelina, 181, 185
Preljubović, Thomas, 181, 184-5, 191
Prespa, 86, 91, 97-8
  St Achilles, 97
Prijepolje, 54
Prilep, 77-8, 92
  Sv. Archangel, 92-3
  Sv. Nikola, 93
Priština, 60-1, 69
Prizren, 72-6, 84-5, 101
  Bogodorica Ljeviška, 74
Proconnesus, 36
Procopius, 25, 124, 134
Psellus, Michael, 86
Pulcheria, 156, 197
Pyrghi, 146, 148-9
  Holy Apostles, 149
Pyrrhus, 188, 191

Quinney, Major George, 79

Radene, Anna, 103
Randolph, Bernard, 152
Raoul of Brienne, 100
Ras, 38, 47, 51, 71
Raška, 40, 47-8, 50, 56, 64
Ravanica, 43-4
Ravenna, 10, 13, 25-6, 28, 30, 33, 35-7, 134, 164,
  239
  Arian Baptistery, 34
  Mausoleum of Galla Placidia, 26-7, 29, 37
  Orthodox Baptistery, 25, 30-1
  San Francesco, 32
  S. Giovanni Evangelista, 25-6
  Santa Croce, 26
  Sant' Andrea, oratory of, 32
  Sant' Apollinare in Classe, 36, 108, 230
  Sant' Apollinare Nuovo, 31, 34-5, 37
  San Vitale, 27-8, 30, 36, 134
Rhodes, Knights of, 191, 228
Robert Guiscard, 99-100
Romanus II, 170-1
Romanus III Argyrus, 127-8
Romanus IV Diogenes, 8
Rome, 7, 9, 16, 19, 25-7, 33, 35-6, 67, 88, 107, 110,
  112, 115, 117, 123, 125, 131, 232, 234-5, 238
Rugovo Gorge, 59, 63-4, 80
Runciman, Sir Steven, 10, 41, 70, 119, 171, 224,
  231, 233

Saadi, 117
St Cyril, 38, 91
St John Damascene, 210
St Methodius, 38, 91

St Romil, 43
St Sava, 47, 48, 54, 56, 63-4, 68, 73
St Simeon the New Theologian, 40
Samuel, Tsar, 77-8, 86-8, 91-2, 103, 125, 137, 156
Sandys, George, 143, 201
Sečenicski Letopis, 43
Selim the Grim, 130, 141
Selvo, Doge Domenico, 13, 100
Sgouros, Pragon, 88
Serbia, 9, 38-9, 41-2, 44-5, 48-51, 57-8, 60-1, 65-7,
  70, 72-3, 85, 94, 96, 198, 203, 227, 239
Serbs, 39-41, 46, 60-2, 71-2, 74, 77, 86, 96-7, 99,
  107, 179, 183-4
Shelley, P.B., 154
Sigismund, Holy Roman Emperor, 232
Simeon Uroš, 181, 184, 191
Simonida, 49, 66, 71-2, 78
Skopje, 71-3, 77-81, 84, 87-8, 99, 122, 179
  Sv. Svas, 81
  Museum of Macedonia, 79
Skripou: Church of the Dormition, 169
Slavs, 60, 85, 105, 110, 113, 156-7, 188, 201, 214,
  220, 226
Smederevo, 41
Sopoćani, 51, 56, 70, 239
Spata, Ghin Boua, 191
Sparta, 9, 155, 202, 204, 220, 226, 238
Steiros, 170
Stephen Lazarevic, 42, 45
Stephen Nemanja, 38, 41, 47-8, 51, 68, 74
Stephen Radoslav, 39, 49, 53, 56
Stephen the First Crowned, 39, 47-8, 54, 64, 74
Stephen Uroš I, 53-4, 56, 64, 71
Stephen Uroš III Decanski, 66-9, 72-3
Stephen Uroš IV Duson, 9, 39, 47, 61, 66-9, 72-6,
  86-7, 178-9, 182, 191, 198, 227
Stephen Uroš V, Tsar, 61, 68, 182
Stewart, Cecil, 179
Strumica, 77
Studenica, 48-9, 54, 64, 74
  Bogodorica, 48-9
  Kraljeva Crvka, 49
  St Nicholas, 49
Suleiman the Magnificent, 217
Sutherland, Capt., 124
Swan, Mr, 202, 238
Symmachus, 33-4
Syros, 160

Talbot-Rice, David, 45, 47, 122, 145
Talbot-Rice, Tamara, 99
Tamberlane, 9, 43, 202
Talygarn, 22
Taticius, 99-100
Tetovo, 83-4
Thebes, 155, 168-9, 182, 230
Theodahad, 35
Theodora, Empress of Justinian, 29, 30, 125, 134,
  165
Theodora, sister of Andronicus III, 39, 68
Theodora, sister of Zoë, 127
Theodora, Despina of Epirus, 196
Theodora, Despina of the Morea, 230
Theodore I Angelus, Despot of Epirus, Emperor of
  Thessalonica, 39, 107, 189-91

Theodore, Despot of the Morea, 202, 228, 232-3
Theodore II, Despot of the Morea, 230, 237
Theodoric, 28, 33-5
Theodosius I, 25-6, 32, 131, 168, 188
Theodosius II, 140, 156
Theodosius the Hermit, 89
Theophano, sister of Basil II, 11, 119
Theophano, wife of Nicephorus I, 156
Theophilus, 119
Theotocopoulos, Domenico (El Greco), 19, 160-2, 166
Thessalonica, 42, 56, 65, 88, 97, 100-1, 106-10, 113-16, 120, 144, 161, 165, 189-90, 199, 227, 239
  Hagia Ekaterina, 115
  Hagia Sophia, 108
  Hagios Demetrios, 109
  Hagios Nikolaos Orfanos, 113, 115
  Panagia Chalkeon, 109
  Paraskevi, 108-9
  Profitas Elias, 111
  Rotunda, 111-2, 115, 165
  White Tower, 114-15
Thessaly, 73, 176, 178-9, 227-8
Thomas, Despot of Clarenza, 230, 237-8
Thomas, Despot of Epirus, 191
Thrace, 132, 161, 227
Tito, 58, 82
Tocco, Carlo, 191, 230
Torcello, 21-2
Tournefort, Sieur de, 145-7, 149
Townsend, Rev.G.F., 84, 134
Traherne, Thomas, 210
Trebizond, 14, 190
Trikkala, 99, 177, 184
Tripolis, 203-5
Trstenik, 45-7
Tsanes, Manuel, 160, 162, 165-6, 180
Turks, 8, 9, 14, 39-41, 43, 45-6, 52, 56, 60-1, 69-70, 72, 74, 77, 99, 107-8, 111, 113-14, 121, 124, 126-7, 129-32, 134, 137-8, 140-1, 144, 148, 157, 163-4, 171, 185, 191-2, 194, 197, 203-4, 217, 225, 227, 236, 238
Tvrtko, King of Bosnia, 61

Ursus, Bishop, 31
Ušće, 48

Valentinian III, 26, 31, 33
Varangian Guard, 99, 120
Vathia, 213
Vavyloi: Panagia Krina, 150
Venice, 8, 12-4, 16-22, 24-5, 35, 46, 96, 99, 100, 107, 111, 125, 160-2, 189, 201, 217, 232, 234, 239
  Accademia, 13
  Correr Museum, 19, 24
  Marciana Library, 14, 232
  Pala d'Oro, 17-8
  St Mark's 13-14, 16, 19-21, 24, 125, 172, 174
  Santa Maria della Salute, 13, 23-4
  Treasury of St Mark's, 16, 18, 114
Venetians, 8, 9, 13-15, 17-19, 26, 100, 125, 143, 148, 203, 216-18, 220, 227
Veneziano, Paolo, 14, 18, 160
Via Egnatia, 85, 91
Vid, Fra, 67
Villehardouin, Geoffroy de, 117
Villehardouin, William of, Duke of Achaia, 190, 214-16, 225, 229
Vinica, 78-9, 79-80
Vitylo, 205, 207-8, 216
Vlachs, 177, 183, 190
Vladislav, King, 53, 55
Voltaire, 7, 9
Vuk, 43
Vukan, 54
Vukašin, 'King', 46, 92

War of Independence, 164, 170, 202-3, 217, 221
West, Dame Rebecca, 12, 38, 57, 63, 71, 73, 89
Wheler, Sir George, 123, 131, 156, 166, 169, 171, 174, 193
Whittemore, Thomas, 127

Yugoslavia, 10, 38, 40-1, 46, 51, 57, 60, 75, 81, 83-6, 90-1, 93, 105, 185, 234

Zeno, 33
Žiča, 47-8, 64
Zitsa, 186
Zoë, Empress, 118, 127-8, 139, 145
Zvečan, 73

BLACK SEA

Constantinople

TURKEY

BULGARIA

Thessalonica

GREECE

ALBANIA

Belgrade

Manasija
Ravanica
Kruševac
Kalenić
Žiča
Studenica
Prijepolje
Mileševa
Sopoćani
Novi Pazar
Peć
Dečani
Prizren
Priština
Gračanica
Sv. Nikita
Skopje
Nerezi
Tetovo
Sv. Andrija
Debar
Prilep
Bitola
Ohrid
Florina
Kurbinovo
Kastoria